Property of-
    Madge S. Keiter

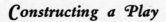

Constructing a Play

Constructing a Play

By

MARIAN GALLAWAY, Ph.D.

*Assistant Professor of Speech · Director of
University Theatre · University of
Alabama*

WITH A FOREWORD BY

Tennessee Williams

NEW YORK · PRENTICE-HALL, INC. · 1950

Dedication

To
E. C. Mabie
and the apprentice playwrights
of Iowa University

Foreword

TEN YEARS AGO AT THE UNIVERSITY OF IOWA I WAS A
student of various branches of the theatrical arts, including
playwriting, and it was there that I became a friend of the
author of this volume. Quite possibly I derived more from
this friendship than I did from any of the actual courses
that I undertook, for Marian Gallaway was one of those
persons who lived and breathed theatre and somehow managed to infect her associates with her own religious excitement about it.

About the actual courses I took I am now a little bit hazy.
I am not sure how much I actually learned in the classrooms
and how much came to me by that process called osmosis,
a gradual soaking-in that occurs involuntarily through the
mere fact of exposure. It was perhaps more in the physical
aspects of the theatre, the courses in stagecraft and the
shop-work backstage, that I picked up the most valuable
training. But I do know that I left Iowa City and my year's
association with the author of this book with a great deal
more theatre knowledge than I had brought there.

If there were, indeed, a set of tools that could be delivered ready-made into the hands of the beginning dramatist, or the novice in any other creative field, it is hard to say whether it would be more of a boon than a detriment. It would relieve him of that vastly prolonged and arduous and solitary exploration of success-through-failure by which most mature workers arrive at their maturity. It would relieve, yes, it would save him. But would it really improve his ultimate worth? There is something in that very history of travail and failure which precedes the coming to flower that adds to the ultimate sweetness of the flower when it has come. It is the difference between the natural and the synthetic, sometimes very slight but always important.

A good instructor in dramatic arts knows very well that there may be instances, not frequent but all the more important for not being so, when studies and rules of construction and even exercises may be virtually useless. Let us suppose that an undergraduate named Jean Giraudoux had enrolled in a playwriting class, not Miss Gallaway's but that of some instructor less cognizant of exceptional instances and the elasticity demanded by them. This instructor would throw up his hands in holy horror, no doubt, when M. Giraudoux turned in his first assignment, for it would almost certainly violate practically every tenet of recognized craftsmanship except that one very liberal rule of stimulating a sensibility to poetic excitement in that part of the audience capable of responding to such stimuli. However, if the instructor did happen to be the author of this book, who is no ordinary instructor, she would realize that she was up against a case where the rulebook must be set aside in favor of some more mysterious sense of order than that which is susceptible to diagrams and outlines. She would not kick M. Giraudoux out of the class, although she might very well despair of giving him much assistance in his intensely solitary struggle toward fruition.

I was once standing backstage, one opening night in Chicago, when close by me passed two very nervous men, a producer and a backer, both suffering from ulcers. The first said to the other, "You know, Louie, I have drunk a quart of prune juice today!" The second replied: "Well, Eddie, it won't do you a bit of harm!"

The problematical and, alas, unlikely Giraudoux in the playwriting class will not be benefited as much as, say, the possible George F. Kaufmann or even Lillian Hellmann, but it will not do him any more harm than a quart of prune juice taken for first-night ulcers. And I would say, with no hesitation, that the number of beginners that can be and will be helped by courses of instruction in the technical aspects of their art make up a vast preponderance. It sometimes appears to me that there is no art whose practitioners as a whole are so technically ignorant and incompetent as writers for the stage. Play after play that you go to see in the course of a season has elements of brilliance which are wasted through lack of common "know-how". Exciting and moving first acts bog down in a morass of inexpert and tedious exposition or the whole thing crashes into ruin by head-on collision with an unacceptable contrivance or unbelievable device. Ah, yes, I know about these things without going far afield. My own backyard is littered with the wreckage of scripts that started upon a sound and exciting promise but collapsed through sheer technical inefficiency on my part. It took me six or eight bad plays to produce a relatively good one, and even now, when I have been at this business for a dozen years, my methods of composition are criminally wasteful. I write three or four drafts when not more than two should be necessary, simply because I did not acquire in my green years the right kind of technical habits.

I am not one of those who deplore all system in the arts, who think them products of a divine sort of anarchy. I prefer Henry James to Henry Miller. I see the excitement of abandonment to impulse, the thrills of anarchy, but I see also, and even more clearly, that mysterious harmony which is beauty and which comes out of a pure design, a clear conception worked out in clarity and order. Sometimes the order may not appear to be order upon the surface; it may have the wild atmosphere of sheer impulse put into action. But if it succeeds, if it creates the effect of beauty, you may be sure that underneath the glittering surface is the inconspicuous but certain structure of bone. Rules are good if only for the exhilarating sense of freedom with which the artist can sometimes finally afford to forget them.

Instruction and exercises of the sort given you in this book cannot make you a playwright. But if you are destined to become one, it is fairly certain that these preliminary studies and exercises wil simplify your period of apprenticeship. It will not clear the forest for you; that is to say, it will not reduce the number of great trees that you will have to pass deviously among. But this it will do: it will chop out a path for you through the underbrush, saving you much confusion and many little abrasions of the skin-surface. What Marian Gallaway is offering is not a way to shortcut your own natural growth but ways to avoid unnatural growth.

—TENNESSEE WILLIAMS

Preface

PLAYWRITING MAY BE DEFINED AS THE ART OF TRANS-
ferring feelings about a human situation from the mind of
a playwright to the mind of an assembled audience. If one
reflects upon the maze of attendant circumstances,—the
subtlety of the creative mind, the complexity of every
human situation, and the heterogeneity of assemblages—it
it not surprising that the transference is seldom complete.
Yet the maze, complex though it is, is not without order
and even egress.

For some years I have watched young playwrights under
fire, in seminars, in rehearsal, and in audience discussions
after performance. The playwright emerges from his experience of communicating, with perhaps some shred of insight into the problems of the specific play on which he has
been engaged. What he does not realize is that year after
year the criticisms are so often repeated and so classifiable
that one can not help thinking they reveal some basic facts
about playwriting.

This conviction is reinforced when one compares the

earliest plays of established playwrights with the work done in their maturity. One can see quite clearly that certain practices develop and certain others appear less frequently as these playwrights learn their craft.

Usually playwrights do not like to regard even their own practices as "techniques" in the sense of having general value. There is a hearty prejudice against the epithet "well-made," which has come to mean merely slick. They prefer to focus the microscope on specific situations and to derive the means of communication from the situation itself. And of course this is what they must do, integrity being the one absolute essential of the artist. Yet this intimate, highly concentrated work has produced a group of practices that occur so frequently under the specific disguise of particular play material as to indicate that they are basic techniques.

Of course it would be absurd to insist that every play embody the whole group of practices that have emerged as skills. Rather, technique should be thought of as a complex of skills of which many may be needed in a single play, all may be useful in the course of a playwriting career, none is incapable of refinement and transmutation in the fiery alembic of the sensitive playwright's mind.

Just as the material of the play determines the particular techniques that will be applicable to it, so the nature of the material and of the playwright's mind determines the steps by which the play is constructed. The artist works as he must. But, since one must start somewhere in setting forth the practices which appear to be useful, it has seemed wise to follow in general the pattern in which apprentice play-

wrights seem to work. Thus, those practices have been presented first which seem to be needed in constructing the
first few drafts of the scenario. The practices which help
to achieve suspense have been placed second because the
inexperienced playwright often brings to a first reading a
script lacking in these devices; and the devices of preparation, many of which are used both consciously and uncon-
sciously in the initial stages of construction, are still most
frequently needed for revision during the rehearsal period,
and have therefore been presented last. Of course one need
not follow this or any other particular order in constructing a play.

One more point should be made. No separate chapters
have been devoted to characterization or to dialogue. I do
not see how plot and character can be regarded separately;
for clarity and credibility are founded on the motives and
capacities of the characters who perform the actions of the
play. And thus at every step the student of the following
pages will be forced to contemplate his characters before
proceeding. No chapter on dialogue has been included because dialogue is really outside the scope of a work purport-
ing to deal only with the construction of the scenario.
Moreover, the definitive chapter on dialogue can not be
written until extensive analysis has been made of the
changes wrought by actors in rehearsal.

Like any other artist, the young playwright may expect
a period of awkwardness until he has mastered his tools.
Therefore I have included separate exercises for the apprentice, which he need not apply to his major work until
or unless he believes them applicable. Moreover, it seems

wise to regard any scenario constructed while studying technique as merely an exercise. Very probably it should not be carried to completion; certainly it should not be forced to completion if, as often happens, the writer has lost his original excitement in the unexpectedly long labor of construction. Yet the loss of excitement need not vitiate the skill acquired in the performance of the exercise. If each assignment has been undertaken with imagination (and the exercise is useless if it is done perfunctorily) the result will be a command of techniques that do not restrict, but rather free the young playwright of the wasteful necessity of re-inventing by trial-and-error the basic devices of playwriting.

For technique is simply the manipulation of the medium to the artist's will. Form, to the playwright, is no more than the final arrangement of characters, action, language, and spectacle into the pattern which seems to the playwright to express what he has to say. And the only rules are those imposed by the medium, by the life-material which the playwright chooses, and by the group mind which he wishes to address.

—MARIAN GALLAWAY

Acknowledgment

Special acknowledgment and thanks are due to Joseph Baldwin of the University of Tennessee for reading and minutely criticizing every part of the book.

Table of Contents

INTRODUCTION

PART ONE: CLARITY

xix

TABLE OF CONTENTS

INTRODUCTION

1

The Playwright as Artist

AN ARTIST IS A PERSON WHOSE EMOTIONS ARE STIMULATED by certain aspects of his environment. If his sensitivity is primarily to sound, he is a musician. If he is mainly sensitive to color, he is a painter; if to form, a sculptor or a dancer or an architect. In whatever field he is sensitive, he involuntarily combines the exciting stimulus with certain of his own experiences and attitudes to create a new emotional experience, the perception of beauty. This is his own private experience, one which few persons or none except himself could get from that particular stimulus.

The work of art—the painting, symphony, statue, cathedral, lyric, drama—is the attempt of the artist to preserve and usually to communicate his experience of beauty. It is perhaps never a photographic or phonographic replica of the stimulus; it is the artist's experience of the stimulus, externalized in some medium satisfying to him. For example, two artists, soldiers, stood in the ruins of Manchester after the last war, aware of acres of desolation, and of hurrying life on the embankment in the distance. Mixed with the sights and sounds of the afternoon were their own powerful personal memories of battle experiences. Suddenly for some unknown reason bells all over the city started ringing. For both men the experience was a thrilling one. One of them based a symphony upon it; the other wrote a brief, bitter lyric poem. Thus one stimulus produced two quite different works of art, because the poet reacted differently from the musician. In other words, a work of art is not a mere duplication of a stimulus, but a fusion of the stimulus with the reactions of the artist and with the medium in which the artist chooses to work.

Practically everyone, no doubt, has had some such experiences of beauty, some intense, some so slight that he allows them to slip quickly from consciousness without pausing at all to discover what they mean or why they seem beautiful. To the artist, however, the stimulus is generally so exciting that he is not content to let it slip from his consciousness. He wants to preserve it, and usually to communicate it.

Frequently an artist will refuse to say why he writes or paints or composes music. His only possible answer is that he must. The experience of beauty is so forcible that he cannot contain it within himself. This reply is undoubtedly part of the truth—in a few cases, the whole truth. To write a short lyric poem or paint a water-color sketch, the work of an afternoon, merely for one's own pleasure, is understandable. But the novelist, the playwright, the composer of an extended piece of music like a symphony, spends from a few months to years upon his creation. Many times during the process he loses the delight of the original experience; yet he continues to probe, to mold, to alter. Can it be that he spends so much time to recapture one past experience merely for his own narcissistic pleasure? Certainly the professional artist knows that he intends to permit someone else to enjoy the work when it is finished. For the artist, the crown of the experience of beauty is the pleasure of sharing it with someone.

It does not seem necessary here to go into an extended discourse on pure aesthetics. However, the above considerations suggest that the creative process has four elements:

1. The artist, an individual with a particular emotional organization
2. A stimulus of any kind whatsoever, capable of exciting the artist
3. The work of art, a fusion of the stimulus with the artist's spiritual nature in the medium that to him best expresses the experience of beauty
4. Someone other than the artist, who appreciates the work of art

Thus a work of art may be called successful insofar as it actually does express the artist's experience of the stimulus to a percipient. All technique in all the arts stems from this double-edged requirement.

The matters spoken of so far are matters which every artist and indeed every craftsman must take into account. The stimuli of the various artists differ; their media also differ. Yet each worker is interested in making something which will appeal to human beings; each in commencing his work must analyze the materials which are to serve his purposes; and each must master the use of his tools.

Drama has been rather narrowly regarded in the schools as a branch of literature, partly because it tells a story, but largely because the only way it could be preserved in the past was in words, the medium of the poet.[1] Actually, the drama is much more closely related to music and the dance than to literature,[2] both in its history and its present manifestation; and its relation to poetry is a historic relation to the old singing poet of the dithyramb. The printed play is no more the drama than the score of the symphony is the symphony, or the dancer's notes the dance, or the architect's blueprint the cathedral. Indeed, the manuscript is precisely a score or blueprint of the actual drama.

Several conditions which govern the composition of a symphony also govern the composition of a drama.[3] The first of these conditions is that the work is not completed by the author.[4] It must utilize the imagination and skill of a director and of the performers who will present the work to the public. It must therefore be clear enough in its purport and strong enough in its passion to dominate the

---

[1] Now, of course, it could be preserved on technicolor-sound film. On this point see Brander Matthews, *A Study of the Drama*, Chapter I. Boston: Houghton Mifflin Company, 1910.

[2] George Pierce Baker compares the play with the novel in his *Dramatic Technique*, pp. 6-13. Boston: Houghton Mifflin Company, 1919.

[3] Percy Goetschius, *The Homophonic Forms of Musical Composition*, p. 1. New York: G. Schirmer, Inc., 1924. See also Arthur Edwin Krows, *Playwriting for Profit*, Chapter II. New York: Longmans, Green & Co., Inc., 1928.

[4] Clayton Hamilton, *"So You're Writing a Play!"*, pp. 31-36. Boston: Little, Brown & Company, 1935.

6

imaginations of all these middlemen; and the dramatist must also control the imaginations of the other artists—designer, costumer, composer, choreographer—who may have to contribute to the completion of the work.

The second condition of drama in common with symphony is that the consumer for whom the work is designed is a group, bound together for the duration of the performance and reacting as a group rather than as individuals. It is well known that a group, at whatever level of intelligence, is less intellectual and more emotional than the individuals who compose it. In other words, like a symphony, the play will stir emotions more effectively than it will provoke thought. Even in a play designed to carry a message, the skillful playwright will induce belief by making the audience *feel* as he wants it to feel, rather than by attempting to convince intellectually. Recent investigations into the psychology of belief have shown that there is a higher correlation between belief and desire than between belief and evidence,[5] a fact known to public speakers since the time of Quintilian, and consciously stated by dramatists at least as early as Corneille.[6]

Further, since the drama is performed to a group rather than read by individuals, and since the audience cannot,

[5] Albert T. Poffenberger, *Psychology in Advertising*, Chapter XXV. New York: McGraw-Hill Book Company, Inc., 1932. See especially p. 540, where he correlates belief and evidence, 0.42; belief and desire, 0.88. See also F. H. Lund, "The Psychology of Belief: A Study of Its Emotional and Volitional Determinants," *Journal of Abnormal Psychology*, Vol. 20 (1925) pp. 63 ff.

[6] Pierre Corneille, "Premier Discours. De l'Utilité et des Parties du Poème dramatique," translated in Barrett H. Clark, *European Theories of the Drama*, p. 147. New York: Crown Publishers, 1947.

like the individual reader, repeat difficult passages, the meaning of the play must be clear enough to be understood immediately. Drama demands even more than symphony in this respect, since one hears a great piece of music comparatively more often, through records and broadcasts, than one usually sees a good play.

Another condition which drama as well as symphony faces is the limit of the audience's endurance, which makes it necessary to complete the performance in something under three hours, with generally some intervals of rest, and some deliberate attempts to restimulate attention after the rest periods.

Like symphony, drama is a complex art. Its tools are those of the architect, the painter, the dancer, the singer, the poet, as well as the specific devices needed to fashion the script, the score of a play. The playwright should be able to use all these tools as freely as the composer of a symphony uses the instruments of his orchestra and the principles of harmony.[7]

The symphonic composer, however, has a musical training that began in childhood. He may not be a highly skilled performer, but he usually plays three or four instruments. He knows the capacities of the various instruments and has had a well-systematized course of study in the principles of musical composition. The playwright, on the contrary, has usually had few opportunities to become trained in the arts of the theatre or even in the fundamentals of dramaturgy. If he has lived in one of our few theatre centers, he may have become acquainted with the

---

[7] Matthews, *A Study of the Drama*, Chapter II.

professional stage, at least from the audience side of the footlights. But good playwrights are sometimes born in Nebraska or Oklahoma or North Carolina, where the opportunity to see plays of any calibre is severely limited. The technique of the cinema, all that exists of the living theatre in many places, is quite different, of course, from that of the stage. And the written play as a sole source of information is far from complete.

The late George Pierce Baker is said to have recommended twenty-nine as a desirable age for a young man to begin his study of playwriting.[8] This recommendation undoubtedly reflects the fact that playwriting demands a rather mature knowledge of human relationships, enough objectivity to allow characters to seem to speak for themselves, and enough stability not to compromise with one's own purposes in the process of translating one's private dream into a work of art for public consumption. Baker's recommendation may have been reasonable in a day when every town had its local stock company, and when the youth could steep himself in the practices of the stage almost as effectively as he can now do in musical records, broadcasts, and concerts. Twenty-nine may become the right age again, when we have developed children's dramatics so that the sixth-grader can learn how to motivate characters and build a scenario from a story. Twenty-nine may be a reasonable age for the playwright to start learn-

---

[8] Professor Baker writes, "I gravely doubt the advisability of such a course for undergraduates . . . In the main I believe instruction in the writing of plays should be for graduate students." *Dramatic Technique,* Preface, p. v.

9

ing his craft, when community theatres become more than adjuncts to the country clubs, and school dramatics in general are more than a pleasant extracurricular activity for a few enthusiasts. At present, however, the playwright may be as naïve, dramatically speaking, at twenty-nine as he was at seventeen.

Yet at twenty-nine, presumably, one may have something of importance to say; even, perhaps, something inspired, which he wishes to set forth in the white heat of emotion. It is a great pity that at this point the artist must pause in the creative process in order to learn his complex medium.[9] There is no surer way of strangling a beautiful conception than by engrafting upon it a mass of suddenly-acquired, ill-digested techniques.

The technique of playwriting is highly complex. The tools are not ready-made like the saws and hammers and drills of the carpenter; indeed, they must generally be remodeled to some extent for each new task. Yet they can be mastered in somewhat the way a young pianist masters scales and chords, taking into consideration that each new combination of notes will require a new fingering. It seems reasonable to let the young playwright, like the young musician, acquire some skill with the devices that are available to him. Then, when he has something of mature significance to say, he will also have at his disposal most of the devices he needs, and will pause in the creative process only to invent such new tools as his special material requires.

<hr>

[9] Krows, *Playwriting for Profit*, p. 23.

ASSIGNMENTS

PLAYS: Henrik Ibsen, *Hedda Gabler,* from *Collected Works,* ed. William Archer. New York: Charles Scribner's Sons, 1908-1927. William Shakespeare, *Romeo and Juliet,* from *Shakespeare's Complete Works,* ed. William Allen Neilson. New York: P. F. Collier and Son Company, 1925. Aristophanes, *Lysistrata,* from *The Complete Greek Drama,* ed. Oates and O'Neill. New York: Random House, 1938.

ADDITIONAL READING: Aristotle, *Poetics,* VI, translated by Ingram Bywater, Modern Readers Series. New York: The Macmillan Company, 1930. George Pierce Baker, *Dramatic Technique,* Preface and Chapters I and X. Boston: Houghton Mifflin Company, 1919. E. F. Carritt, *Philosophies of Beauty,* selections from Bernard Bosanquet, Andrew Cecil Bradley, Benedetto Croce, and John Dewey. New York and London: Oxford University Press, 1919. Gustav Freytag, *The Technique of the Drama,* Introduction. Chicago: Scott, Foresman & Company, 1904. Clayton Hamilton, *"So You're Writing a Play!"* Chapters I and V. Boston: Little, Brown & Company, 1935. Arthur Edwin Krows, *Playwriting for Profit,* Chapter II. New York: Longmans, Green & Co., Inc., 1928. John Howard Lawson, *Theory and Technique of Playwriting,* Introduction. New York: G. P. Putnam's Sons, 1949. Ephraim Gotthold von Lessing, *Hamburgische Dramaturgie,* No. 34 in Barrett H. Clark, *European Theories of the Drama.* New York: Crown Publishers, 1947. Brander Matthews, *Playwrights on Playmaking,* Preface and Chapter I. New York: Charles Scribner's Sons, 1923. Brander Matthews, *A Study of the Drama,* Chapters I, II, and IV. Boston: Houghton Mifflin Company, 1910. W. T. Price, *Analysis of Play Construction,* Chapter I. New York: W. T. Price, Publisher, 1908.

2

What the Playwright Makes: Climax

IT IS USELESS TO STUDY THE TOOLS OF AN ART OR CRAFT unless one has a fairly clear notion of the sort of things these tools can create. A composer does not use arpeggios simply because he happens to like arpeggios; nor does a carpenter use a plane merely to see the curled shavings. A craftsman uses his tools in relation to the object he wants to make.

A carpenter makes a tangible object which can be used to support weight. The work of a painter stands framed, a triumph over space. The poet's words lie in a bound volume to be conned again and again. But the work of the playwright vanishes while it is being created; and the purchaser of a ticket, which costs a little more than a book, is often at a loss to say just what he bought for his money—two hours of anaesthetic, or illumination, or amusement, or ennui.

The playwright himself cannot always say just what he makes. Sometimes he simply tries to reveal a character,[1]

---

[1] Baker, *Dramatic Technique*, pp. 82-88, "the illustrative action."

or to tell a story, or to write beautiful dialogue,[2] or to amuse a particular audience. Sometimes he wants to explore or complete an emotional experience, or to prove a thesis.[3] Sometimes he tries only to make money. All these aims may be accomplished through the drama; yet none epitomizes what the playwright actually makes.

What, then, does the playwright make? What does the audience buy?

Some people purchase the printed play, it is true. But, as a rule, the sale of the book is in proportion to the success of the performance; and the purchasers of the printed play are far fewer than those who buy tickets. Evidently, then, a play does not exist chiefly to be printed, but to be produced.

The theatre audience leaves with no evidence of what it has purchased, save the program, which, perhaps significantly, concerns itself far more with the performance than with the author or the script. Presumably, then, what the audience buys is received and consumed inside the theatre, under the direct stimulation of the scene, the actors, the environing crowd. The individuals in the audience do not buy the production; they buy something which the production does to them, something intangible, but positive— an experience. Painter and lyric poet may deny any intent to communicate through their works; but the playwright who does so denies the very medium in which he professes to work.[4]

---

[2] Matthews, *A Study of the Drama,* p. 251.
[3] Baker, *Dramatic Technique,* p. 43.
[4] This is most forcibly stated by Francisque Sarcey in his "Essai d'une

Yet to say this is to say very little. Obviously the audience-consumer gets a different experience from *Ghosts* than from *Charley's Aunt* or *Peter Pan* or *Cyrano de Bergerac*. If one is to arrive at any principles which will help and not confuse the playwright, one must distinguish common elements in all the diverse experiences of playgoing.

The common elements are not hard to find. Three plays widely different in their forms and in their effects have been chosen as examples.

The first, nearly 2,500 years old, is still one of the funniest comedies in the world, *Lysistrata*. In this play, the protagonist, Lysistrata, hopes to end a long war between Athens and Sparta. She has a plan so simple and so deeply rooted in the fundamental needs of human life that one almost thinks it might be used today. The women simply refuse to yield themselves to their husbands until the men agree to lay down their arms. Lysistrata's plan gains credibility, and Lysistrata herself gains sympathy as she whips her selfish, libidinous, and tricky women into line. When the women take over the Acropolis, one believes that the plan has a sporting chance to succeed. Then the plan is tested. A little girl named Myrrhine has given us some of the heartiest laughs in the play by the ruses she employs

---

Esthétique de Théâtre," translated in Clark, *European Theories of the Drama*. See also William Archer, *Playmaking: A Manual of Craftsmanship*, pp. 3-15. New York: Dodd, Mead & Company, Inc., 1937; Aristotle, *Poetics*, VI, translated by Ingram Bywater, Modern Readers Series. New York: The Macmillan Company, 1930. Baker, *Dramatic Technique*, pp. 16-46; Matthews, *A Study of the Drama*, Chapter XII; Allardyce Nicoll, *The Theory of the Drama*, pp. 119-123. New York: The Thomas Y. Crowell Company, n.d.; and Hamilton, "So You're Writing a Play!" Chapter III.

for seeing her husband. Myrrhine's husband, Cinesias, arrives and attempts to enjoy her. Partly through loyalty to the cause, and partly through feminine coquetry, Myrrhine defers the love-making by insisting on one elaborate luxury after another, until Cinesias is as exhausted with desire as the audience is with laughter. At the end of the scene Myrrhine has won the battle for Lysistrata, and there is nothing to do but dictate the terms of peace to the Laconian envoys, already beaten by nature as badly as Cinesias was. The curtain closes on the pious singing of the women; and the audience rises with a tremendous sense of well-being, as if it had had a glimpse of a better world, in which problems could be settled in some broadly human way, without the bickering and treachery of the world as we know it.

Romeo and Juliet, a play almost 300 years old, is probably the most moving love-tragedy in the English language. Attracted at once to the boy mawking through his first puppy love and to the girl blushing at marriage as "an honor I dream not of," the audience is utterly charmed by the first courtly meeting between them; and when, on her balcony afterward, it is clear that they must love or die, one is deeply moved to wish that they might live. The climax of the "upward movement," as Freytag calls it, is the moment when Juliet hastens to "shrift" to marry her lover. After this, fear follows upon fear. Romeo avoids the duel with Tybalt only to be forced into it by Mercutio's death. He is banished, and even as he desperately steals his marriage night, Juliet's father promises her to Paris. The dreadful potion works, but before Juliet is in the tomb, the Friar's plan miscarries and Romeo's Page falsely informs him that Juliet is dead. Romeo arrives at the tomb in a frenzy of grief to embrace his love and end his own life. He is forced to add another murder to his crimes when he finds Paris at the tomb. Now, whether Juliet awakes in time or not, there is no help for the lovers. Romeo's farewell,

> Eyes, look your last!
> Arms, take your last embrace! And lips, O you
> The doors of breath, seal with a righteous kiss
> A dateless bargain to engrossing death!

is one of the most heartbreaking speeches in all drama. The irony of Juliet's awakening a moment later quickly becomes emotion again as she finds the vial in Romeo's hands and cries,

> O churl! Drink all, and leave no friendly drop
> To help me after?

Her quick decision upon the approach of the watch resolves all anguish in her death. The lovers belong to each other now in the only way that means forever. No further accidents of life can separate them or cause them pain. As the audience begins to recede from its grief, there is a last sharp moment of pity as the fathers of the pair compound their long and meaningless and tragic feud.

It is impossible to describe the effect of a great tragedy to someone who has not experienced it. Anyone who has experienced it recalls the lingering sense of pain like that of a wound which has healed, and the wonderful reaffirmation of the dignity and beauty of human beings.

The last example, *Hedda Gabler,* is a play about fifty years old. Hedda impresses one at first as a vicious woman, because of her rude treatment of kindly Aunt Julie, and because of her general restlessness. But little by little it becomes clear that she suffers the desperate exasperation of a potentially powerful person in an environment which has no use for her powers. Through irritation at Tesman's pedantry and Thea's female littleness, one gains an admiration for Hedda, a sympathy for her terrible barrenness, and for the indignity of her bearing a child to Tesman. Her experiment with Lovborg is cruel, selfish, wrong; but in her place one might be driven to destroy simply because it was impossible to create. When at last Hedda finds that her fate lies in the hands of Brack, the smooth opportunist, the elaborately respectable small-town lawyer; and that even her legitimate small place is filled by a woman small enough to fill it, it seems utterly right that she should reject the whole situation and take her own life. Whatever Ibsen may have meant by "an act of free beauty," [5] the audience leaves the theatre with a broader vision of the right of the human personality to fulfill itself in the society in which it moves.

These are not run-of-the-mill plays. They have been deliberately chosen to give the young playwright a glimpse of the highest experience the theatre can offer. But if they are not commonplace, neither do they exhaust the possible examples. One might have studied *Oedipus Rex,* or *Mac-*

---

[5] In Act IV, Hedda, speaking of Lovborg's suicide, says, "It gives me a sense of freedom to know that a deed of deliberate courage is still possible in the world—a deed of spontaneous beauty."

beth, or *The Vikings of Helgoland,* or *Street Scene,* or *Our Town,* or a dozen others. The three which have been outlined, however, reveal the essence of the great theatre experience and suggest the means by which the experience may be made to occur.

The fundamental feeling of which one is aware upon leaving the theatre after one of these great plays is a deep satisfaction with life. In some manner, cruelty, suffering, and frustration yield to the great positive values. One's own personal problems dwindle in importance, while the personal self assumes the dignity of all humanity.[6] Aristotle calls the experience *katharsis,*[7] and Freytag describes it in transcendental terms.[8] The fact that it occurs indicates a tendency of the human mind to seek wholeness and rightness in the universe, a tendency fostered by religious and philosophical teachings from the most primitive to the most recent times, whether the unity is expressed as "God moves in a mysterious way," or "The electron is the basis

---

[6] August Wilhelm Schlegel, *Lectures on Dramatic Art and Criticism,* p. 69. London: George Bell & Sons, Ltd., 1894. Schlegel writes: "The satisfaction, therefore, which we derive from the representation, in a good tragedy, of powerful situations and overwhelming sorrows, must be ascribed either to the feeling of the dignity of human nature...or to the trace of a higher order of things impressed on the apparently irregular course of events, and mysteriously revealed in them; or perhaps to both of these causes conjointly."

[7] *Poetics,* VI. This is the nearest Aristotle comes to explaining the effect of climax.

[8] In Freytag's words, one experiences a "rebound of vital forces," a "feeling of security," and "the radiance of broader views and more powerful feeling which has come into his soul...like a transfiguration upon his being." Gustav Freytag, *The Technique of the Drama,* p. 88. Chicago: Scott, Foresman & Company, 1904.

of all animate and inanimate existence." It is apparently a function of the mind of man to seek unity in the cosmos, and a function of the artist to provide a glimpse of some sort of unity.[9] The extent to which the playwright can provide the experience depends largely upon his power to conceive it, upon the breadth of his vision and the depth of his sympathy, upon his ability to see in a particular individual the mirror of humanity.

The glimpse of underlying unity and rightness in the cosmos is the essential feature of a dramatic climax. It is present in the three plays just discussed, and to a greater or lesser degree in every play that can be said to achieve a climax. The process by which climax is achieved is also broadly common to all plays that succeed in moving an audience. The audience begins by becoming interested in a character or characters. Interest becomes sympathy, probably at the moment when the character first vigorously expresses some deep need or desire. As the attainment of the desire is withheld, tension on stage increases, while the personal desires of the audience become sublimated or concentrated in the desire of the protagonist for his objective.[10] And the audience identifies itself with the protagonist at least to the extent of wishing with him. Finally,

---

[9] That a world of chaos is not acceptable to theatre audiences is indicated by the scant popularity of the "slice of life" drama and the rapid passing of *expressionism* and *constructivism* as such, soon after the novelty of their presentation wore off. See Schlegel, *Lectures on Dramatic Art and Criticism*, pp. 243-44.

[10] This is *empathy*, a motor response. See Herbert Sidney Langfeld, *The Aesthetic Attitude*, Chapter VI. New York: Harcourt, Brace & Company, Inc., 1920; and John Dolman, *The Art of Play Production*, Chapter II. New York: Harper & Brothers, 1928.

as the protagonist either gains or fails to gain his objective, the deep satisfaction of climax occurs.

The process implies that the basis of rapport between audience and protagonist is desire.[11] If individual desire differentiates one man from another, it also enables men to understand, love, and pity each other. Or, as Hegel puts it, desire is the universal element in a play, the element of common humanity to which the audience responds. The intensity of the response seems to depend largely upon the force of the desire, and to some extent upon the propriety of the object desired. Again, it is evident that the ability of the playwright to conceive strong passion, deep desire, determines how powerfully he can create the empathies which end in climax.

So far it has been maintained that the playwright's goal is an audience experience, climax; that the process by which the experience is achieved can be described in very general terms; that in some way the experience of climax involves a perception of universal humanity; and that desire plays a basic role in effecting the experience.

A further examination of the role of desire in creating climax leads us to Hegel's difficult and frequently neglected but highly rewarding *The Philosophy of Fine Art,* and to a definition of dramatic action. Although there is no space in a brief text on playwriting to outline the history of dramatic criticism,[12] a rather careful glance at this great

---

[11] Matthews, *A Study of the Drama,* p. 94.

[12] Every student of playwriting should be familiar with Clark, *European Theories of the Drama;* Brander Matthews, *The Development of the Drama.* New York: Charles Scribner's Sons, 1904; John Howard

work will afford insight into the problem of what actually constitutes a dramatic action, and how a dramatic action results in climax.

To Hegel, the whole universe is dramatic; that is, capable of sudden, violent, and often fatal change. The root of the dramatic is the complexity and instability of every phenomenon. A simple illustration is the eightpenny nail, a finite object possessing the characteristics of shape, size, color, weight, hardness, smoothness, temperature, sharpness. The nail also embodies certain essential interconnections between these properties. If the temperature is much altered, the nail melts or becomes brittle. A variation in size —length or thickness—alters the weight. Sharpness depends on shape and hardness. If oxidation changes the color, both hardness and smoothness are affected. Nor do these internal relationships complete the description of the nail. The eightpenny nail also has certain external connections in time and space. It came as ore from a certain place. It was fashioned by men. Other men fashioned the machines that were used to fashion the nail. It was sold by a retailer. It will be used in a barn or a home or a factory. Thus the nail exists not merely as the sum of its characteristics, but as a system of relationships. The phenomenon "nail" is only the sensuous embodiment of a complex abstract unity.

Man, like the simpler phenomena, is also a complex entity exhibiting certain properties and relationships. Like the nail, an individual man is the sensuous embodiment of

Lawson, *Theory and Technique of Playwriting,* Parts I and II. New York: G. P. Putnam's Sons, 1949.

universal mankind. This concept has a double implication for the playwright. It implies that what the theatre audience responds to in the character on stage is the human being, the abstract man, the man like oneself and like all men. It also implies that the only way of evoking this abstraction is through the sensuous properties of an individual.

To Hegel, each object in its perfect balance of relationships is beautiful. But this harmonious beauty is fraught with possibilities of destruction by its very complexity. Each element in the entity is continually striving to assert itself above the other elements, and the entity as a whole wishes to assert itself above other entities in the cosmos. One may object to attributing will to inanimate objects like the nail, but one can readily see the application of Hegel's theory to the extreme complexity of the internal and external relationships of man. One may find it difficult to recognize an act of will in the sharpness of the nail driving into wood, but it is easy to see that some element of will is involved when a man with indigestion behaves rudely to his wife. In the sphere of human relationships, which Hegel regards as the sole province of art, it is evident that with a failure of a portion of the system, the whole human being is somehow changed, and his relationships with the world outside himself also change.

For Hegel, then, the source of beauty is a harmonious balance between the various properties and relationships of man.

Fundamentally, man is striving to assert and to extend his finite ego through infinity. In so striving, he collides with other entities or forces of the world outside himself. The collision may be within physical nature—a small man trying to dominate taller ones, a cripple trying to compete with normal men; it may be in the conditions of human life—a racketeer trying to suborn an honest senator, an *émigré* trying to live in a strange environment, a chauffeur trying to win the love of an heiress; or it may be in the violation of some intrinsically right and just human relationship—an impoverished father murdering his family, a self-centered mother monopolizing her grown sons' affections, the seduction of a friend's wife. In any case, the collision of one individual with the universal breaks up the initial harmony, and a vigorous emotional reaction is set up. Two distinct spheres of interest, torn from their original harmony, confront each other in conflict, and the reestablishment of harmony becomes a prime necessity, as much for the onlooker as for the opposing forces.

One or both forces now engage in some sort of action toward restoring the harmony. This action may be of any kind. It may be merely physical—Othello threatens Iago and strangles Desdemona to regain his self-esteem; Macbeth murders Duncan to gain the throne; Ellen of *Ladies in Retirement* murders her hostess in order to get a home for herself and her sisters in their old age. The action may be social—Billie Dawn of *Born Yesterday* uses her new education to defeat the racketeering junk dealer who keeps her; Mary Tilford of *The Children's Hour* uses the gossip of her school chums and her grandmother's influence to destroy a schoolteacher she dislikes. It may be a spiritual action—George of *Of Mice and Men* uses the promise of a home to keep his feeble-minded friend Lennie in line; Mr. Manningham of *Angel Street* drives his wife insane in order to search for the jewels without interference. Whatever the nature of the action, if it is occasioned by a breach in the balance of relationships of a human being, and is directed toward repairing the breach and restoring the balance, it is a true dramatic action.[13]

The re-establishment of harmony may be brought about by the suppression of the individual or by his asserting himself as the true expression of the universal. The former is the common ending of a tragedy, the latter of a comedy.[14]

---

[13] Georg Wilhelm Friedrich Hegel, *The Philosophy of Fine Art*, Vol. I, p. 288. London: George Bell & Sons, Ltd., 1920. Summarizing his point of view, Hegel says: "Glancing now at the main position we have arrived at... we have found that circumstances, conditions, and relations... create the situation by virtue of the *temperament* or passion which experiences them.... We have further seen that the situation breaks up this determinate form in opposition, obstruction, development, and disruption, so that the emotional life feels itself compelled ...to react *with energy* against this disturbing and restraining influence, which stands in the way of its objects and passions. It is here... that the action, strictly speaking, commences, when, that is to say, the contradiction has fully asserted itself, which was already implied in the fully determined situation. Inasmuch as, however, the action which is based on the collision disturbs the unity of that which was opposed to it, it calls into being by its antagonism the opposing force of that which it confronts, and consequently the action is immediately confronted with *reaction*... We are here presented with two distinct spheres of interest, both of which have been rent, as it were, from the harmony they originally possessed, and confront each other in conflict. Such by the contradiction which is involved in them, make a *resolution* of the discord necessary. This movement, regarded as a homogeneous whole, belongs no more to the province of the mere situation, and its conflicts; we are carried now into that portion of our inquiry to which we have already given the name of the genuine action."

[14] This statement is modified in Chapter VII of this text.

Romeo and Juliet had to die because certain external circumstances did not permit the assertion of their love; yet by their death they asserted the wrongness of these circumstances and the eternal value of love. Lysistrata established harmony by asserting her individual will in accordance with a universal need. Hedda revealed that no harmony could exist between herself and her environment, and that therefore her individuality had to be submerged. In any case, the final harmony is more durable than before, because the threatening element has been either assimilated or suppressed by the universal.[15]

Three generalizations emerge from this discussion of what the playwright makes. First, the common denominator, the universal factor which moves audiences, is not thought, not unpurposive activity, not the mere writhing of passion, but will, the effort of an individual to assert his

---

[15] John Howard Lawson, a Hegelian in philosophy, emphasizes the point that as man and his environment are socially conditioned, so the inseparable form-content of a play is socially conditioned. Perhaps it is this fact which makes the mid-twentieth century concern itself with the desires of middle-class individuals rather than with the great actions of an Oedipus or an Eisenhower; and which accounts for the extremely diverse and unconventional forms to be found on the contemporary stage. We see with the microscope what the Greeks saw with the healthy but naked eye. We make much of *minutiae*, where the Greeks saw larger relationships only. We see the wrinkle at the corner of the mouth, where the Greeks saw the mass and angle of the whole head. It seems probable that the late-twentieth century will see in much larger terms, because of the broad concepts being forced upon us by science and economics; and that the individual will receive sympathy only as he broadly expresses universals. Whatever attitude the playwright takes, he will have to shape his plays to express the life and mind which he is trying to set forth, in terms that will be comprehensible to the generation he addresses. See Lawson, *Theory and Technique of Playwriting*, Part I.

individuality and to find his own harmonious place in his milieu through such an assertion. Second, the action by which he tries to do this is a dramatic action. Third, the playwright's end product, a dramatic climax, is an intense experience of satisfaction for the audience in the final establishment on stage of a harmony broken or threatened during the play. These two elements exist in every dramatic climax—harmony of an abiding nature on the stage, and intense satisfaction in the audience.

Climax is not the sole pleasure of playgoing. Of course one enjoys wit, beauty of language, the mere spectacle, the recognition of the human being in the actor on stage, the momentary thrill of suspense or release of tension in laughter. One frequently enjoys simply the anaesthetic effect of a play. But surely the most intense pleasure to be gained from the theatre, the pleasure which keeps classics perennially on the stage, is the delighted perception of universal order and unity revealed in the fate of one small set of individuals at the climax of the play.

With this goal in mind, and some knowledge of the process by which the goal is achieved, one may now proceed to an examination of the practices which playwrights have devised, the techniques, the tools, for transmuting the raw material of human life into the moving theatre experience, climax.

ASSIGNMENTS

PLAYS: Maxwell Anderson, *Elizabeth the Queen*. New York: Longmans, Green & Co., Inc., 1928. John Van Druten, *The Voice of the Turtle*. New York: Random House, 1944. Tennessee Williams, *The Glass Menagerie*. New York: Dramatists Play Service, 1945.

ADDITIONAL READING: William Archer, *Playmaking: A Manual of Craftsmanship*, Chapters I and XV. New York: Dodd, Mead & Company, Inc., 1937. Aristotle, *Poetics*, VI-XV, translated by Ingram Bywater, Modern Readers Series. New York: The Macmillan Company, 1930. George Pierce Baker, *Dramatic Technique*, Chapter II. Boston: Houghton Mifflin Company, 1910. John Dolman, *The Art of Play Production*, Chapter II. New York: Harper & Brothers, 1928. Gustav Freytag, *The Technique of the Drama*, pp. 84-103. Chicago: Scott, Foresman & Company, 1904. Georg Wilhelm Friedrich Hegel, *The Philosophy of Fine Art*, Vol. I, pp. 209-288. London: George Bell & Sons, Ltd., 1920. Herbert Sidney Langfeld, *The Aesthetic Attitude*, Chapters V and VI. New York: Harcourt, Brace & Company, Inc., 1920. John Howard Lawson, *Theory and Technique of Playwriting*, Parts I and III. New York: G. P. Putnam's Sons, 1949. Brander Matthews, *A Study of the Drama*, Chapters VII and XII. Boston: Houghton Mifflin Company, 1910. Francisque Sarcey, "Essai d'une Esthétique de Théâtre," from Barrett H. Clark, *European Theories of the Drama*. New York: Crown Publishers, 1947.

3

The Playwright's Background

BEFORE WE DESCRIBE THE SPECIFIC TOOLS WITH WHICH A playwright fashions his materials, it must be recalled that the playwright in common with other artists has the double task of understanding his material so that his own response to it is clear and valid, and of translating this material and response into an audience response. As an artist it is not his function to be dominated like a vaudeville clown by what the audience wants; he must control the audience, leading it to want what he wants to give.

A book about the devices used to construct plays cannot be expected to deal with all the means by which the playwright learns about his complex stimulus, human life; nor can it deal exhaustively with a great number of psychological techniques for probing the playwright's attitudes; and it will make only a few general assumptions about the mind of the audience. Yet a little may be said here of these matters, for they are a basic part of the playwright's resources.

The stimulus of the playwright is human life, so complex even in its mere physiological organization that scientists cannot agree on the relative effect of heredity and environment in shaping character; so subtle in its psychological aspects that a recurring fragment of an old experience may alter the total overt behavior pattern of an individual; so precarious in its social ramifications that a kind old lady in New York may die of pneumonia because of a coal strike in Tennessee.

The initial stimulus for writing a play may be any aspect of human experience;[1] but, in the light of the foregoing chapters, the essence of the stimulus is the desire of an individual to bring some perverse element of his life into harmony with the whole. Analysis of a few of the stimuli which have moved playwrights to write plays makes this point clear.

One playwright is moved to write about a character he knows, as Tennessee Williams was in composing *The Glass Menagerie*, a play about himself and certain members of his family. The underlying desire here is, of course, the mother's wish to bring back "the good old days" for her children.

Another is moved to dramatize the life of a historical character,[2] as was Maxwell Anderson in writing *Elizabeth the Queen*. Here the essence of the play is very clearly

---

[1] For a good discussion of the initial stimuli of plays, see Baker, *Dramatic Technique*, Chapter VII.

[2] This is a particularly difficult assignment, and one that should rarely be attempted by an inexperienced playwright. The many plays written about Abraham Lincoln and never produced illustrate this point.

Elizabeth's desire to retain her lover without giving up the prerogatives of a monarch.

Van Druten, in writing *The Voice of The Turtle*, seems to have been moved by a situation: a young actress gives a night's lodging to a stranded soldier and has an *affaire* with him. Beneath this situation Van Druten discovered the desire of both the soldier and the girl for matrimonial security.

Sometimes a play begins with an idea, and it is difficult for the playwright to find the desire which transforms an intellectual conviction into emotional, theatrical terms. One example of such a play is *State of the Union*. The authors began, no doubt, with the conviction that one cannot touch pitch without being defiled. Grant Matthews, the protagonist, wants to gain political office and still retain his integrity. The underlying desires, mutually incompatible, are concretized in his mistress on the side of politics and his wife on the side of conscience.

As a last example, Sheridan's *The School for Scandal* may well have begun with a scene, the famous screen scene; but underlying the play is the desire of honest old Sir Peter for the affection of his frivolous young wife.

All these examples show that whatever the initial stimulus may have been, when it was fully probed by the playwright, it revealed a core of desire, of maladjustment, of disturbed harmony that must be resolved. To discover the precise desire, the precise maladjustment inherent in a given stimulus requires thought, imagination, patience, exhaustive knowledge of the true nature of the stimulus in its environment of space and time.

Above all, a play is a report on life. An inaccurate report is either unethical or ridiculous. With this in mind, the playwright's background cannot be simply the theatre and its allied arts. The sources of the playwright's knowledge of his stimulus are manifold: his own life and the lives of his friends, the techniques and conclusions of psychology, the resources of history, the daily news, the habit of probing motives and cataloguing responses of human beings, living a great many places, and doing a great variety of jobs. One playwright gets this information in college, another in the public library, another on the water-front of New York, New Orleans, or San Francisco. There is no "must" about how an artist learns his world, no time at which he can say, "Now I know enough." Boundless curiosity and inexhaustible patience are the best aids of the playwright in the pursuit of knowledge of his stimulus. Finally, insofar as most of the tools described in subsequent chapters force the playwright to probe and thus amplify his knowledge of the material, these tools, too, help him to understand the whole of a particular experience.

But it has been said that a work of art is not a mere duplication of experience. What characterizes a work of art is the artist's particular attitude toward the world and especially toward the material on which he is working. He dares not be indifferent; for a play has as its aim the emotional satisfaction of the audience. Unless the play expresses emotion, it can hardly be expected to excite an audience.

Moreover, the artist must not only become excited about his material; he must perceive some relationships between the material and the common needs of humanity. He must assert some life values through it, whatever life values he holds. This is not to say that he must have an unalterable set of values; but he must be clear and honest as to what he approves or dislikes in humanity at the moment of writing.

The artist's responses, like those of any other individual, are conditioned by his particular biological organization, his innate spiritual qualities (intellectual capacity and emotional habits), and the environments to which he has been subjected. These factors largely determine his artistic purposes and accomplishments. It is because of his fundamental nature that he will see a beautiful woman, for example, as material for a poster or for a ribald joke, or as a symbol of bliss or terror or frivolity. It is because of his fundamental nature that life and its relationships seem to him comic or terrible or pathetic.

Freytag writes,

> Therefore, in answer to the question, how the poet must compose his action...the advice, meant in all seriousness, is given that he need trouble himself very little about it. He must develop in himself a capable and worthy manhood, then go with a glad heart to a subject which offers strong characters in great conflict...What is, in truth, dramatic will have an earnest tragic effect in a strongly moving action if it was a *man* who wrote it; if not, then assuredly not. The poet's own character determines the highest effects in an elevated drama more than in any other species of art.[3]

This is not to say that any teacher should set himself up as a critic of the young artist's soul. Undoubtedly only a Shakespeare could produce a *Lear*; but Van Druten's deli-

---

[3] Freytag, *The Technique of the Drama*, p. 85. See also Hamilton, *"So You're Writing a Play!"*, pp. 23-24.

cate talent has value too. Nor should one infer from Freytag's grandiose statement that an untested talent is forever limited. As the young artist gains understanding of the many-faceted world, often his sympathies and antipathies deepen. He gains power to react more forcibly to stimuli as he becomes aware of more stimuli and more meanings of stimuli. Occasionally a deeply moving experience will alter even his very modes of thinking and reacting.

The teacher must not lose sight of the fluid state of the young artist's nature. As confidant, then, rather than as mentor, he may be able to help the young artist discover just what, at a particular moment of his soul's growth, a given stimulus means to him; and he may be able to reinforce the artist's conviction that this moment's meaning is important.

One of the grave dangers of teaching artists is that this fundamental relationship is forgotten by both teacher and student. The teacher receives an impression of some sort from the imperfectly expressed work of the beginner, and honestly tries to determine what would improve it. The student, eager to improve, and embarrassed by his own inadequacy at expressing sometimes very subtle and complex experiences, allows his original intent to become biased by the all too clearly expressed suggestion of his teacher. The result is frustration. The student finds himself striving to utilize perhaps irrelevant suggestions, getting farther and farther away from his original purpose, losing interest in the task, and, worst of all, losing confidence in himself. The first requisite of a productive relationship between the artist and his teacher is that both must insist upon the work expressing the *artist's* intent. Any so-called technique which does not proceed from absolute clarity on this point is false and destructive.

Knowledge of the stimulus, then, and knowledge of his own intentions with regard to it are the inalienable property of the artist and must form the inviolable core of the play. The amount and quality of these two kinds of knowledge determine whether the writer is a genius or a hack, what he will write about, and to what extent he is potentially able to construct a great dramatic character-situation. There are no short cuts to this knowledge. The playwright must acquire it in his own way and in his own time. The most that a teacher can do is to give him a few tools for understanding and sharing his experiences, and to insist that he be true to his own best abilities.

When the playwright has full knowledge of the material which impels him to write and understands his own feelings and thoughts about it, the aesthetic experience is complete. But the task of externalizing, of communicating, of making a work of art from a raw experience of beauty, has yet to be done.

Before even beginning to shape the materials, the artist must put himself into the mind of the persons who will view his finished work. How much information do they already have that will help them to understand and empathize in the characters? How quickly can they learn and how can they be made to retain the story and its background? What life values do they hold that will color their responses for or against what the playwright means to say? How different is the spirit of the audience from that of the playwright himself? What has the audience in common with the playwright? How can the playwright make the audience respond as he wishes it to respond?

For the playwright should remember that it is he who wants to make a communication, and that he must make it in easily comprehensible terms. The playwright who refuses to consider his audience is like the priest of Cortez who preached to the Indians in Spanish and even baptised them, only to realize with pain and horror that they still sprinkled the heart's blood of captives on their ancestral pyramids. He is like an Afghan coming to New York with a message and insisting that New York learn his native language in order to hear the message. Nothing can be accomplished without learning the language of the people with whom one wants to communicate.

The playwright's sources of information about the audience are manifold. First, of course, he has his own direct experience as part of theatre audiences, by which he may to some extent gauge and interpret the responses of other members of those audiences. His acquaintance with a wide variety of individuals also helps him to know the sort of people he will address, although individuals behave differently from crowds.[4] Most helpful is the habit of observing mass behavior at plays, concerts, rallies—in fact, everywhere a crowd gathers. It is especially important for the young playwright to form the habit of listening to the audience at his own plays. In this way he will catch a thousand signals—shifting position, smoothing hair, whis-

---

[4] William McDougall, *The Group Mind*, pp. 31-40. New York: G. P. Putnam's Sons, 1920.

pering, the volume and kind of laughter—that will indicate the response to a play more accurately than will the multitude of verbal congratulations that pour in after the performance.

These direct sources of information about audience response serve to test information which the playwright may gather from indirect sources. Three of these indirect sources deserve special mention: works on public speaking,[5] psychological experiments on mass behavior,[6] and the statistical research that is being done by advertising firms to discover and classify the likes and dislikes of the consumer.[7] A few of these works are listed in the bibliography at the end of the chapter, and should be read thoughtfully by any artist who wants to make his living through the favor of the public.

The radio advertisers have a wise adage which the playwright would do well to remember: "It is not the taste of the angler that determines the bait to be used, but the taste

[5] For example, William Phillips Sandford and Willard Hays Yeager, *Principles of Effective Speaking*, Chapters III and XV. New York: Thomas Nelson & Sons, 1934; Lew Sarett and William Trufant Foster, *Basic Principles of Speech*, Chapters VI, XII, and XVIII. Boston: Houghton Mifflin Company, 1936; and A. Craig Baird, *Public Discussion and Debate*, Chapter XII. Boston: Ginn & Company, 1937.

[6] Daniel Starch, Hazel M. Stanton, and Wilhelmine Koerth, *Controlling Human Behavior*, Chapters II, XI, XXIII, and XXIV. New York: The Macmillan Company, 1936; McDougall, *The Group Mind*, Chapters II and IV; H. L. Hollingworth, *The Psychology of the Audience*, Chapter VIII (very valuable). New York: American Book Company, 1935; Merl E. Bonney, *Techniques of Appeal and Social Control*, Chapter I. Menasha, Wisconsin: George Banta Publishing Company, 1934.

[7] Poffenberger, *Psychology in Advertising*, Chapters I-V; Daniel Starch, *Principles of Advertising*, Chapters XII, XIII, and XVII, New York: A. W. Shaw Company, 1925.

of the fish." This does not mean that the playwright should compromise in what he has to say. The material and the playwright's feelings about it must be kept inviolate. But like the fisherman, the playwright must find the bait that will make the audience swallow the barbed hook of his creation. The more wary the fish, the more carefully must the bait be chosen.

Knowledge of the outside world, of his own soul, and of the audience must come to the playwright as opportunity presents itself. Meanwhile he may go into the theatre to study his two basic instruments, the stage and the actors who will body forth his written symbols.

Most young playwrights resist studying scenery and working on stage crews. But at least a superficial knowledge of the stage is indispensable to one who writes for the theatre. Through such knowledge he becomes aware of the power of visual stimuli in gaining attention, conveying exposition, and creating illusion. A study of the stage reconciles him as nothing else can do to the fact that a play is the work of a group rather than of the dramatist alone. A knowledge of the stage also helps the playwright to retain his morale in the apprentice days when he is peddling script, for he understands that part of the difficulty of selling plays is the enormous cost of the production in money and man power. Above all, to know the resources of the stage enables him to grasp with confidence an idea that he might otherwise reject as too difficult of execution, and to eliminate highly complex requirements that are not really essential for expressing his idea.

Often a young playwright is surprised by the way his

lines sound from the mouths of actors. Sometimes he is surprised to discover that a character is different from what he appeared in the moment of writing, and cannot be played as the playwright expected, even though the playwright himself selected the cast. The inexperienced playwright blames the actor; the experienced writer knows that the fault is in the play. He tries to write *for* the actor. He creates his effects not by words alone, but by pauses and pantomime, the living voice of the actor, and the actor's body moving in space.

One of the best ways to learn the value of the actor is to act or direct a good bit while learning to write. Especially valuable to the young playwright is directing the imperfect plays of other young writers. But even if opportunities to act and direct do not occur, the young playwright should attend many rehearsals of all sorts of plays and all rehearsals of his own plays.

The purpose of this introduction has been to place the study of plot construction in its proper relationship to the other factors that go to make a play—the world of stimuli, the reacting soul of the artist, the revealing medium, and the responding audience. Now without seeming to overemphasize the importance of technique, yet with an appreciation of the function of craftsmanship, it is possible to begin a study of those devices belonging specifically to the playwright.[8]

---

[8] Clayton Hamilton quotes Robert Louis Stevenson: "Get to see the world entirely through technical spectacles, to see it in terms of what you can do. Then, when you have anything to say, the language will be apt and copious." *"So You're Writing a Play!"*, p. 26.

What follows is a complex of basic tools, in the use of which a good many specific skills can be developed. About three-fourths of these skills are evident in some combination or other in every successful[9] play. The apprentice playwright should practice the use of these tools as the young pianist does his scales. He should master them *as tools,* as devices to use in solving problems, not as rules which he must follow. These tools do not substitute for the qualities of the artist; but to master them may save the artist time, energy, and the heartbreaking frustration of working by the trial-and-error method.

ASSIGNMENTS

PLAYS: Maxwell Anderson, *Winterset.* Washington, D. C.: Anderson House, 1936. Elmer Rice, *Street Scene.* New York: Samuel French, Inc., 1929. Lynn Riggs, *The Cherokee Night,* from *Russet Mantle and the Cherokee Night.* New York: Samuel French, Inc., 1936.

ADDITIONAL READING: George Pierce Baker, *Dramatic Technique,* Chapter VII. Boston: Houghton Mifflin Company, 1919. Henrik Ibsen, *From Ibsen's Workshop, Collected Works,* Vol. XII, ed. William Archer. New York: Charles Scribner's Sons, 1908-1927. Albert T. Poffenberger, *Psychology in Advertising,* Chapters I-V. New York: McGraw-Hill Book Company, Inc., 1932. William Phillips Sandford and Willard Hays Yeager, *Principles of Effective Speaking,* Chapters III and XV. New York: Thomas Nel-

---

[9] See above, p. 4.

son & Sons, 1934. Lew Sarett and William Trufant Foster, *Basic Principles of Speech,* Chapters VI, XII, and XVIII. Boston: Houghton Mifflin Company, 1919. Starch, Stanton, and Koerth, *Controlling Human Behavior,* Chapters II, XI, XXIII, and XXIV. New York: The Macmillan Company, 1936. Starch, Daniel, *Principles of Advertising,* Chapters XII, XIII, and XVII. New York: A. W. Shaw Company, 1925.

PART ONE: CLARITY

HEGEL DECLARES, "... a poet creates for the sake of a public, and primarily for his own nation and his time, both of which should be able to enter into such a work of art with intelligence, and feel at home."[1] And again, "Works of art are not composed primarily for the mere student or the professor, but with the express purpose that they shall be intelligible on their face, and a source of enjoyment without anyone having to undertake first a circuitous route of extensive historical investigation. For art is not addressed to a small and select circle of the privileged few, but to the nation at large."[2]

It has been shown that the first step toward the playwright's goal of climax, the satisfaction of the audience, is to evoke a feeling of sympathy for some character or characters. But ordinarily the basis of sympathy is understanding. A person is thought a fool if he does things which other people do not understand. Examples abound on every side of antagonism and scorn not only toward eccentric persons, but even toward average people who

---

[1] Hegel, *The Philosophy of Fine Art*, Vol. I, p. 357.
[2] *Ibid.*, p. 369.

assert tastes in conflict with those of their associates. A person who dislikes movies or enjoys long walks or prefers conversation to bridge is looked upon with mild resentment or patronizing indulgence by his acquaintances. The real friends of such a person are the people who understand him. It seems unlikely, then, that a play could arouse much sympathy, and far less that it could evoke empathy, unless the audience understands the characters and their actions and relationships. A wise playwright will see to it that his play is clear.

Just as a musical composition has a basic rhythm and motif, just as a painting has a basic design, or a fine building a skeleton of joists and beams, a fine play has a strong and definite central structure or design or skeleton. Usually the skeletal structure of a play is fairly simple. It rests upon five bases, each of which is as integral to the play as the joists of a building are to its form and strength. There is a desiring individual or group of individuals, the protagonist of the play; there is the object desired; there is a factor which makes the objective difficult to obtain; there is a definite ending to the story; and there is a clear and logical course of action leading to this ending.

This basic structure is present in the three plays which have been shown to have powerful climaxes. Lysistrata wants to end the war between Athens and Sparta; she is hindered from doing so by the weakness of her women and by the laws of the state which place government in the hands of the men; she wins her objective by the simple expedient of restraining the men from their wives until peace has been made. In *Romeo and Juliet* the scheme is slightly more complex. Romeo and Juliet wish to remain together forever; they are held apart by a feud between their families; they attempt two plans, but are defeated by circumstance, and win their objective only in death. Hedda Gabler wants to assert her dominating personality; she is thwarted by the littleness of the society in which she lives; she fails in an experiment with Lovborg, which places her in the power of the law, in the person of Judge Brack; finding her situation intolerable, she kills herself.

The basic skeleton is disguised in many ways, but whether the play is in one act or ten scenes, whether it is realism, or expressionism, or fantasy, whether it is tragedy or comedy, a slight amount of probing will reveal this particular skeleton in all successful plays.

Five questions must be asked and definitely answered by the playwright before he can begin to construct a scenario: Whom is the play about? What does he need to make his life harmonious? What impedes his getting it? Does he get it? How does he succeed or fail? Without answers to these questions, no amount of fine dialogue or clever situations or tender characterization will give the glimpse of unity which is fundamental to the experience of climax.

4

The Protagonist

IT HAS BEEN SHOWN THAT THE SYMPATHY OF THE AU-
dience is aroused, sustained and transformed to empathy
by some individual or group of individuals whose affairs
may be said to provide a focus for the play. This individual
or group is the protagonist, an indispensable element of the
basic structure of the play. Whether the protagonist is to
be one individual or a group, a great hero or a common
man, depends on the playwright's interests and upon his
attitude toward life. In any case, the audience must know
clearly whom the play is about.

There are, of course, many differences between Oedipus
devoting himself to purging the evils of his city and Joe
Bonaparte of *Golden Boy* craving to "be somebody." But
these differences are more significant to the student of theatre history than to the playwright. It is more interesting
to the playwright to realize that the great heroes of clas-
sical and Shakespearean tragedy have characteristics in
common with the proletarian fighter of *Golden Boy*. Probably these characteristics—credibility, attractiveness, voli-

tion,[1] and integration—are the ones which make them good foci of dramatic plots.

A good protagonist is, of course, always lifelike. He seems to have been produced by a certain environment, he reacts credibly to his experiences and to other characters, and he seems to function by the laws of cause and effect. In a good play it is always possible to find the answers to the questions, "How?" and "Why?" in regard to his actions.

One of the easiest means of gaining credibility is the careful building up of the environment of the characters. Moe and Hennie of *Awake and Sing* seem to be real people largely because they are surrounded by a tremendous mass of authentic environmental detail—the family, the flat with its ugly furniture, the modes of speech, the janitor and the little dog, and the jobs which take the various members of the family into the surrounding city. So solidly credible is this play that one is actually taken in by the quite illogical optimism of Ralph at the end of the play. Even *Our Town*, which does not require a realistic setting, makes use of environmental detail for credibility. The vital statistics of Grover's Corners elicited by the Stage-Manager, the drugstore, the schoolbooks, the alcholic organist, the pantomimed shelling of beans, all serve to deepen the audience's feeling that it knows George and Emily as it knows its next-door neighbors.

[1] "Volition" is synonymous with "desire," a goal-oriented conscious experience in which the individual is energized to initiate, sustain, or change behavior. See Paul Thomas Young, *Emotion in Man and Animal*, pp. 87-88. New York: John Wiley & Sons, Inc.; London: Chapman & Hall, Ltd., 1943.

More difficult, but even more important in building credible characters is care in making the relationships between characters true and consistent. We believe in George and Emily not only because we recognize Grover's Corners and its inhabitants, but also because of the quiet evening talk between Dr. and Mrs. Gibbs after choir practice, the homely breakfasts, the parental concern for the children, George's talk with his father-in-law on the wedding morning, and many other touches which have nothing to do with the progress of the story, but add immeasurably to the livingness of the two main characters through their relationships.

Even a quite inexperienced playwright usually tries to utilize the laws of cause and effect in planning the actions of his characters. But the two devices just mentioned, the use of environmental detail and the careful use of relationships, provide emotional bases of belief, and are therefore among the playwright's best devices for making his characters credible.

Examples of incredible protagonists are not hard to find among the plays of students, even though the student may be destined to become a master of his art. An early play of Maxwell Anderson, *White Desert*, is based on jealousy between husband and wife. Michael takes Mary to a remote place immediately after marrying her. There are few environmental details beyond the fact that the cabin is isolated and snowbound in winter. Their only neighbors come to play bridge of a winter evening, and Sverre, the neighbor, neglects his own wife to banter with Mary. Afterwards, Michael, having possessed Mary before marriage, is tor-

tured with the thought that she might some day be unfaithful with Sverre. Mary declares that she has given
herself to no man except Michael, but admits having had
impure thoughts both before and since marriage. Upon
this admission, Michael becomes as morbidly jealous as Ben
Jonson's comic Kitely. From this point on cause and effect seem to be out of proportion. Mary reveals a need for
independence as sudden and extreme as Michael's jealousy.
As a means of asserting her independence, she seduces
Sverre at the first opportunity. Later she is afflicted with
pangs of conscience and confesses. Michael agrees to forget, but neither he nor Mary is able to forget, and Mary
decides to leave. Michael shoots her as she crosses the yard,
and accepts the consolation of Sverre and Sverre's wife.

There is nothing essentially impossible about the story of
White Desert. Yet the play suffers from lack of environmental detail, paucity of relationships through which to
reveal the characters, and apparent disproportion between
motive and action, or between cause and effect.

Another frequent cause of the protagonist's seeming incredible in the plays of beginners is that the young writer
seeks the eccentric rather than the familiar, the emotionally unstable rather than the normal. Young writers are
often preoccupied with sex aberrations, religious emotion-
alism, romantic criminals, intensely individualistic characters. One of Maxwell Anderson's first plays, *Sea-Wife*, is
about a woman with delusions from puerperal fever. Another, *Outside Looking In*, is about a young murderess who
has decided to go straight. One might also name a string of
plays by young men not yet known—about a Renaissance

priest who tries to work miracles, about a young man with a leaning toward homosexuality, about a woman who walked the streets in order to buy dope for her malingering old mother, about a bawd who yearns for the consolations of religion.

As a matter of fact, there are some great plays about psychopathic characters. Hamlet, Electra, Mio, and Faust all have their unhealthy aspects. But it is hardly necessary to point out that in each of these cases the playwright had the skill not only to make the protagonist credible and sympathetic, but actually to infuse him with deeply universal qualities. On the whole, however, the seriously unstable protagonist appears less frequently in the work of the mature writer than in the plays of younger ones.[2]

The young playwright sometimes rejects one of his most practical aids to credibility, the comments and questions of director and cast in rehearsal. He becomes offended or feels that the performers are not making enough effort when they fail to understand his characters. After a verbal explanation, he expects the actor to supply the omissions of the script. The professional writer, however, knows that questions and misunderstandings would not arise if the script were clear. For every "How?" and "Why?" which he explains verbally, there must be a clear answer in the script. Unless the answer is there, the actor's art may prove inadequate to make the half-written character convincing, and the play will fail to move the audience.

---

[2] Baker, *Dramatic Technique*, pp. 64-67; Barrett H. Clark, *A Study of the Modern Drama*, p. 130. New York: D. Appleton-Century Company, Inc., 1938; Freytag, *The Technique of the Drama*, pp. 49-61.

The young playwright has, then, three devices by which he may add to the credibility of his protagonist: making the environment clear and credible; providing the protagonist with clear, consistent relationships with other characters; and seeing that cause and effect are proportionate in the protagonist's actions and reactions. He has a further device at the rehearsal stage, the questions and comments of the performers. Finally, if he must treat of psychoneurotic or eccentric characters, he must be particularly careful to make these characters credible.

The term *protagonist* means one with whom the audience suffers. To suffer with a person, one must be able to care what happens to him; that is, one must find him attractive in some way.[3]

The simplest way of getting a favorable first response is, of course, to make the character physically attractive. This was Ibsen's way in *Hedda Gabler*, and it is the Hollywood way; it must be said that it often works. Mere physical beauty, however, is usually not enough to keep an audience interested in a character throughout a serious

---

[3] Barrett H. Clark writes: "If we do not care what happens to the characters, then the play fails." *A Study of the Modern Drama*, p. 104. See also Freytag, *The Technique of the Drama*, pp. 64-66, 308-311. The evil protagonist, such as Mrs. Phelps of *The Silver Cord*, Regina Giddens of *The Little Foxes*, and Creon, the protagonist in the last half of *Antigone*, usually has some redeeming quality. Mrs. Phelps has an appealing manner and a strongly maternal spirit that attract one until one realizes that she is selfish and possessive in her love. Regina Giddens had the beautiful body of Tallulah Bankhead, and she had also the streak of self-interest that probably every human being would find at the core of his nature if he probed honestly. Creon had his conscience as guardian of the city, his affection for his son, and the bitter disappointment over his son's death.

play. Nor is physical beauty always necessary. It may even be used to create antipathy rather than sympathy.

More important than physical beauty is some sort of moral or spiritual beauty. Anderson's aging Elizabeth is beautiful because of her intense need of love; Cyrano de Bergerac, whose nose is so long as to make him ridiculous, is beautiful because of his capacity for devotion and self-sacrifice; black-skinned Othello is beautiful because of his dignity, strength, honesty. In other words, the protagonist may possess some admirable quality, and that quality will clothe him in beauty.

Even the spiritually base protagonist—that is, one who violates common tastes and standards of behavior—may be made to seem beautiful by the possession of some counteracting characteristics. Macbeth, whom we should abhor as a murderer, gains our pity because he is reluctant to commit his first crime, because he has a strong sense of decency,[4] and because he experiences terrible remorse after murdering Duncan. Hedda, beautiful, but restless, cruel, and scornful, gains our pity through her barren pride and the gnawing sense of her own futility.

A protagonist usually appeals to the audience if he has a social objective; that is, if he seeks an end that will benefit someone else as well as himself. Lysistrata and Oedipus and Dr. Stockman of *An Enemy of the People* have the good of their cities at heart. The warden of *The Criminal Code* wants to save a young convict from the brutalizing

---

[4] Act I, Sc. 7: "Besides, this Duncan hath borne his faculties so meek, hath been so clear in his great office, that his virtues will plead like angels, trumpet-tongued, against the deep damnation of his taking off."

effects of prison. Charlotte of *The Old Maid* wants the happiness of her daughter.

One important fact to remember is that a character will appeal to an audience if he has powerful and understandable needs and desires. Human needs are manifold, as can be seen from lists of "drives" in texts on psychology, public speaking, and advertising. To say that a protagonist must possess some of these drives is not to limit the playwright, but to send him ranging through the whole of human nature for such drives as are appropriate to his particular protagonist. A strong desire, even if it is unsocial, will move an audience more quickly than any other single device for making the protagonist attractive.

Plays have been written and occasionally have lasted, in which the protagonist was unattractive. But an unskilled beginner who writes unattractive protagonists is courting the disfavor of his potential audience. It is a good plan upon finishing a script to ask oneself a few elementary questions: Does the protagonist, for example, offend common tastes and beliefs? Do the other characters react to him in such a way as to create the impression that he is a likable person? Does he behave attractively to the other characters? Has he any attractive qualities beyond mere physical beauty? For he must be revealed as attractive by some standards, if he is to secure the approval of the audience; where approval is withheld, there can be little sympathy, and hence no climax.

Not only must the protagonist be credible and attractive; but, what is more important, and more difficult, he must also be volitional, dynamic. One statement is true of humanity as a whole: human beings are not satisfied. They want one thing or another from the moment of birth until they close their eyes for the last time. What they want—food, love, personal dignity, the extension of the ego in some fashion—differs from time to time as well as from person to person. But it is impossible not to react with sympathy to the spectacle of a human being in intense need. So universal is desire, whatever the objective, that sympathy is certain to occur for a desiring individual, whether it be Oedipus crying in his blindness for a place to lay his head, or Myrrhine concealing a helmet under her robe and pretending pregnancy in order to be with her husband. As a corollary to this statement, the strength of the audience response is just about proportionate to the intensity of the protagonist's desire. He does not have to be intelligent, purposive, or aggressive; he has simply to want something badly enough to experience discomfort because of the lack of it. It is the quality of volition which makes a character dynamic.

Great protagonists desire intensely.[5] After railing and swearing at Essex and sending him away, Elizabeth cries, "Now what can come between us out of heaven or hell or Spain or England?"[6] The Warden of *The Criminal Code,* learning that his daughter loves the young convict, redoubles his efforts to save the boy, crying, "I'd turn

---

[5] Hegel, *The Philosophy of Fine Art,* Vol. IV, p. 309. Hegel points out that the absence of dramatic quality in oriental plays is due to the oriental fatalism which denies value to personal volition.

[6] Maxwell Anderson, *Elizabeth the Queen.* New York: Longmans, Green & Co., Inc., 1931.

the demons out of hell—for you." Othello is driven mad by the loss of his faith in Desdemona.

There are several devices by which protagonists can be made to seem volitional, none of them infallible, but all useful upon occasion.

First, if the objective is extremely desirable, the audience will wish the protagonist to attain it. The desirableness of the objective is the basis of the easy response of the audience in the boy-meets-girl situation, in Stockman's struggle with his fellow-townsmen to get a pure water-supply, in Lysistrata's campaign to end war. The audience simply reinforces the protagonist's expressed wish with a strongly concurring wish of its own.

If the protagonist suffers because of his need of the objective, he seems volitional. Examples abound: Juliet's "Is there no pity sitting in the clouds"; Elizabeth's anguish as she waits for Essex to send the ring that will gain his pardon; Dr. Haggett's shaking hands as he moans, "This morning I was a peaceful country doctor filled with gentle thoughts of a medical description.... Look at me now." [7]

Again, if the protagonist takes risks to secure his objective, it is evident that his need is great. Juliet takes the sleeping potion in order to be faithful to Romeo. Mio of *Winterset* faces a criminal gang to remove the stigma from his father's name. Antigone risks her life in the forbidden burial of her brother. Mrs. Maurrant of *Street Scene* risks her husband's brutal rage to "get a little something out of life."

---

[7] Sidney Howard, *The Late Christopher Bean*. New York: Samuel French, Inc., 1933.

Another very simple means of making the protagonist seem volitional is to give him a plan for achieving his objective. This is the method advocated by Brunetière in his definition of drama as "the spectacle of a will striving towards a goal and conscious of the means which it employs." [8] Juliet's taking the potion is part of her plan for reunion with Romeo. Hedda tries to achieve "an act of free beauty" through her experiment with Lovborg. Lysistrata uses all her skill toward the success of her campaign. On the other hand, Anderson's Elizabeth is an opportunist, and the plan which activates her story is that of her political opponents. Othello has no plan, although Iago has. Thus, purposiveness, while undoubtedly desirable in some cases, is not so fundamental as other factors in making the protagonist seem volitional.

A good dramatist uses the very structure of his play to reveal the volitional nature of his protagonist. The pattern varies in detail, but in its broad outlines it can be perceived in every powerful play. First, somewhere early in the play, there is a scene or group of scenes which reveals a fundamental disharmony either within the protagonist or between the protagonist and his environment. The insistent revelation of disharmony, Hegel's "collision factor," [9] results in a clear and vigorous statement by the protagonist of precisely what he thinks he needs to readjust himself. The rest of the play is a series of incidents which alternately promise and withhold the adjustment, thereby mak-

---

[8] Ferdinand Brunetière, "La Loi du Théâtre," translated in Clark, *European Theories of the Drama*, pp. 404-410.

[9] See above, p. 22 f., and below, p. 68.

ing it seem more desirable and the protagonist more volitional. This is exactly what one does when one shows a child candy and then withdraws it from the child's reach. It is the teeter-totter principle used by Scribe and his followers. Candy or objective seems more desirable, and child or protagonist and audience desire more intensely, as the process is prolonged to a point just short of exhaustion. Skill in plot construction lies not so much in eliminating this threadbare but useful pattern as in making it seem to proceed from the deepest roots of character and situation.

Oddly enough, the young playwright has the most difficult time in making his protagonist seem to desire strongly. An example may be taken from a student's play. Maurya, a rich dilettante, stands in the shadow of her deceased brother, a great pianist. Fancying herself a patron of the arts, Maurya's most driving desire is to dominate the life of her brother's son, Paul, by providing him with a musical education in Vienna. When Maurya's husband uncovers an *affaire* between Maurya and her Russian butler, the following scene takes place:

PAUL. Maurya, is this true?

MAURYA. Does it offend your petty morals?

PAUL. Morals don't bother me. But deceit and faking and the shell of pretense that goes with them...

MAURYA. Then take your prying mind away from here. I've tried to help you—and been balked at every turn. Now I'm tired... All you do is chatter a lot of high school patriotism about America this and America that. (Scornfully) America—of all places in God's creation.

PAUL. I don't stick up for what this country is or has been, but I'm mighty interested in what it can be, after we take a damn good physic to get rid of the filth that has stuck in our guts for years.

MAURYA. Such delicate similes are out of place in polite society.

PAUL. Well, they're at home where I'm going.

MAURYA. For heaven's sake hurry up and go. I've put up with enough prattle and silliness already—even to being called mother.

Maurya seems to have no need either for her husband or for the Russian lover; and she turns her nephew away at the first open conflict with his scruples, although he is said to be connected in her emotions with an old frustration, and is the center of practically all her plans in the play.

Some explanation must be found for the fact that a young playwright often fails to make his protagonist dynamic. The most obvious reason is that of the many young men who wish to write plays, a rare few have the capacity to desire strongly. To paraphrase Freytag, they have not all developed a worthy manhood. They have not the greatness of soul needed to conceive powerful desire.

Yet even where the capacity exists, the early plays may fail to exhibit strongly volitional protagonists. Probably a degree of maturity is needed before one perceives the force of a single powerful desire. To the young man life offers such a range of possible satisfactions that no one possibility could absorb his whole will, nor could the failure of any single possibility be utterly tragic for him. Yet until he has himself experienced, either actually or in imagination, a driving need for some objective, he is unready to write an important play.

A few not wholly mechanical aids have been given above. One must further be sure that the protagonist is actually the desiring force in the play, and, if possible, must give him the initiative in attempting to secure the objective. If, because of his nature or his situation, the protagonist cannot initiate the action, then he must certainly furnish some resistance to the forces which threaten his life harmony. In any case, the playwright must either write with a poet's passion, or he must in cold reason avail himself of any devices he can master to make his protagonist volitional. For this quality of volition is the surest mark of the skilled playwright.

Finally, the question has been asked, "Why must there be a protagonist?" and "Why cannot the protagonist be several persons or a group of persons rather than an individual?" In the school of the well-made play it was inconceivable that a play should not have a hero.[10] However, beginning with Gerhardt Hauptmann's *The Weavers,* from time to time there has been a play in which a group seems to take the place of the hero. It would be wise to attempt to understand why they succeeded or failed. The protagonist of *The Weavers,* first of the modern plays with a group protagonist, is, of course, the whole body of workmen protesting against social injustice. Although these men differ from each other as personalities, they all represent one human need, the need to assert the worth of human labor. The unity of their will is clear. With even less differentiation, the dead soldiers in *Bury the Dead* are one in their will to resist lying down. One might also men-

---

[10] Freytag, *The Technique of the Drama,* p. 304 f. "The drama must have only one chief hero, about whom all the persons ... arrange themselves. ... The unity of its action is essentially dependent upon this."

tion the once-popular living newspaper, *One-Third of a Nation*, which was without a central character, but in which many characters, very simply drawn, personified one single drive of humanity, the right to be housed as human beings rather than as animals.

In *The Cherry Orchard* there is a slight focus of interest, perhaps, on Madame Ranevsky, or on Gaiev, but the whole family takes the place of the conventional protagonist. The members of the family are definitely characterized as individuals; but they have two strongly fundamental characteristics in common: their will to preserve the *status quo*, and their charming incompetence to lift a hand for themselves—in other words, the same objective and obstacle. The family, as a unit, personifies White Russia, as clearly as Cathleen ni Houlihan represents Ireland in Yeats's play.

In America, Elmer Rice's *Street Scene* centers around the effect of a slum environment upon the Maurrant family. However, since the daughter, Rose, alone combats the environment, it seems fair to consider her as the emphatic point of the story, the protagonist.

More recently, *Our Town* has been cited as a play without a protagonist. However, without conventional emphasis, Emily definitely focuses the emotions of the audience, even before the last scene makes it clear that she is the protagonist of the play.

All these plays have had more or less popular appeal. On the other hand, Lynn Riggs's beautiful *Cherokee Night* was not popular, partly because of its unfamiliar milieu and unconventional time sequence, but largely because the audience could not synthesize the seven or eight individually interesting psychotic characters into one malajusted half-breed Indian, the abstraction for whom Riggs apparently wished to find a solution.

As the thought of the late nineteenth and early twentieth centuries probed and exalted the individual soul, so the mid-twentieth century seems to be trying to comprehend the interdependence between people and peoples, to understand the group mind and the group needs. Thus it seems likely that a group protagonist must emerge as an acceptable dramatic protagonist. However, we do not seem to have found the techniques for making the group protagonist sufficiently clear to induce sympathy; and audiences in this country still prefer plays in which someone "has the lead."

The young writer whose view of life leads him to write of groups rather than of individuals must cope with several specific difficulties, if he is to secure the concentration of audience sympathy that results in climax. If the protagonist is a group, each member of the group must be lifelike enough to command sympathy. In the theatre as in life, one does not feel either strong sympathy or strong antagonism toward a stranger. In order to form an attitude, one must know the person's views, or better yet, his wishes; one must know his general background, his father, wife, son, friends; his tastes, manners, language peculiarities; his ways of reacting to situations and to people. In common experience, the more intimately one knows a person, the more one cares what happens to him, be it good or ill. But the ripening of an acquaintance takes time, and the dramatist has only a limited time at his disposal. Obviously he cannot develop a dozen or more representatives of the group very thoroughly. He must therefore employ the highest skill of the cartoonist, selecting with care the exact details that will most quickly make the character seem alive. And unless the playwright has superlatively keen discrimination, the characters are likely to remain cartoons, instead of becoming three-dimensional living personalities.

If the protagonist is a group of two-dimensional members, each member is likely to be merely an instrument for conveying the intellectual concepts of the playwright, an abstraction, a mass mind, not a mass will. Public speakers and successful advertisers know that persuasion and belief are not achieved solely—not even mainly—by logic. A real conviction springs from emotional stimuli. Even the rankest cold classicist, Corneille, admits [11] that although a play may be didactic its lesson must be conveyed through the passions of the main character. Ibsen was aware of this in constructing *An Enemy of the People,* and carefully surrounded Dr. Stockman with emotional appeals of an extremely fundamental kind, so that the audience responded to his campaign not with cold approval but with passionate assent. In using a group protagonist, the playwright

---

[11] "I do not mean to say that when an actor speaks he can not inform the listener about many things, but he must do so through the passion which moves him and not through simple narration." Corneille, "Premier Discours. De l'Utilité et des Parties du Poème Dramatique," in Clark, *European Theories of the Drama,* p. 147. This thought is echoed by Arthur Hopkins in *"How's Your Second Act?"* p. 8. New York: Samuel French, Inc., 1931: "In the theatre I do not want the emotion that arises out of thought, but thought that rises out of emotion. The emotional reaction must be secured first."

must see to it that the group represents a common will or need, not merely a common idea.

If, in using a group protagonist, the playwright succeeds in making each member seem lifelike and volitional, each separate character may seem to need a story of his own, as did the characters of *Cherokee Night*. Since one play can tell only one main story well in two and a half hours, the playwright must be sure that his details reinforce each other to emphasize the main theme of the play. This can be done by giving the members of the group a common objective, as will be shown in the next chapter.

The group protagonist is not common on the American stage. On the other hand, in love stories and a few other kinds of stories, the double protagonist is not uncommon. In *Romeo and Juliet,* to name only one example, it is really impossible to insist that either Romeo or Juliet is the protagonist. In *You and I,* an early play of Philip Barry, a father and son seem to be about equally important. It should be noted, though, that in some plays which seem to have a double protagonist one of the two lively and empathic characters is really the objective, which the other is striving to gain. This is surely true in *Elizabeth the Queen,* where Essex is not only one of Elizabeth's objectives, but also part of her obstacle. The difficulties of using the double protagonist are the same in kind if not in extent, as the difficulties of using the group protagonist. If the playwright wishes to use a double protagonist, he must make both characters equally lifelike, equally moving, equally expressive of the central theme of the play.

In conclusion, a protagonist seems to be needed in a play

as a focus for the emotional responses of the audience. A group or a double protagonist is not impossible; but it is far more difficult to create a lively and integrated group in the time at the dramatist's disposal, than to build one fully imagined and carefully presented individual, with the characteristics of credibility, attractiveness, and volition.

An artist will not seek the easiest way, nor count the cost of his labors. But he may with a good conscience follow the route of the beginner in the other arts; that is, begin with the simpler tasks and progress to the more difficult ones as he acquires the skill to perform them.

1. Analyze:
    a. What means are used to make Elizabeth of *Elizabeth the Queen* credible and attractive?
    b. Who is the protagonist of *The Glass Menagerie*? Support your answer.
    c. How is Sally of *The Voice of the Turtle* made attractive?
    d. Discuss the protagonist of *Cherokee Night*.
    e. Who is the protagonist of *Street Scene*? Justify your answer.
    f. What devices make Mio of *Winterset* volitional?

2. Which is the best protagonist, and why?
    a. A well-dressed woman passes a bakeshop, murmurs, "It's nearly lunchtime," and rearranges her furs as she hurries on.

b. A thin, ragged boy passes a bakeshop, presses his nose to the pane, swallows, and goes on.

c. A well-dressed woman passes a bakeshop, pauses and looks in the window, murmuring, "I wonder if that would tempt him?" There is tension about her eyes as she enters the store.

3. Invent scenes to make the following protagonists attractive and volitional:

a. Father Damien.
b. François Villon.
c. John L. Lewis.
d. A notorious swindler.
e. Eva Braun.
f. The postman.
g. A big businessman.
h. Your least interesting aunt.

ASSIGNMENTS

PLAYS: Anton Chekov, *The Cherry Orchard*, from *Chief Contemporary Dramatists*, ed. T. H. Dickinson. Boston: Houghton Mifflin Company, 1930. Clifford Odets, *Golden Boy*, from *Six Plays of Clifford Odets*. New York: Random House, 1939. Thornton Wilder, *Our Town*. New York: Coward-McCann, 1938.

ADDITIONAL READING: William Archer, *Playmaking: A Manual of Craftsmanship*, Chapters III and V. New York: Dodd, Mead & Company, Inc., 1937. Aristotle, *Poetics*, XIII-XV, translated by Ingram Bywater, Modern Readers Series. New York: The Macmillan Company, 1930. George Pierce Baker, *Dramatic Technique*, pp. 64-67. Boston: Houghton Mifflin Company, 1919. Ferdinand Brunetière, "La Loi du Théâtre," and Henry Arthur Jones, "Critique of Brunetière's Law," in Barrett H. Clark, *European Theories of the Drama*. New York: Crown Publishers, 1947. Pierre Corneille, "Premier Discours. De l'Utilité et des Parties du Poème Dramatique," in Barrett H. Clark, *European Theories of the Drama*. New York: Crown Publishers, 1947.

Gustav Freytag, *The Technique of the Drama,* pp. 48-66, 308-311. Chicago: Scott, Foresman & Company, 1904. Georg Wilhelm Friedrich Hegel, *The Philosophy of Fine Art,* Vol. I, pp. 236-263. London: George Bell & Sons, Ltd., 1920. John Howard Lawson, *Theory and Technique of Playwriting,* Part II, Chapter I, and Part III, Chapters I and II. New York: G. P. Putnam's Sons, 1949. F. H. Lund, "The Psychology of Belief: A Study of Its Emotional and Volitional Determinants," *Journal of Abnormal Psychology,* Vol. 20 (1925), p. 63 f. Allardyce Nicoll, *The Theory of Drama,* pp. 145-158. New York: The Thomas Y. Crowell Company, n.d. Albert T. Poffenberger, *Psychology in Advertising,* Chapter XXV. New York: McGraw-Hill Book Company, Inc., 1932. Paul Thomas Young, *Emotion in Man and Animal,* Chapters II, III, VIII, X. New York: John Wiley & Sons, Inc.; London: Chapman & Hall, Ltd., 1943.

5

The Objective

THE MOST MOVING QUALITY OF A GOOD PROTAGONIST IS
the quality of volition. Yet, as Stanislavski points out,[1] it is
impossible merely to desire in the abstract. One must desire
something. The very existence of a desire implies a potential means of satisfying it, an objective. This objective is
one of the three fundamentals of a play.

Hegel[2] regards man as a complex system of balances
fraught with potent and dangerous elements of disruption
from within and without. A perfectly adjusted individual
is inconceivable. A bad cold, an unappetizing meal, or a
new face in the office forces the individual to recognize
new wishes within himself. Sometimes the wish is not very
strong; the readjustment is a matter of a few days or a
few minutes. On the other hand, any one of these common
stimuli may actually alter the life of even a well-adjusted

---

[1] Constantin Stanislavski, *An Actor Prepares*, Chapters III and VII.
New York: Theatre Arts, Inc., 1936.
[2] Hegel, *The Philosophy of Fine Art*, Vol. I, pp. 263-267, 272-274,
283-288.

individual. If, for example, the cold became severe, if pneumonia set in, or tuberculosis, the individual would inevitably suppress his former wishes and concentrate his will on the sole effort to live. He would stop work. He might even leave the cold city and seek dry sunshine in a more clement part of the earth. If the new face at the office was very attractive or very disagreeable, he might perhaps set up a whole new system of personal relationships. Unattractive meals have been the source of serious friction in families. Whether the adjustment will be easy or difficult depends on how effectively the new stimulus disrupts the relationships of the individual in his universe; but in any case an adjustment must be made to each new stimulus.

The factor which reveals a breakdown in the internal or external harmony of the individual and a need for readjustment is the collision factor, the factor which starts the play.[3] It may be anything from an earthquake to a storm in a teacup, from a chance word to an act of God. It is not the objective; it merely indicates to the individual that his life is unendurable under new or newly recognized conditions.

Once this collision factor has revealed the breakdown, the individual begins to seek a way of readjusting himself. The particular means which he selects to bring about the

---

[3] Hegel, *The Philosophy of Fine Art*, Vol. IV, p. 263, "Insofar, however, as dramatic action rests essentially on a definite state of collision, the right point of departure will lie in the situation, out of which the future devolution of that conflict, despite the fact that it has not, as yet, broken out, will none the less in its further course issue." See also Freytag, *The Technique of the Drama*, pp. 121-125. See also above, p. 22 f.

readjustment is his objective. A man whose wife is a shrew may want to seduce his stenographer, or he may wish to reform his wife, or he may wish to escape women altogether. Whatever means seems most likely to restore his equilibrium will be his objective.

In the discussion of what dramatic action is, not enough attention has been paid to the objective. Dramatic action has been defined as crisis,[4] shock,[5] a will striving toward a goal,[6] the executed will,[7] the presentation of an event for its effect on a human soul,[8] an action which arouses emotion.[9] There has been much discussion of unity of action, of the point at which a play should begin, and of how it should end. Much light will be thrown on all these problems by simple reference to what the protagonist wants.

A dramatic action begins[10] with the intrusion of some factor which destroys the peace of the protagonist, forcing him to recognize the disruptive elements and to seek a means of regaining harmony. The action proper is the effort of the protagonist to attain the means by which he hopes to regain harmony. The play ends when he succeeds or clearly cannot succeed in this aim. In other words, the

---

[4] Archer, *Playmaking: A Manual of Craftsmanship*, p. 36.

[5] Nicoll, *The Theory of Drama*, p. 38.

[6] Brunetière, "La Loi du Théâtre," in Clark, *European Theories of the Drama*.

[7] Hegel, *The Philosophy of Fine Art*, Vol. IV, p. 252.

[8] Freytag, *The Technique of the Drama*, p. 19.

[9] Baker, *Dramatic Technique*, p. 46.

[10] This is not to say that the curtain must rise on the entrance of the collision factor, for there may be some reason to delay this factor until other points have been established, or the collision may have occurred before the opening curtain.

core of the play, the element which gives it unity, which determines its beginning, middle, and end, is the objective, the means by which the protagonist hopes to regain his disrupted harmony. A unified dramatic action is the pursuit of one such objective.

The objective is important not only as a device to give the plot unity and a goal, but also as a means of characterizing the protagonist. What an individual wants is a strong clue to what he is. A clear illustration of this point can be seen on any college campus in the girls whom boys select as companions. One tall, handsome lad seems to avoid girls; when at last he is seen talking frequently with a girl, she is pale, quiet, unsophisticated, self-contained, honest. Another lad selects a noisy hoyden as his favorite feminine companion. Still another is usually seen with a rich-skinned, seductively dressed, stupid girl. Certainly one knows a good bit about these boys by studying the girls they select as companions.

In adult life a man's choice of profession characterizes him to a large extent. A physician's nature is essentially different from that of an insurance salesman. But one is sometimes driven into a profession by pressures other than his own inclination; whereas, once he has an income, his pleasures are clearly his own choice. Thus a man's hobbies especially characterize him. A man who will spend hours on a golf course improving his stroke is quite a different person from the one who uses his Saturdays to chaperone a Boy Scout camp, or read Proust, or build a radio, or study a symphony, or get drunk. The thing for which a man will spend money, energy, and irretrievable time—that is, the thing he wants—tells more about him than any single factor.

This is true even of people who are muddled in their aims. A student in premedical school wants to be an actor; yet he keeps grinding through uncongenial science courses. Another student cries that she is unpopular because she does not know how to dance and play bridge; yet she does nothing to acquire these basic social skills. Instead, she reads a great deal, and defiantly seeks the company of another student who is regarded as socially undesirable. What these individuals think they want is indicative of their characters to some extent; but one cannot understand them fully without discovering what keeps them doing the thing they say they do not want to do. Behind their unwilling expenditure of time and energy, there is a want more powerful than the want they express. In the case of the medical student, perhaps he wants to prove that he can complete the thing he started, or to please his parents, or to acquire the security and prestige of a lucrative profession. In the case of the maladjusted girl, perhaps she wants to understand the functions of humanity in the universe, or simply to distinguish herself from the social butterflies by being "different." It can be seen that the character of either of these students is of one sort if he is motivated by one of these wants, quite different if another want motivates him. What he really is depends on the want which actually governs his actions.

In analyzing an acquaintance, one determines what the person wants by what he does. The converse of this proposition is also true, and of great use to the playwright. What a person wants determines what he will do. Thus the objective of the protagonist not only characterizes him, but also helps the playwright to decide what incidents are to be used in the play.[11] Charting the main events of a play is something like tramping the streets of a city. If one knows his goal, he can discover how to get there, and make his journey with economy of time and effort, and with a feeling of satisfaction. If there is no goal, or a vague one, his activities are at best merely a pleasant but meaningless ramble; at worst, a series of exhausting frustrations. There can be no meaningful action without a goal.

To summarize, the objective supplies unity, beginning, middle, and end to the plot of the play; it characterizes the protagonist; and it helps in selecting the incidents which make up the course of action. The careful analysis of the objective is one of the most rewarding tasks of plot construction.

One cannot say what kind of thing the objective must be. The old melodrama often centered around "the jewels" or "the letter" or some other "prop" which served as the concrete externalization of what the protagonist was trying to get or to protect. In the dramaturgy of our time the objective is generally less obvious, but it is none the less definite.[12] Cyrano wants honor; Hedda wants to estab-

---

[11] Lawson, *Theory and Technique of Playwriting*, Part III, Chapter III.

[12] Hegel, *The Philosophy of Fine Art*, Vol. I, p. 292. "Such are the supreme motive forces of art. They are the eternal religious and ethical modes of relationship, status, personal character, and in the world of romance, before everything else, honour and love." This is elaborated in Vol. IV, p. 295.

lish her own dignity, as does Joe Bonaparte of *Golden Boy;* Hauptmann's weavers want bread; Regina and the Giddens family want money; Amanda of *The Glass Menagerie* wants a certain type of experience for her daughter; Jacobowsky wants a native land. It is hardly worth while to classify objectives, for they are as varied as the solutions of the problems which confront human beings.

Whatever the objective may be, however, it should be clear, specific, unified, dynamic, and in some way attractive.

The objective should be clear and specific.[13] Everyone has experienced baffled irritation with a friend who was unhappy and maladjusted but did not know what he needed to overcome his maladjustment. A protagonist on the stage who has no specific objective is equally irritating. Skilled dramatists guard against this sort of irritation by certain quite definite practices. Even when the protagonist himself does not know exactly what his objective is, the audience is carefully informed, through some wish which the protagonist himself expresses in the simplest possible language in the first third of the play. Romeo says, in the first balcony scene, "My life were better ended by their hate, than death prorogued wanting of thy love." In *Winterset*, Act I, Scene 3, Mio tells Carr that he must prove his father innocent *if he is to have a normal life*. In *Paris Bound*, a long scene in Act I overemphasizes Mary's deter-

---

[13] Lawson, *Theory and Technique of Playwriting*, p. 167. "The will which creates drama is directed toward a specific goal. But the goal which it selects must be sufficiently realistic to enable the will to have some effect on reality. We in the audience must be able to understand the goal and the possibility of its fulfillment."

mination not to monopolize the affections of her husband. In the first scene of *Dark of the Moon*, the Witch-Boy demands to be made human so that he may marry Barbara Allen. In *Our Town*, Emily insists, "But mama, you've got to say something about me. Am I pretty enough—to get anybody—to get people interested in me?" And Mrs. Webb replies, "You're pretty enough for all normal purposes." In *The Cherry Orchard*, the wish to keep the orchard is mentioned several times in Act I, and just before the first-act curtain Gaiev protests, "I swear on my honor . . . the estate shan't be sold. . . . Call me the basest, vilest of men if I let it come to an auction." Anya replies, "How good you are, Uncle, and how clever. I'm at peace now. Quite at peace! I'm happy."

For some reason the beginner finds it extremely difficult to make a clear and definite statement of what the protagonist wants. Yet such a statement is made in every important play, as early as possible, several times, and in terms that the audience could not possibly misunderstand. Some of the common arguments of young playwrights against being definite about the objective may be answered.

It is objected that human beings seldom have such definite motives. Possibly the objection arises because young men themselves are unstable as to their own most compelling interests, especially young men of great and varied talents. But even a young man will understand the pursuit of a temporary aim—courting a girl, gaining a particular honor, making a fraternity—with as much intensity as if it were a life aim; and he will recognize in the pursuit of such an objective some deeper aspect of the character pur-

74

suing it. In the same way a playwright can utilize a strong minor objective of his protagonist, one that can be convincingly gained or lost in the "two hours' traffic" of the play, and through it he can reveal the most basic struggle of the character to achieve life harmony.

It is objected that limiting the objective limits the scope of the play. Actually, the scope of the play is greater or less not according to the number of actions it includes, but according to the insight of the dramatist in making the single action of his play reveal depths of character, and, indeed, of humanity. The scope of the play is the extent to which it succeeds in revealing universal human desire through the desire of one individual for one objective.

Another argument occurs frequently. The young writer wants to be subtle. Fearing that a plain statement in simple language will be too crass, he falls into obscurity. Subtlety for the playwright is the ability to make a very little say a great deal, to convey broad revelations of character through apparently commonplace actions. It is never obscurity in conveying the revelation. Certainly if any portion of the play must be clearly presented and understood, it is the protagonist's objective.

The first requirement of a good objective, then, is clarity. The objective must also be unified. Unity of action has already been defined as limiting the play to the pursuit of one objective. In general, this objective is quite simple.[14]

---

[14] Hegel, *The Philosophy of Fine Art*, Vol. IV, p. 253. "The movement of the drama is not thrown upon the background of a national existence essentially complete in its envisagement of every conceivable variety of class, age, sex, activity, and so forth, but on the contrary

A simple objective is not only easy for the audience to understand and for the dramatist to reveal; it also furnishes a single clear goal toward which all the hope and fear of the audience can be directed.

Occasionally one finds the objective complex. In *Winterset,* for example, Mio says that he has been driven out of schools and hounded from place to place because his father was convicted of murder. He cannot live unless he proves his father was innocent. When, however, Miriamne reveals that she loves him, he is willing to abandon the vindication of his father, for he has found the means to life harmony. Evidently, then, his objective all along was "to be accepted as a human being by his fellows." The vindication of his father was only a means to this end.

Similarly, *Tomorrow and Tomorrow* seems to have a complex objective. In the first scene Eve admits to her husband that she is restless and unsatisfied, and that she wants a child to give her stability. The first half of the play is devoted to getting her the child—by a lover, as her husband is sterile. The rest of the play is concerned with making the child accept Eve's husband as his father. The play has unity if the objective is correctly perceived: Eve wants a complete marriage.

A double objective, that is, two mutually incompatible objectives held simultaneously, creates a strong situation. The old conflict between love and duty, successful to the point of banality, was of this kind.[15] It is precisely this

rivets our attention throughout on *one* fundamental purpose and its achievement."

[15] Nicoll, *The Theory of Drama,* p. 172.

conflict of desires that made *Elizabeth the Queen* such a strong play. Elizabeth could not be happy without Essex, nor could she have him without violence to her conscience as a monarch. A popular play of Barry, *Paris Bound,* also has a double objective. Mary vows on her wedding day not to be jealous, because she realizes that one human being cannot utterly possess another. But when her husband is unfaithful, she is both fond and conventional enough not to be able to endure sharing him. In both *Elizabeth the Queen* and *Paris Bound* the over-all objective is to suppress one or the other objective.

The danger of a beginner's using the double objective is that the character may tend to ratiocinate and do nothing, to be stalemated. Probably the principle behind the successful use of the double objective is that the two objectives must be equally desirable, mutually exclusive, and simultaneously held; and that the character must be so strongly moved by each of them that he will act upon each alternately.

The pitfall into which a beginner slips in attempting a complex objective is that his plays do not seem to have the organic unity of *Winterset* and *Paris Bound.* He centers his attention on securing one minor objective at a time, and fails to indicate that the various minor objectives are related to a major objective which comprises all the others. He thus seems to be writing a group of short plays instead of one long one.

A student's play offers a clear example of the failure to integrate the entire play by means of a single objective. The protagonist was one of the first settlers of Kansas, a calm, sturdy man, who attacked his problems as they came. Among the several problems he settled in the course of the play were the establishment of law and order among the cattlemen who overran the wheat fields; the discovery of a wheat that would not be either frostbitten or driven out of the ground by dust storms; the negotiation of credit for the famine-ridden farmers who had bad luck with their wheat; the grinding of the durum winter wheat; and finally a plague of grasshoppers. The play might have been unified through a single passionately held objective, to stay on the land. But as this was lacking, the accomplishment of each of the minor objectives seemed the end of a one-act play.

The point to be insisted upon is that a carefully determined objective gives unity to the play. For even a highly skilled dramatist this objective is frequently simple; but even if the objective is complex, it is always unified.

A further characteristic of a good objective is the capacity of causing action; the objective should be dynamic. It should be important, something which the protagonist really desires, and without which he suffers. And it should not be too easy of attainment. The reasons for this are fairly obvious. Unless the objective is important enough to cause the characters to do something, there will be no action of any kind. If the lack of the objective does not particularly matter to the protagonist, the audience will care no more than he whether or not he achieves it, and there will be no climax. If the objective is something the protagonist could have by merely taking it, no tension of hope and fear can develop in the audience, and again there will be no climax.

From Oedipus, whose passion to serve his state caused his ruin, to Othello, who went mad and slew his wife when he could no longer believe in her fidelity, nearly every strongly moving play has a dynamic objective. The more intensely necessary and the more difficult of attainment the objective is, the more emotional tension is created and the more satisfaction the audience experiences in the attainment of it or in the well-prepared failure to attain it.

A few instances may be cited of successful plays in which the objective is not dynamic. Among the chief of these is *The Cherry Orchard*, which depends for its appeal upon the utter charm of the characters. Like *The Cherry Orchard*, *Our Town* balances the abstractness of Emily's motive, to fulfill her destiny, by Thornton Wilder's magic power of evoking the universal through the particular. *The Glass Menagerie* has particular problems of interpretation, since it promises in a long confidential introductory speech to be about the desire of a young factory worker to produce some kind of artistic work; but in performance, Laurette Taylor's acting dominated the play and it became the halfhearted and abortive effort of the mother to provide her crippled daughter with some of the glories of her own vanished past as a Southern Belle. If this is the major objective of the play, Amanda did all that was consonant with her character to achieve it.

On the other hand, many unproduced plays are without a dynamic objective, and some have even reached the stage with this weakness. A thoroughly scholarly play about the

youth of Abraham Lincoln was produced and ran for
some time with Federal Theatre backing. In this play Lincoln stated frequently that he had no wish to do anything
but settle down and read. His mother gave him some good
advice and sent him as far as New Salem. There, his love
for Ann Rutledge spurred him to seek a legal career in
order to be worthy of her hand. But upon the death of
Ann, there was no further reason, so far as the playwright
had shown, for Abe's continuing his career, and, in truth,
the protagonist had a complete spiritual breakdown. Yet,
because the audience knew that Lincoln did go on, the
dramatist felt that he must end the play with Lincoln
setting out for Springfield. If Ann had left Lincoln with
an ambition or purpose of some sort, or better, if Lincoln
had within himself some driving force,[16] one could have
believed in his spiritual recovery. All that the playwright
gave him was a kindly, garrulous neighbor, who reminded
Lincoln, as he must have reminded himself, that Ann
would have wanted him to carry on. When he set out for
Springfield, one felt that he did not carry with him the
spirit that created the great Lincoln tradition. He had no
objective.

Sometimes a character just wants to be left alone. If
he wants to be left alone badly enough to do something
about it, the material can make a play. But the protagonist
can be no more dynamic than the objective which the
playwright finds for him. The inability to conceive an objective worth seeking with the whole force of one's being

---

[16] Such as Sherwood supplied in *Abe Lincoln in Illinois*—intense com-
passion for humanity.

is a weakness of some importance in a playwright. Many skills are needed to counteract this weakness.

Finally the objective must be attractive in some way. Nothing will so easily give the protagonist the quality of attractiveness and volition as an objective which the audience recognizes as praiseworthy or desirable. It may be something so fundamentally desirable as a man's need for a woman, an objective found with more or less emphasis in nearly all modern American plays; or a mother's desire to benefit her child, as in *Lady Windermere's Fan* and *The Glass Menagerie;* or the need of a home, as in *Jacobowsky and the Colonel.* It might be some spiritual or intellectual or social need, such as Othello's need to retain his faith in Desdemona; or Stockman's crusade to purify the water system; or Grant Matthews's need to retain his integrity in politics in *State of the Union;* or the Warden's effort to save Bob in *The Criminal Code;* or Paula Tanqueray's attempt to become respectable; or Oedipus's wish to rid Athens of the plague. All these objectives are desirable on their face, and they do much to gain admiration or at least sympathy for the protagonists who hold them.

Occasionally a play holds the audience although the motives are decidedly objectionable. An example of this is *The Little Foxes,* which had the advantage of Tallulah Bankhead's skill in the sordidly selfish but highly volitional character of Regina. Another example is *The Silver Cord,* Sidney Howard's drama of a disarmingly attractive mother who wants to dominate her sons. Still another is *Golden Boy,* in which the very understandable and highly volitional protagonist throws away a creative talent in order to cut a figure in the eyes of the world. Two factors might account for the audience's accepting these plays. First, the characters and situations are utterly credible and life-like. Second, there seems to be a sort of confessional fascination in viewing on the stage faults which one secretly knows to be one's own.

The point is that if the protagonist is to seem attractive, as he must if the audience is to care what happens to him, one simple means of making him so is to provide him with an attractive objective. If the objective is unattractive, doubly skillful use of other factors must counteract the weakness.

The objective, then, is one of the most important elements of the play. It provides the chief source of unity; it is the best means of characterizing the protagonist; it helps in selecting the main events of the play. Whether it be material or spiritual, social or selfish, it must be clear, unified, dynamic, and attractive. Occasionally, good plays have objectives lacking in some of these characteristics; but a beginner will need unusual talent if he ignores the usefulness of the objective in creating those tensions of hope and fear which are resolved in a clear and satisfying ending.

1. Analyze:
   a. What devices can you find in *Both Your Houses* that make Alan's objective dynamic?
   b. Who is the objective of *The Criminal Code,* and what makes him attractive?
   c. What makes the objective of the Witch-Boy credible in *Dark of the Moon?*

2. For the following protagonists find a clear, dynamic objective and a way to make the objective appealing to an audience of (*a*) businessmen, (*b*) farmers, (*c*) university students, (*d*) church members:
   a. Shakespeare.
   b. A man who inherits a farm and likes farming.
   c. A pioneer in the American Midwest.
   d. The mother of a soldier killed in the war.
   e. A woman who married five old men, all living, none divorced.
   f. St. Augustine.
   g. A gangster.
   h. The old-maid daughter of a moderately rich elderly widow.
   i. A woman whose husband lets her know she bores him.
   j. A man of mediocre ability who had a great ancestor.

ASSIGNMENTS

PLAYS: Maxwell Anderson, *Both Your Houses.* New York: Samuel French, Inc., 1933.   Martin Flavin, *The Criminal Code.* New York: Liveright Publishing Company, 1929.   Howard Richardson and William Berney, *Dark of the Moon.* Manuscript controlled by Select Theatres Corporation, 234 West 44th St., New York.

ADDITIONAL READING: William Archer, *Playmaking: A Manual of Craftsmanship*, Chapter XXII. New York: Dodd, Mead & Company, Inc., 1937.   George Pierce Baker, *Dramatic Technique, Chapter II*. New York: Houghton Mifflin Company, 1919. Gustav Freytag, *The Technique of the Drama*, pp. 19-27, 121-125. Chicago: Scott, Foresman & Company, 1904. G. W. F. Hegel, *The Philosophy of Fine Art*, Vol. I, pp. 263-288, Vol. IV, pp. 250-295. London: George Bell & Sons, Ltd., 1920.   John Howard Lawson, *Theory and Technique of Playwriting*, Part III, Chapter III. New York: G. P. Putnam's Sons, 1949.   Allardyce Nicoll, *The Theory of Drama*, pp. 45-57. New York: The Thomas Y. Crowell Company, n. d.   Constantin Stanislavski, *An Actor Prepares*, Chapters III and VII. New York: Theatre Arts, Inc., 1936.

6

The Obstacle

IF VOLITION IMPLIES AN OBJECTIVE, IT ALSO IMPLIES SOME-
thing which inhibits the will from reaching out and
instantly achieving the thing desired,[1] since the desire becomes extinct as soon as the objective is achieved.

A gourmet, eating, may continue to eat with zest, may
actively desire each new item on the menu; but when he
has tried all the hors d'oeuvres he wants, he will desire the
soup, and then the entree, the roast, and so forth. He enjoys what he has, but he can hardly be said to desire it. A
man may be intensely aware of felicity in the possession
of his wife; a parent may be ecstatic over the perfection of
his child; a collector may rejoice in some precious object,
an inventor in the solution of a problem, a politician in the
success of a campaign, a minister in saving souls. In each
case the achievement of one wish may lead to another. But

---

[1] Hegel, *The Philosophy of Fine Art*, Vol IV, p. 253 f. "... the end
and content of an action is only dynamic by reason of the fact that
... it calls into being in other individuals other objects and passions
opposed to it."

the feeling of intense appreciation of an object one possesses is quite a different mental state from the wish which precedes the attainment of the object, or from the sense of fear and loss when the object is threatened. Desire is an awareness of the lack of a particular object.

If the objective is lacking, there must be some reason that it is lacking. The reason is the obstacle. It appears, in one form or another, in every play.

It is almost a truism that the more one is restrained from his desire, the more eager he is to accomplish it.[2] A child, forbidden to do something, will be strongly inclined to do it. The difficulty of a task, the aloofness of a girl, will challenge the ego of a spirited youth. Likewise, a protagonist, faced with an obstacle, will find his desire piqued and intensified. Thus the obstacle reinforces one of the most important qualities of the protagonist, the quality of volition. Further, since the audience empathizes with the protagonist, the presence of an obstacle acts directly to increase the tensions of hope and fear in the audience, and thus makes the climax doubly satisfying.

Moreover, as Archer points out, as soon as the objective has been achieved, the play is over.[3] Therefore, some element of impediment is needed to justify prolonging the

---

[2] Up to a possible saturation point. Cf. Percival Wilde, *The Craftsmanship of the One-Act Play*, p. 198 f. Boston: Little, Brown & Company, 1938.

[3] William Archer declares that conflict is one of the most dramatic elements in life and that "There is nothing more futile than a play in which we feel that there is no real obstacle to the inevitable ending, and that the curtain might just as well fall in the middle of the first act as at the end of the third." *Playmaking*, pp. 31-35.

play for two hours or more. If John Brown suddenly realizes that Mary Jones is the girl for him, if he immediately asks her to marry him and she accepts, and they marry at once, there is no play. If, however, Mary's father strongly objects, or John's mother lays an elaborate scheme to make him dislike Mary, or if Mary reveals that she is not the girl John thought her, or John discovers that he cannot support Mary or that he wants something else more than marriage, we have material for *Coquette, The Cassilis Engagement, The Silver Cord, The Damask Cheek, You and I,* or some other play. The need for the obstacle can easily be perceived in the boy-meets-girl situation, but it is equally necessary in any sort of play.

What the obstacle is to be in a given play depends, of course, on the material from which the play is to be fashioned. Certainly the "villain" of melodrama has passed away as such; and yet very often a person is the obstacle.[4] Sometimes this is a disagreeable person, like Trock in *Winterset.* Sometimes it is an excitable and rather irresponsible person like old Capulet, who is not at all vicious or malevolent. Sometimes the person who represents the obstacle is even attractive, like Gray in *Both Your Houses* or the naïve MacManus in *The Criminal Code.*

Another sort of obstacle arises from the objective behaving independently. This is true of Essex in *Elizabeth the Queen.* Essex might have been a suitable king consort, except that he opposed Elizabeth's government, and finally

---

[4] Cf. Freytag, "... and as the hero must be endowed with a strong life ... the opposing power must be made visible in a human representative." *The Technique of the Drama,* p. 104 f.

even staged a *coup d'état* against her. The independent objective is the obstacle in *The Voice of the Turtle,* in which Sally's plan to keep her lover by letting him feel free is defeated by the fact that Bill wants to belong to one woman. The Witch-Boy in *Dark of the Moon* is defeated by a streak of superstitious terror in Barbara, his objective, aggravated by her fanatical family and neighbors.

Occasionally the obstacle is a mutually exclusive double objective,[5] such as that of *Elizabeth the Queen* and *Golden Boy.* Elizabeth wants to keep both throne and lover. Joe Bonaparte wants to be both a violinist and a prize fighter. Neither can have both.

The obstacle in most of Odets' plays and in Elmer Rice's *Street Scene* is the environment in which the protagonist lives. In *Ghosts* it is the effect of the elder Alving's past, for which Mrs. Alving is trying to atone. In *Children of the Moon,* the obstacle is a streak of insanity in the family. In *Tomorrow and Tomorrow* it is Gail's sterility. In *The Cherry Orchard* the incompetence of the group protagonist provides the obstacle. *Our Town* hardly seems to have an obstacle until the third act reveals that the objective is to enjoy the intense beauty of life and the obstacle is mortality. The obstacles in this group are the twentieth-century counterparts of the Greek concept of Fate.[6]

Finally, in a mystery play the obstacle seems to be the ingenuity of the playwright in deferring the discovery of

---

[5] See above, p. 76 f.

[6] "Inward liberty and external necessity are the two poles of the tragic world," says Schlegel, in his *Lectures on Dramatic Art and Criticism,* p. 67.

the murderer. In this type of play the audience is the protagonist, and the objective is the answer to the question, "Who dun it?"

Thus the obstacle is not necessarily the old-fashioned villain of the melodrama, or, indeed, a person at all; nor is it fate as exemplified in Greek Tragedy. It is whatever stands between the protagonist and the thing he desires.

Whatever the obstacle, it should be something that furnishes the protagonist with opposition worthy of whatever kind of powers he possesses. Any contest is more exciting if the contestants are well matched than if one contestant is clearly better than the other. In a play the protagonist should have about a fifty-fifty chance to gain what will mean to him permanent stability.

The contest may be equalized in a number of ways. In a wrestling match or prize fight, for example, brute force is opposed to brute force, and the contestant who has a little strategy or a little luck will win. In football, a heavy line may be balanced by fast ends. In battle, a large army may be balanced by the superior equipment of the opposing forces. In all these cases, the conflict is primarily between brute force and brute force.

In a thriller like *Frankenstein* or *King Kong*, intellect opposes itself to brute force. In *Mary of Scotland*, Mary's feminine appeal is opposed to the intellect of Elizabeth. Iago's cold intellect struggles against Othello's passion. In *Elizabeth the Queen*, Elizabeth's passion is opposed to the intellect of her counselor, Cecil; to the pride of her lover, Essex; and to her own integrity as a monarch. In *John Gabriel Borkman* and *The Silver Cord* the conflict is between two strongly emotional forces. In *Street Scene* strong desire is opposed to the impersonal force of the environment.

If an audience sees that the protagonist is straining against windmills, it is likely to lose respect for him, unless the play is supposed to be a farce. An example of this loss of stature occurs in an unpublished play about Paul Bunyan, the legendary giant-logger of the Northwest. The obstacle in this play is King Pete of Europe, a whippersnapper of a fairy-tale king, done out in tinsel and called "Your Royal High Muck-a-Muck." He does nothing but issue wordy manifestos and conspire in a stagey way with three henchmen, whom he leaves behind to accomplish his fell purposes. King Pete exits at the end of the first act and never appears again. He does not participate in the real showdown of the play. And the result is that Paul Bunyan, the great logger and prime orator, is a verbose dunderhead.

On the other hand, since the Greeks, an overwhelming obstacle has been dangerous to a play. Dozens of examples could be cited from the writings of apprentice playwrights. One of the most obvious is the story of a young man with a political career ahead of him, who discovers at the end of Act I that he has a malignant cancer. Another is about a woman who wanted her daughter to have an education but was inevitably defeated by the daughter's wildness and by her own poor background, unrealistic attitude, and savage temper. The commercial failure of *Cherokee Night* may have been partly due to the fact that there was no solution for the characters except the impossible one of turning back the clock.

However, examples can be found of plays that held the stage in spite of containing almost insuperable obstacles. Elmer Rice set the Maurrants against an almost overwhelming environment and produced *Street Scene*. Anderson faced Mio with the implacable viciousness of the underworld and produced *Winterset*. Chekov faced attractive characters with their own irremediable incompetence and produced *The Cherry Orchard*. The secret behind these successful plays with almost overwhelming obstacles lies in the fact that these protagonists are given some chance to win, so that the audience is maintained in a state of suspense. Above all, these playwrights were able to evoke sympathy for their protagonists. In such cases, surely the audience empathizes so strongly as to add the straining of its own hope to the desperate struggle of the protagonist.

If the obstacle is not strong enough to cause much of a struggle, it will take the dexterity of a Van Druten to prolong the play interestingly for two hours. If, on the other hand, the obstacle is so powerful that the protagonist has hardly a chance, as is the case in *Winterset,* no less skill than Maxwell Anderson's can keep the audience hoping and fearing until the final curtain.

It is important that however complex the obstacle may be, the elements be integrated, so that the protagonist will struggle against only one opposing force throughout the play. There are many plays in which the obstacle is simply a person, or a social force, or a psychological factor, or some other definite single impediment. In a great many plays, however, the obstacle is complex. In *Elizabeth the*

Queen the obstacle has at least three elements which operate together to impede Elizabeth's permanent adjustment. These elements are Elizabeth's simultaneous devotion to her lover and her kingdom, the independence of her lover, and the machinations of her counselor, Cecil. These are not three single obstacles, attacked one after the other. Cecil's machinations succeed because of Essex's character; Elizabeth's problem exists because of Essex's character; yet if Cecil were content to let her solve her personal problem in her own way, she might, no doubt, have endured quarrels and reconciliations to the end of her days. No element of this complex obstacle could be removed without altering the situation. And every element is clear by the end of the second scene. The obstacle is tightly integrated. In *The Criminal Code* the obstacle is the system in which Bob is caught, a system represented partly by Gleason, who brutalizes the prisoners; partly by MacManus, who naïvely delights in the regimentation; partly by Galloway, who tries to aid Bob's escape; and partly by the political system which delays Bob's parole until too late. The system—prison regimentation, prison philosophy, prison management—ruins Bob. The Warden does not have to combat one element after another, but from the beginning he combats the integrated strength of all three elements.

An example of lack of unity because the obstacle changes has already been given.[7] The protagonist of this play tries to make Kansas land profitable, but he is impeded first by the cattlemen, then by a dust storm, then by a plague of grasshoppers, then by the mills being unable to

---

[7] See above, p. 77 f.

grind the tough winter wheat. The play seems to be a series of one-act plays, not a coherent whole. Another example is Paul Green's *The Field God*, in which Gilchrist is prevented from the enjoyment of a normal love life with Rhoda, first by the fact that his ailing wife, Etta, is alive. Etta dies at the end of Act II. In Act III, Gilchrist and Rhoda are married, but their morbid consciences prevent them from enjoying their life together. The third act seems like a new play.

The audience is baffled and irritated if it is allowed to think that the conquest of a certain obstacle will result in equilibrium for the protagonist, and then is forced to witness a further struggle before he regains his life harmony. An obstacle which has more than one element must be not merely the sum of its parts, but a fusion, an integration of its parts. And if it is at all possible, all the elements which are important should be revealed to the audience within the first third of the play.

If the obstacle is a person, he must arouse some sort of emotional response in the audience. A play is not a debate in which the audience tries to formulate opinions by a dispassionate appraisal of two speakers' reasons. A play is a clash of wills and desires, in which the audience takes sides according to its likes and dislikes. A conflict of views is not drama unless the arguments threaten the well-being of the participants, affecting the audience not through reason so much as through the emotions.[8] A clear illustration of this principle occurs in *Valley Forge*, Act I, Scene 3, as Washington discusses with his generals whether or not to con-

---

[8] See above, p. 62.

tinue the war. Sterling and Varnum reply reasonably, and the scene is about to become boring when Tench cries out, "This whole damned war is treason to King George." No doubt the arguments have been important; but Tench, in his passionate need to believe in Washington, cuts through reason to what the audience can understand—passion; and the scene becomes highly exciting again.

It appears to be easier to write an obstacle against whom the audience directs hostile feelings than one for whom the audience feels sympathy, if one may judge by the fact that contemporary playwrights use the antipathetic obstacle about twice as frequently as the sympathetic one. We dislike Elizabeth's counselor, Cecil, because he is deceitful, and Trock because he is cynical and cruel. We hate the fanatical preacher in *Dark of The Moon* for driving Barbara to betray the Witch-Boy.

On the other hand, the obstacle is not always antipathetic. Moody, the unscrupulous manager who exploits Joe Bonaparte in *Golden Boy*, is deliberately made pathetic by his love for Lorna, and by comparison with Fuselli, who is much more unscrupulous than Moody. Gray, in *Both Your Houses*, is a devoted father and a delightful gentleman. Even MacManus, the inspector of *The Criminal Code*, is almost attractive because of his naïve pride in the perfection of the prison system; while the criminal who sends Bob the knife does so out of a rudimentary sense of loyalty. In *Tomorrow and Tomorrow*, it would be impossible not to like Gail, the sterile husband.

In short, drama does not occur because a character thinks something right or wrong; it occurs because he wants something intolerably. The protagonist must feel passionately even more than he must think clearly. The obstacle must be an obstacle to the achievement of a desire, not merely a personified opinion. Thus it seems wise to ask the beginner to align sympathies for the protagonist and against the obstacle until he has learned to make his protagonist extremely volitional and attractive and the objective extremely desirable.

It has been pointed out in this chapter that one of the three bases of a play is the obstacle, the element of impediment that prevents the protagonist from simply taking what he wants. It has been shown that the obstacle may be a person, an environmental factor, a psychological factor, a factor of heredity, a past action. However complex the obstacle may be, it must be integrated, if the play is to have unity. It must be fairly well-matched to the protagonist, and it must be capable of evoking some emotional response from the audience.

Before going further, it may be well to summarize the last three chapters, since, no matter what may start the mind of the playwright working, he must settle these points before going very far in the construction of the scenario.

The basis of a play is threefold: a protagonist, the thing he needs to establish a harmonious relationship with life, and the impediment that stands between him and his objective. For a beginner, it is a good plan to try to reduce the play to its simplest terms: A wants B, but C stands in the way. The terms A, B, and C may be quite complex, but if they are clear, the scenario can proceed in a logical direction toward the achievement or failure to achieve the objective; that is, a course of action can now be planned toward the climax the playwright wants to achieve.

Certain varieties of this pattern have been touched upon and may be brought together here. In the comedy pattern and especially in farce, one of the three elements is likely to be trivial. The protagonist may strive very hard to achieve a trivial objective, as in *Three Men on a Horse;* or he may be striving toward a strong objective and fighting windmills, as Christy was in *The Playboy of the Western World,*[9] or he may be a weakling himself, like Vice President Winterbottom, buffeted by strong opposition toward or away from a strong objective.

In the "slice-of-life" play, the obstacle is generally an environmental or a psychological factor, the protagonist may be a group, and the objective is likely to be abstract.

In the propaganda play, the playwright wants to rouse the audience for or (usually) against something. The protagonist, individual or group, is generally the mouthpiece of the playwright himself; the obstacle is whatever the playwright is against; and the objective is audience response. Therefore the last curtain falls on a crisis, leaving the audience unsatisfied, and forcing it to supply the climax by asserting its conviction after the play.

In the mystery pattern the murderer is usually the formal obstacle, and the detective or whoever exposes the murderer is the protagonist. But in a good mystery play

---

[9] Old Mahon's delight when Christy agrees to go "like a gallant Captain and his heathen slave" is evidence that he actually wanted the boy to stand on his own feet all along.

often the audience does not know murderer from detective until the end of the play. Thus the actual situation which produces climax is somewhat odd. In the beginning of the play a group of characters, some innocent, some guilty, raise the question, "Who dun it?" The audience picks up the question not so much because of strong empathy with any character as because of its own curiosity. In other words, the audience itself takes the function of protagonist, and often uses more ingenuity than the characters to find the answer. The characters and the audience are thrown off scent, not merely by what the murderer does, but by all sorts of things which the other characters do, and which happen to the other characters. Thus one may say that the obstacle in the play is the ingenuity of the playwright himself in devising the chain of perplexing actions that baffle the audience. The pattern of the mystery play, then, is: The audience seeks the answer to a question, but is impeded by the playwright.

If this appears to be reducing playwriting to a formula, it should be remembered that the formula has been shown to be capable of almost infinite variation both of complexity and of emphasis, and that no element of the formula is "mechanical" if the playwright has drawn faithfully from life for his materials.

Every music teacher knows how eagerly the young student demands a "piece" before he has learned how to play a smooth scale. Every teacher of painting knows the insistence of his students to paint life before they understand the principles of light and shade. The playwright is always too ready to attach the gilded cornices of words to his shaky beams and timbers of plot. Like pupils in the other arts, the playwright should master his scales, chords, and arpeggios; his brushes and oils and varnishes; his saw, plane, and hammer; his basic tools. With them, he may begin to fashion whatever beauty is in his own soul.

EXERCISES

1. Analyze:
   a. What is the obstacle in *Counsellor-at-Law*, *The Glass Menagerie*, *The Voice of the Turtle*?
   b. In what ways are protagonist and obstacle well matched in *Winterset?* In *Dark of the Moon*?
   c. What empathies are created, and how, for the obstacles in *Both Your Houses*, *The Criminal Code*, *The Patriots*?

2. Construct obstacles for the following:
   a. A pretty young stenographer in Minnesota has weak lungs and wants a heavy winter coat.
   b. A lawyer is running for the legislature.
   c. A schoolteacher wants to accept a good position in a distant town.
   d. Two men want to marry the same girl. The girl is the protagonist.
   e. A group of miners demands a wage increase.
   f. A fifteen-year-old girl has learned a serious piece of scandal about someone she idolized. State her objective as well as her obstacle.
   g. A fifteen-year-old boy determines to go into the Navy.
   h. A young wife wants her husband to be proud of her.

THE OBSTACLE

i. A factory-owner wants to replace an incompetent foreman.

j. A doctor wants to spare a patient the knowledge that she has borne an idiot child.

ASSIGNMENTS

PLAYS: Sidney Kingsley, *The Patriots*. New York: Random House, 1943. Elmer Rice, *Counsellor-at-Law*. New York: Samuel French, Inc., 1931.

ADDITIONAL READING: William Archer, *Playmaking: A Manual of Craftsmanship*, pp. 23-33. New York: Dodd, Mead & Company, Inc., 1937. Henry Arthur Jones, "Introduction to Brunetière's Law" in Barrett H. Clark's *European Theories of the Drama*. New York: Crown Publishers, 1947. Arthur Edwin Krows, *Playwriting for Profit*, pp. 85-102. New York: Longmans, Green & Co., Inc., 1928. Brander Matthews, *The Development of the Drama*, pp. 1-37. New York: Charles Scribner's Sons, 1904. Brander Matthews, *A Study of the Drama*, pp. 92-108. Boston: Houghton Mifflin Company, 1910.

7

The Ending of the Play

DRAMA, ACCORDING TO GEORGE PIERCE BAKER, IS THE "presentation of an individual or group of individuals so as to move an audience to responsive emotion of the kind desired by the dramatist and to the amount required."[1] To secure this response means, of course, that the dramatist himself must know what emotion and how much emotion he wants the audience to feel. In the words of John Howard Lawson,

> To act without conscious purpose is irrational; to change one's purpose while one is trying to accomplish it shows weakness and confusion; also that the purpose was not sufficiently analyzed before the act was undertaken. If it turns out that the purpose can not be accomplished, then the act must be abandoned.[2]

The mere selection of certain material implies some attitude toward it. This does not mean that every play is a thesis play. Perhaps one only wants to say, "Is it not sad that a family feud should drive two lovers to their

---

[1] Baker, *Dramatic Technique*, p. 46.
[2] Lawson, *Theory and Technique of Playwriting*, p. 184.

death?" Then one's purpose in writing would be to leave the audience aching with sadness at the death of the lovers. Perhaps one wants to say, "Jealousy can drive a man insane," or "Manners often obscure important emotions," or "The son of a criminal should not have to suffer for the crimes of his father." All these observations or "root ideas"[3] have been used as themes of plays. They are, obviously, of different degrees of profundity. It is not necessary to be particularly profound in writing a play. But whatever the material, the dramatist uses it because for some reason it has meaning and importance for him, and he wants to convey this meaning and importance to an audience.

The dramatist's point of view toward his material is the inevitable result of his experiences in his milieu. Willynilly, what he writes will express this point of view. If he is a shoddy thinker, or maladjusted to his times, or ignorant, or vulgar, his viewpoint will be revealed in his work. Likewise, if he has a concrete and logical attitude, a well-constructed play will reveal it.

The value of knowing his own point of view becomes clear to the playwright when he attempts to determine the ending of his play; for the right ending is the one which most clearly expresses the playwright's attitude toward the material. If he himself is uncertain of what he means, it will be extremely difficult for him to find

---

[3] *Ibid.*, p. 182. Every student of playwriting should be thoroughly familiar with Part III, Chapter III of this invaluable book. See also Baker, *Dramatic Technique,* p. 78 f.; and Ephraim Gotthold von Lessing, "Hamburgische Dramaturgie," No. 34 in Clark, *European Theories of the Drama.*

an ending satisfactory either to himself or to an audience.[4]

How seriously the wrong ending might destroy the essential meaning of the play may be shown by a few examples. The fundamental idea behind *Paris Bound* is that sexual infidelity may be quite unimportant. The play ends with Mary and her husband going on happily together after a sexual lapse on his part. If Mary had refused to take Jim back, the play would have meant just the opposite of what Barry evidently intended. If she had allowed herself to be carried away by the musician who taught her how basic the sexual urge is, the play might have meant that a woman has as much right to sexual freedom as a man. Any one of these ideas might have been conveyed by this story. By selecting the ending as it stands, Barry made clear the idea which to him was fundamental in the material.

In *Street Scene,* Elmer Rice simply wants to point out that one's life prospects are determined to a large extent by his environment. He allows Rose to take her little brother to a better neighborhood after the grim events which almost crushed them. If he had thrown her into the arms of the boy who loved her, the meaning might have been "Love conquers all," "Even love cannot save people from the tragic effects of a bad environment," or simply, "Misery loves company." If Rose had gone to the man who wanted her for his mistress, again the meaning of the play would have changed to "One is at the

---

[4] For an opposite opinion, see Matthews, *A Study of the Drama,* pp. 195 ff. Note that this view is based on the plays of and around 1910, a transition period.

mercy of his environment." But Rice evidently believed that one can escape one's environment, and therefore he allowed Rose and her brother a ray of hope in their removal to a better neighborhood.

The last example will show how an inconclusive ending leaves the meaning of the play obscure. In *Both Your Houses*, Alan McClean, a new member of Congress, is shocked at the extravagance and venality of the politicians who make our laws. He tries to reduce to absurdity a uselessly expensive bill by insisting that it include every ridiculous trailer that has been proposed. But the bill passes with all its trailers. Disgusted, McClean asks if honesty in government is possible, and is frankly told, "No," by the committee leaders. McClean then warns that such a system will produce revolt among the American people. He does not say what he intends to do, but goes out, followed by the daughter of his chief opponent. The last speech of the play is a cynical condemnation of political swindlers by a political swindler who is too old to be caught up with in his time, he says. McClean's secretary replies, "Maybe." Presumably Mr. Anderson's purpose in showing up the system was to make the American people revolt. But Alan McClean, the protagonist, the voice of every honest man in the audience, walked out. Hence, the total result upon the audience was not so much a disposition to fight the system as a feeling that nothing could be done about it.

These examples show that the meaning of a play determines how the play should end. The playwright must decide with absolute clarity just what the material means to him, and what he wants it to mean to the audience.[5] In his training period he should form the habit of stating his meaning in a single sentence, the root idea,[6] and he should see that the ending of his play expresses this idea and no other. Of course it is not to be assumed that the playwright will know the significance of his material at the outset of the construction process. He may; but it is more likely that he will see the significance only after he has probed quite deeply into the material. That is, he may be well along in the scenario before he knows exactly what he wants to say through this particular material. But the point is that before the scenario is complete he must see what it means in order to write the proper ending, and to make all the preparation needed for that ending.

Whether the theme is highly important or only very slight, the audience wants to know what happens to any of the characters in which it becomes interested. The skilled dramatist learns to focus interest and deepen sympathy for a few main characters, and to answer scrupulously any questions with regard to their fate. Primarily he emphasizes the protagonist, the obstacle, and the objective, if these are characters, and a very few minor characters; and he writes at least a suggestion of an ending for their stories.

As to the fate of the protagonist, there are, as Jacobowsky says, two possibilities: either he gets his objective, or

---

[5] Brander Matthews discusses the aims of the playwright, especially from the point of view of moral effect, in A Study of the Drama, pp. 225-231. See also Krows, Playwriting for Profit, pp. 61-64; and Nicoll, The Theory of Drama.

[6] Lawson, Theory and Technique of Playwriting, p. 182.

he does not. This is not necessarily a distinction between comedy and tragedy. The happy ending is, of course, that in which the protagonist gets what he wants and thereby finds equilibrium and happiness. Sometimes, however, the protagonist gets what he wants, but is prevented from enjoying it by a simultaneous catastrophe This is the ending of *Romeo and Julet*, in which the lovers achieve their objectives of being together forever only in death. It is the ending of *Oedipus*, who succeeds in ridding the state of the plague only through his ruin. It is the ending of *The Criminal Code*, in which the Warden secures Bob's pardon, but only after the prison has had its inexorable effect upon the boy. A play well designed toward this type of ending evokes the most intense pity.

The other alternative is that the protagonist does not get what he wants. Here again there are at least two possibilities. If the protagonist has failed to arouse sympathy, or if the objective does not seem desirable, the audience may feel the protagonist's failure served him right. This sort of ending leaves the audience cold, and produces no climax. In *The Left Bank*[7] the protagonist, Claire, an American *émigrée* in Paris, wants to provide a normal home for her adolescent son. Claire is not a very dynamic person; she yields in situations where one thinks she should stand up for her convictions. Her self-centered amoral husband is the obstacle. The son is the objective, talked about quite a bit, but never seen, and therefore not very appealing. When Claire divorces her irresponsible husband in order

---

[7] Elmer Rice's play, which ran for a year in the reflected glory of *Counsellor-at-Law*.

to be with the boy, one feels that she took a long time to reach a fairly easy decision. Claire is too little, and not attractive enough, and her objective is too little known to permit the audience to feel any great concern for her well-being.

If, on the other hand, the sympathetic protagonist fails to achieve a desirable objective through some factor not his own fault, pity is extremely keen, especially if defeat seems unavoidable.

In this connection it may be suggested that the term *inevitable* has been overworked and perhaps not clearly understood by students. Surely it is exasperating to watch the protagonist suffer if one feels that his suffering could have been avoided. But the playwright who "stacks the cards" against his protagonist usually does not build sympathy, but rather tends to make his protagonist seem a fool or a poor worm undeserving of sympathy. The *inevitable*, as applied to a play, does not mean card-stacking. It means that the protagonist has powers of some kind strong enough to cope with his obstacle, except in the single instance when he is beaten. To say that a fatal flaw in his character defeats him, or that fate defeats him, must not imply that he is a weakling. If the play ends with the failure of the protagonist, the best way of arousing sympathy for him is to let his defeat seem the logical outcome of his strong opposition to a force *somewhat* beyond his control.

In summary, the protagonist may get his objective and live happily ever after; or get his objective and with it catastrophe; or he may fail to get his objective for some logical reason beyond his control. In any case, his actions throughout the play lead him at least plausibly, and *if possible* inevitably toward this ending.

If the obstacle is a person, he may be made to suffer, he may go unpunished, he may be made happy, or he may reform.

Usually an unattractive obstacle is made to suffer in some way. The wicked villain of melodrama and the anti-social obstacle of today's drama suffer in response to a primitive desire of the audience personally to inflict punishment on any individual who deliberately makes life difficult for a well-meaning person. Richard III is killed in battle; Iago is turned over to justice; Jud Fry of *Oklahoma!* is killed with his own frog-sticker. The punishment is not always pointed. Trock, the remorseless criminal of *Winterset,* tells in his opening soliloquy that he is already dying of tuberculosis contracted in prison. This fact serves to motivate his almost unbelievable ruthlessness, but it also means that he will not long survive his misdeeds. Anderson does not play up the punishment after the first unforgettable speech, because part of his thesis in *Winterset* is a cynical reflection that justice is trampled by the law courts; but Trock gets punished and the audience is glad. Sometimes the suffering of the obstacle consists merely in mental pangs. In *Holiday,* Julia has to suffer the embarrassment of a broken engagement, a check to her vanity, and some personal disappointment for standing between Johnny and Linda. In *Golden Boy* the protagonist is killed, but Moody, the obstacle, loses not only his best money-maker in the death of Joe, but also the mistress of whom he is deeply fond. Many of the best plays written today and more of the merely popular ones have some form of punishment as the fate of the obstacle. Yet one can point to a few instances in which the obstacle is not made to suffer. In *Elizabeth the Queen* the obstacle must triumph. Elizabeth pronounces one mighty threat against Cecil; but at Essex's death she merely says, "It's your day, Cecil, I dare say you know that. The snake in the grass endures." In *Counsellor-at-Law*, Cora, the snobbish, unfaithful wife, goes away with her lover unmolested, and the political rival is simply quieted with the threat of blackmail.

Once in a while the obstacle is actually left happy. This is the case in *Tomorrow and Tomorrow*, when Eve gives her child to the husband whose sterility almost destroyed her interest in life. In this play the husband is definitely made attractive, and the audience would find it intolerable if he should be made to suffer. A reward, however, is rare for an obstacle who inhibits an attractive protagonist from achieving the objective which the audience wants him to achieve.

Finally, the obstacle may reform. Montoya, the fanatic old conservative in *Night Over Taos*,[8] beaten by the march of time, yields to it, but retains his honor by committing suicide. Usually the reform of the obstacle is not acceptable to the psychology-wise public of today. In *Broken Dishes*[9] a far-fetched coincidence shows up the hollowness of the mother's bragging and forces her to

[8] Written by Maxwell Anderson.
[9] Written by Martin Flavin.

reform; but one does not think the reform permanent. Particularly irritating is the reform of Reverend Henry, the big bad Negro who causes all the trouble in Paul Green's *Potter's Field*.[10] From his first appearance he is sinister. But in the last act, without warning, he appears as an evangelistic figure, almost holy. Such a metamorphosis is hard to believe.

A thorough study of the ending of the obstacle's story suggests that the most satisfactory thing to do with a wicked person is to punish him in proportion to his wickedness. If he is viciously antisocial, he should be jailed or executed. If he is merely selfish or irresponsible, he should be spanked in some way. The audience appreciates justice and wants to see it administered. But again, the fate of the obstacle must not violate the playwright's point of view toward his material.

The subordinate characters of a play are usually introduced to supplement the main story thread. But if they have any intrinsic interest for the audience, they must be given an ending to their stories. This fact was recognized by the producers of *Oklahoma!* in revising Lynn Rigg's *Green Grow the Lilacs*. Ado Annie and the Peddler became so entertaining in *Oklahoma!* that Ado Annie had to catch a husband, and the Peddler to get caught under the rose.

How much time must be devoted to the fate of the subordinate characters, and whether their story is to be ended before or after that of the main characters, depends

---

[10] Early version of *Roll Sweet Chariot*, which does not alter either the character or the fate of the Reverend Henry.

on what final emotion the playwright wishes the audience to take away. Sometimes this question cannot be answered until well along in the rehearsal period or even after a few performances.

One more point must be made. A climax is the satisfaction of the audience in the re-establishment of a broken or threatened balance of relationships. The audience must feel that the story "came out right." This feeling of satisfaction does not occur fortuitously. It requires the highest skill of the playwright. Lawson expresses the importance and difficulty of this matter in his excellent chapter, "Unity in Terms of Climax":

> Every detail of the action is determined by the *end* toward which the action is moving ... the climax is the concrete realization of the theme in terms of an event. In practical playwriting this means that the climax is the point of reference by which the validity of every element of the structure can be determined.[11]

The playwright who "has a story but can't decide how to end it" may be glad to know that there are only a few possible endings, and that the one to be used depends on the meaning he himself attaches to the material. Some of the specific difficulties of young playwrights may shed further light on the problem of the ending.

One of the most baffling difficulties of young playwrights comes from a too-solemn respect for fact. The playwright takes his story, let us say, from life, perhaps from the life of a person still living. The actual story is not ended, and the student shrinks from inventing an

---

[11] Lawson, *Theory and Technique of Playwriting*, p. 178.

ending. The first suggestion in this case is that the biographer or the novelist may have to write the whole life of the character, but the playwright needs only one significant action that reveals the character as the playwright sees him. This is the course Tennessee Williams followed in writing *The Glass Menagerie*. Instead of trying to tell the whole story of the mother and her son and daughter, he selected the one dramatic moment of an undramatic life, the moment when the daughter had a gentleman caller; and he built his play toward the mother's failure to get the young man for her daughter. In this one action Mr. Williams was able to epitomize the whole life of his three characters.

A good many historical plays fail because the young writer knows too much. Scholarship must, of course, be complete and honest, since the more one knows, the better he understands his characters in their milieu. But the time for scholarship in playwriting is long before writing, so that the material is assimiliated and the significant facts rise into prominence; and after a tentative scenario has been made and the playwright knows just what facts he will need in his play. Reading while building the scenario often results in cluttering the play with incidents which obscure rather than clarify. In selecting material for an historical play, it is necessary to find one significant action to express whatever the playwright wants to express. In two hours it is impossible to present a hero's entire life.

Another point to remember in using material from life or history is that one has excellent precedent for adding, omitting, rearranging, even distorting material in order to preserve the meaning and emotional effect that the playwright believes legitimate. Shakespeare heads a list which includes Anderson,[12] Sherwood,[13] Kingsley,[14] and Shaw.[15] The playwright is an artist with a certain point of view to get across. He is free to use his materials in any way that does not actually falsify those materials. Again it should be pointed out that careful scholarship must provide the basis for tampering with fact. The playwright must answer two questions: "Can the material mean what I want it to mean?" "Can the audience be made to believe I am right?"

Sometimes the young playwright has not established his own attitude toward the material. He writes fact, merely fact, not the fusion of stimulus and personal attitude which is basic to the creation of a work of art. For the artist there is a distinction to be made between fact and truth. Fact is what actually happened, and the report of it is a photograph which any good craftsman could make. Truth in art is fact fused with feeling and meaning. It is inconceivable that George Washington should have actually said after a battle, "The spirit of earth moves over earth like flame." Yet this is one of the high moments of *Valley Forge*, and it is entirely true in the light of our image of Washington as a great leader. Truth, one might almost say, is not a report of speech or action;

---

[12] *Elizabeth the Queen, Mary of Scotland, Anne of the Thousand Days, Valley Forge.*
[13] *Abe Lincoln in Illinois.*
[14] *The Patriots.*
[15] *Saint Joan, Ceasar and Cleopatra, The Devil's Disciple, Great Catherine, The Man of Destiny.*

it is a revelation of the significance of the speech or action.

One of the most common reasons that the young play-wright cannot find the right ending to his story is that he is not clear as to the basic character-situation, especially the objective. He wants simply to present characters in a static rather than a dramatic way. Unless the characters can be presented as needing something or defending some threatened essential, there is no play in the material.

Finally, one of the young playwright's most cherished wishes is to be subtle. He has a taste for the inconclusive ending. Some caution against oversubtlety has already been given in discussing the objective. This caution applies equally well to the ending of a play. If the playwright decides to make a very little say a great deal, he will find that he has to prepare the audience to get his meaning. For example, *Counsellor-at-Law* ends with the Counsellor hurrying off to a case with his secretary after Cora has left him. It is not necessary to write a love scene, for Regina has revealed her love for Counsellor Simon to the young man who was courting her. She has revealed a thoroughly feminine hatred of Simon's wife. She has been extremely solicitous about his well-being. She has been kind to his mother, in contrast to Cora's snobbery. And finally, she saves him from suicide. There is no further need to prove what the audience already knows. The "subtle" ending is entirely clear.

For the ending of the play, more than any other single element, shows what the playwright means by his story, and satisfies the curiosity and concern of the audience in the fate of the characters. In constructing a play, it is not necessary to "start from the end," [16] but one must know where he is going before charting his course.

EXERCISES

1. Analyze:
   a. What are the means by which the ending of *The Criminal Code* is made satisfying?
   b. What is the theme or meaning expressed by the ending of *The Criminal Code*? Justify your answer.

2. Determine your reaction to the following situations; then find the ending that will express your reaction and will also satisfy an audience:
   a. An educated Negro in South Carolina wants to establish a school for Negroes in his county. He has a complex obstacle: his own poverty, the apathy of the farm group he wants to educate, and the indifference of the white school board.
   b. A boy who has talent but no ambition decides to run for the legislature in order to spite the girl who refused to marry him. Find the obstacle and the ending.
   c. An old farmer divides his rich farm land between two sons to avoid income tax. He gives the best land to his older son, although he loves the younger son best. Find the farmer's

---

[16] Lawson, *Theory and Technique of Playwriting*, quoting Ernest Legouve and Percival Wilde. But see Wilde, *The Craftsmanship of the One-Act Play*, pp. 61, 79-88.

objective, something to make the old man attractive, an adequate obstacle, and the right ending.

d. Napoleon Bonaparte, after becoming Emperor, married Josephine Beauharnais, a widow with children, because of her distinguished appearance and noble blood. She frankly married him for the security he could give her children. Find protagonist, objective, obstacle, and ending.

ASSIGNMENTS

PLAYS: Paul Green, *Johnny Johnson*. New York: Samuel French, Inc., 1937. Oscar Hammerstein, and Richard Rodgers, *Oklahoma!* New York: Random House, 1943. Lynn Riggs, *Green Grow the Lilacs*. New York: Samuel French, Inc., 1931.

ADDITIONAL READING: William Archer, *Playmaking: A Manual of Craftsmanship*, Part IV, pp. 321-368. New York: Dodd, Mead & Company, Inc., 1937. George Pierce Baker, *Dramatic Technique*, Chapter XX. Boston: Houghton Mifflin Company, 1919. Brander Matthews, *A Study of the Drama*, Chapters IX and X. Boston: Houghton Mifflin Company, 1910. Allardyce Nicoll, *The Theory of Drama*, pp. 119-137, 185-213. New York: The Thomas Y. Crowell Company, n.d. Jean Racine, "First Preface to Britannicus," in Barrett H. Clark, *European Theories of the Drama*. New York: Crown Publishers, 1947. Percival Wilde, *The Craftsmanship of the One-Act Play*, Chapter X. Boston: Little, Brown & Company, 1938.

8

The Course of Action

SKILL IN PLAYWRITING HAS BEEN CALLED "CONCEALING the skeleton." Many a young playwright, however, attempts by fine writing and busy scenes to conceal the fact that there is no skeleton in his play, with the result that the audience is left baffled instead of moved.

The term *skeleton* is an apt description of the relation of the story to the play. As the muscles of the body move the bones, so the spirit behind the story moves the story and makes it seem alive; but just as the muscles could accomplish nothing without the stiffening power of the bones, so no amount of lyrical spirit can give coherent action to a play that lacks story.

The skeleton of a play is a course of action, or story, an apparently causal and logical system of events which accounts for the protagonist's either gaining or failing to gain his objective, and which brings him from his initial instability to a state of more or less permanent harmony.

The term *logical* is not strictly accurate, since belief is not solely a mater of logic. Any preacher or political speaker[1] knows that he may argue with flawless reason for hours without inducing belief in his audience; but that if he can touch a fundamental human desire, if he can appeal to the basic hopes and fears of people, he can convince them of almost anything.[2] The basis of a sermon or a political harangue or a play must be logical and honest if it is to command respect; but if it is to be convincing it must also be emotional. Thus one can only say that the skeleton of a play must be apparently causal and logical.

This concept gives the dramatist the right to include in his play any material which he believes necessary and important. His problem of preparing the audience may be doubly difficult if some of his material is illogical; but he can use anything short of deliberate violence to the material, if he can make it *seem* logical to the audience.

The course of action is not merely a chronological series of events, but a causal system. It is incorrect to say that it is a chain of cause and effect, for it is not necessary for each event to be caused by the event preceding it and to produce the one following it.[3] True, each event must have

---

[1] A. Craig Baird, *Public Discussion and Debate,* Chapter I; and Alan Monroe, *Principles and Types of Speech,* Rev. Ed., Chapters VIII and XVIII. Chicago: Scott, Foresman & Company, 1939.

[2] Hollingworth, *The Psychology of the Audience,* p. 109 f. Quoting W. D. Scott, he writes, "The orator who has welded his audience into a homogeneous crowd should never be guilty of attempting to reason with them, for by the very process of forming them into a crowd he has deprived them of the power of critical thinking."

[3] Lawson, *Theory and Technique of Playwriting,* p. 121. On p. 231 of the same work, Mr. Lawson says, "The notion that a play is an unbroken line of cause and effect is a dangerous one, because it prevents

its clear cause. But the important point is that every event belongs to a system of causes that produce one final event, the re-establishment of equilibrium.

The incidents or steps of the course of action can usually be joined by one of three connectives, AND, BUT, and THEREFORE. A prevalence of AND in the early part of the play is likely to indicate solid motivation, plenty of causes; a prevalence of THEREFORE indicates effect, logical coherence; a prevalence of BUT means peripetia, suspense, and is particularly good toward the end of the play. The connective AND THEN is practically never necessary in a well-integrated play. Of course time is involved to some extent in all action. But the important action hinges, generally, not on time but on other actions, on character, or on both. The student playwright should examine the incidents he wishes to include, not on the basis of their chronological order, but on the basis of their use in the causal system.

Analysis of the course of action in two plays will illustrate the important fact that the course of action is a system rather than a chain of causes. In *Elizabeth the Queen* two major causes underlie the story as a whole, Cecil's plot and Essex's pride. It is Essex's pride that provoke's Cecil, and makes Essex fall into the trap. It is Essex's pride and the Queen's apparent silence *together* which cause the *coup d'état*—a development further than Cecil

---

the piling up of diverse forces driving toward the climax." See also Krows, *Playwriting for Profit*, p. 60. Krows writes: "A play is not a prolonged story, but an evolved story." For the effect of the "chain" structure, see Paul Green's *Johnny Johnson*. New York: Samuel French, Inc., 1937.

had planned. Elizabeth throws Essex into prison partly because she fears his arrogance may cost her the throne, partly because it gives her feminine satisfaction to triumph over her lover. Her attempt to save him is caused, of course, by love and remorse. Essex's refusal to accept her desperate offer of the kingdom is caused as much by his pride as by his sense of England's need. But actually he dies because he and Elizabeth are politically incompatible, because Cecil intervened, because Essex committed an act of treason, and because his honesty and his pride forbade him to live a bad king. Thus Cecil's plan succeeded and Elizabeth lost her lover as the result of a system, not a chain of causes.

The same relation of story elements is revealed in *Green Grow the Lilacs,* a play based on only two incidents. Here again it is clear that, although one happening leads to another throughout much of the play, nearly every event has more than one cause, if not in the action, at least in the *status quo.* Laurey had to go to the party with Jeeter because she was afraid to refuse him, because the particular coquetry that she and Curley used made them pretend to be independent of each other, and because in asking Aunt Eller to go to the party, Curley forced Laurey's hand. Laurey fired Jeeter because she was afraid of him, because he was in a position where he might harm her, and because he did try to harm her. The whole combination of circumstances up to this point threw Laurey into Curley's arms. It is unnecessary to go further to show that causation in this play, too, is more than a chain; it is a system.

SCHEMATIZED COURSE OF ACTION
ELIZABETH THE QUEEN

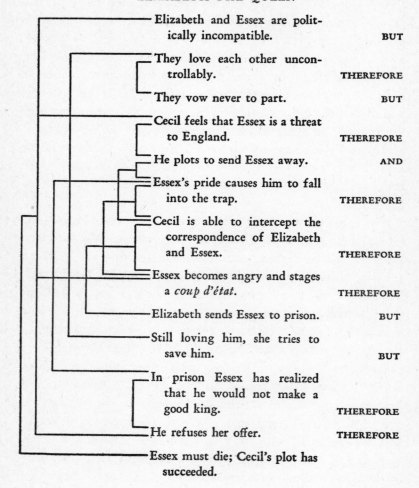

Elizabeth and Essex are politically incompatible. — **BUT**

They love each other uncontrollably. — **THEREFORE**

They vow never to part. — **BUT**

Cecil feels that Essex is a threat to England. — **THEREFORE**

He plots to send Essex away. — **AND**

Essex's pride causes him to fall into the trap. — **THEREFORE**

Cecil is able to intercept the correspondence of Elizabeth and Essex. — **THEREFORE**

Essex becomes angry and stages a *coup d'état*. — **THEREFORE**

Elizabeth sends Essex to prison. — **BUT**

Still loving him, she tries to save him. — **BUT**

In prison Essex has realized that he would not make a good king. — **THEREFORE**

He refuses her offer. — **THEREFORE**

Essex must die; Cecil's plot has succeeded.

SCHEMATIZED COURSE OF ACTION
GREEN GROW THE LILACS

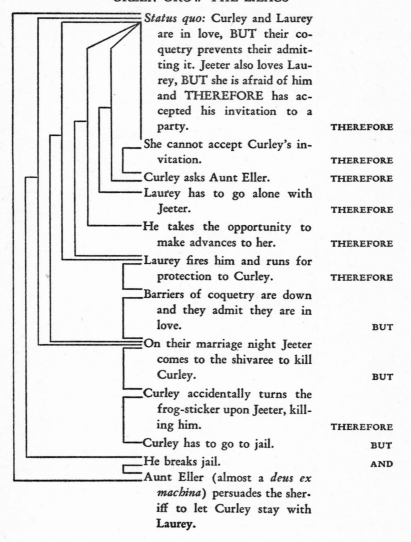

Status quo: Curley and Laurey are in love, BUT their coquetry prevents their admitting it. Jeeter also loves Laurey, BUT she is afraid of him and THEREFORE has accepted his invitation to a party.

She cannot accept Curley's invitation.

Curley asks Aunt Eller.

Laurey has to go alone with Jeeter.

He takes the opportunity to make advances to her.

Laurey fires him and runs for protection to Curley.

Barriers of coquetry are down and they admit they are in love.

On their marriage night Jeeter comes to the shivaree to kill Curley.

Curley accidentally turns the frog-sticker upon Jeeter, killing him.

Curley has to go to jail.

He breaks jail.

Aunt Eller (almost a *deus ex machina*) persuades the sheriff to let Curley stay with Laurey.

THEREFORE

THEREFORE

THEREFORE

THEREFORE

THEREFORE

THEREFORE

BUT

BUT

THEREFORE

BUT

AND

The late George Pierce Baker distinguishes the story or course of action or skeleton of a play from the plot of a play by saying that the story is "what the play boils down to when you try to tell a friend as briefly as possible what it is about." [4] The story is only part of the plot. It is what happens to the characters, what they do. The plot, as expressed in the written or mental scenario, is the story *arranged and amplified* by the playwright, in order to make the audience respond as he wishes it to. The scenario contains all the acts and scenes in order, with at least a general indication of what is to be done in each: all entrances and exits, preparatory material, suspense devices—in short, everything but the dialogue and the stage manager's plots.

Before one can begin to plot a play, he must have some sort of story. There is no rule as to how much story is needed. *Elizabeth the Queen* has not so much story as *King Lear* or *Richelieu* or *Under the Gaslight;* but it has quite a bit more than *Green Grow the Lilacs.* Van Druten's stories are often very slight. By actual count of pages, only one-third of Elmer Rice's great *Street Scene* is story. There is little elaboration of story in *The Cherry Orchard* or *Ghosts* or *Our Town.* But even *Life With Father,* frankly a loose collection of anecdotes, needed the scrap of story about Father's christening to indicate the play was ended, and to bring down the curtain on something like a climax. The story need not be elaborate if the writer has mature insight into his characters and skill in building great scenes from many details. But to a young

---

[4] Baker, *Dramatic Technique,* pp. 57-61.

writer, inventing a story is much easier than developing characters and scenes.[5] The purpose of this chapter is to show that once the initial character-situation is established, a story is not difficult to construct.

A course of action may be described as either positive or negative. It is positive when the protagonist takes the initiative, directing his actions consciously toward a goal which he sets for himself. Macbeth begins to act immediately upon conceiving the desire to become King; his course of action is positive. The course of action is negative when the protagonist has to defend himself against a threat to his well-being. In such a case some other character may have the positive course. Othello does not act until Iago goads him to fear Desdemona's infidelity; Othello has a negative course of action, while Iago's is positive. Sometimes the course of action is a combination of both positive and negative elements. In *Winterset*, for example, Mio comes to New York to vindicate his father, and actually pushes his investigation in the face of recognized danger from Trock. But Trock is also positive, and forces Mio to a defensive position. There is surely no rule requiring a playwright to make his protagonist take the initiative. On the other hand, as has been pointed out, one of the surest ways of making a protagonist appealing is to make him highly volitional; and one of the easiest ways of making him volitional is to make him take the initiative in the action.

When an individual wants something very much, as the protagonist of a play does, it is natural for him to

---

[5] In spite of Aristotle, *Poetics* VI. See below, pp. 298 ff.

make a plan to get it, using whatever resources he may possess. If the course of action is positive, and the protagonist "conscious of the goal and of the means which he employs," the plan will be his. In *Both Your Houses,* Alan plans to defeat the politicians by packing the bill under consideration so full of expensive trailers that Congress will not pass it. In *The Criminal Code,* the Warden plans to secure Bob's release, while the criminals carry out another plan, complicating matters. In some plays the course of action is thus the plan of the obstacle or of some other character. The villain, Iago, plans to drive Othello mad. Lord Cecil of *Elizabeth the Queen* plans to prevent Elizabeth from reconciling her two objectives, Essex and England.

Sometimes the characters and the situation are such that none of the characters can provide a usable plan. The course of action in this sort of situation is a complex of circumstances. In *Street Scene,* for example, the tragedy of the characters is that they have not the mental or moral strength to combat their environment. Even Maurrant's return to check up on his wife seems an act of sudden impulse rather than a deliberate plan. Likewise, in *Green Grow the Lilacs,* Jeeter is a constant threat to Laurey; but one feels in his action only the sort of deliberation of which a maniac would be capable, even when he appears at the shivaree. Like Maurrant, he appears to act upon overwhelming impulse. Maurrant happens to succeed, and Jeeter happens to fail.

A course of action based on circumstances is perhaps more difficult to construct than one which can be built around a clear-cut plan, since it is hard to make this kind of a course of action seem logical. But, well constructed, the course of action based on circumstance has the advantage of seeming as untheatrical and as real as life itself.

The requisites of a good course of action are that it shall seem to lead logically to the ending the playwright has devised; that it shall seem to proceed without the obvious interference of the playwright; and that it shall reveal the protagonist as dynamic, volitional.

One of the most effective ways of learning any task is to watch someone else do it. Thus a case study may serve to suggest to an inexperienced playwright how to utilize the principles studied so far in constructing a course of action for his own play. The method given here is not by any means the only method; but it has the advantage of achieving clarity, the first requirement of a play. For the beginner, this method may serve until he has developed his own technique.

The student began,[6] as many young playwrights do, with a character, his aunt, whom he wished to make his protagonist of his play. He knew the following facts about her:

> She is unmarried, about 58, not pretty, but has charm, dresses well, is very active. Her nieces and nephews enjoy going to her house for supper. She lives alone, but has many friends. She plays cards, will drink, occasionally tells a shady story, more to be a

[6] Clayton Hamilton declares that there are only four ways of starting a play: from an abstract idea or theme, from an idea of a character, from a striking situation, or from a feeling of an environment. *"So You're Writing a Play!"*, pp. 79-93.

good sport than because she is interested. She has a good sense of humor even in regard to herself. She is a good businesswoman, executrix of a moderately large estate left by her mother, to whom she devoted the years when most of her friends were rearing families; but she is not a martyr. Her public works include Red Cross, church committees, Girl Scouts, and an orphanage of which she is president. She is always doing things for people, visiting the sick, staying with the bereaved, helping her young relatives financially and spiritually.

She has had at least three romances, but does not seem to have any regrets or complexes about marriage. She has two humorous faults: she falls down often, but never hurts herself; and she gets in a good many minor traffic accidents, but never admits she is to blame.

Summarizing, she has plenty of money, no apparent wish for a husband or children, seems perfectly balanced, not dramatic.

If this woman was to be used as the protagonist of a play, it was necessary to find some angle of her life that was unsatisfactory, that would reveal her as volitional. The student investigated her three romances as far as he could, without meeting anything that seemed significant. He tried inventing a love story about her, but his inventions not only seemed banal; they seemed to be false, to distort the character of his aunt as he knew her. He simply could not see her as disappointed in love. He reported being "stuck," and the following colloquy took place:

Q. What does she most want?

A. Nothing. She has everything she wants.

Q. What would make her desperately unhappy if she lost it?

A. She's got to be doing things for people. That seems to be the main thing with her.

Q. Is it a compensation for anything?

A. She just asks, "I wonder if she'd like me to do—" whatever it is. A kind of matter of conscience. The golden rule.

Q. Is she particularly interested in any of her nieces or nephews?

A. She helped me out of a jam, and I haven't felt any difference, I mean in our getting along together. And as to dying—she lost her mother and didn't go to pieces. She lost a brother and got through it. She's got fortitude.

Q. Is there any public work she particularly likes?

A. Probably the orphanage, because she does most of the work around there. The committees are lazy, and they put off doing things.

Q. Would she care if she were put off the board?

A. I guess it would be the worst slap she ever had. She has done a lot of good for the home—Say! That's the angle. Something happens to throw her out of the home.

Q. What could happen?

A. Well, once she fired an incompetent matron—

Next day he produced his first statement of the objective:

Among her public works is an orphanage for which she has worked twenty years, her influence being toward humanity and progress, while the rest of the board were reactionary. The home is her child. Her next move is a delicate one, to get rid of the old, incompetent matron and introduce one with training for the job. The old matron is a relative of a rich board member, a descendant of the founder. It will be a tough job to get the old lady out at the risk of offending the rich board member. Objective: she wants to be useful; to improve the home by getting a competent matron; to give the best to her child.

The student readily saw that it would be hard to make this objective seem vital enough to upset the aunt's equilibrium, and very easy to let sympathy get away from the aunt to the poor old lady who was to be thrown out of a job. He had to find a way of convincing the audience that firing the matron was a vital necessity to the aunt. Probably, he agreed, the flaw in the objective was the statement that the home was her child. Ordinary people could not understand that an institution could mean so much to a person, even though that person had given the best years of his life to creating the institution. The objective would have to be more personal.

The student returned after several weeks with quite a bit more information about the situation as a whole, and the following statement of the objective:

> Among her public works is an orphanage, for which she has worked twenty years, her influence being toward humanity and progress, while the rest of the board are reactionary. In the home is a girl, sixteen, over the age limit. She has been there since infancy, and Miss Stacy has practically brought her up. Miss Stacy would have adopted her except that her mother did not want to be responsible for a strange child of questionable parentage. Now that Miss Stacy's mother has died, and the girl is almost grown up, Miss Stacy thinks it is too late to adopt her. But Miss Stacy still considers herself the child's guardian, loves her, and intends to get her a job and a husband. Without being sentimental about it, Miss Stacy hopes to satisfy a deep feminine need to provide for her child. Objective: to see that the girl has a happy normal life in spite of her institutional background.

This was still too vague, but it was obviously a more attractive objective than to fire the matron. The problem now was to find an obstacle that would make the objective more concrete. The student was sure that he still wanted to tie the matron into the story, and that she was on the side of the obstacle, as was the rich board member. What he needed was a way of tangling the girl's story with that of the matron. In a day or two he came back with this statement of the obstacle:

> The board, headed by the matron's wealthy relative, want to get rid of the girl because they are not authorized to care for girls over sixteen. But Miss Stacy compromises, allowing her complaints against the matron to go unspoken as long as the girl is allowed to remain peaceably. But when the matron is caught stealing and involves the girl in her crime, the girl's name must be cleared at any cost. The rich board member withdraws her support, and the home will go on the rocks. The obstacle is complex: The rich board member wants her poor relative to have a job; the board is averse to change, particularly if it involves inconvenience to a member of a "leading family"; and a scandal will cause withdrawal of public support.

He was now able to state the character-situation in clear, brief terms:

> Miss Stacy (Protagonist) has sublimated her mother impulse in service to humanity, the orphanage. Her particular concern is for one of the orphans, Ebba (Objective). But Ebba gets involved in the peculations of the matron, a poor relative of the rich board member (Obstacle), so that firing the matron is impossible without hurting Ebba, whom Miss Stacy loves; and without wrecking her lifework, the orphanage, by a scandal.

Phrasing the author's purpose was the next task to be accomplished. Of course the first statement was that he wanted to gain sympathy for Miss Stacy; but that was merely the general objective of any play, to gain sympathy for the protagonist. He then said he wanted the audience "to pity the wise, courageous, love-hungry woman who had her only love satisfactions taken from her." His sense of humor rescued him from this violence to his aunt's character. There could be nothing sentimental about the response to her. He tried again. "I want them (the audience) to recognize her potentialities for good." This was cold, intellectual. After several more attempts he produced the statement of purpose that guided him through the writing of the play:

> I want the audience to feel that Miss Stacy must be allowed to utilize her capacity for service.

Here was a Hedda in reverse, a successful Hedda. It began to look as if he had material for a play. The ending was easy to find. If the audience was to feel that Miss Stacy must be allowed to serve the orphanage, she had to be successful in her objective of getting a new matron. If she was not to be pitied, Ebba must be happy at the end of the play. And through the downfall of her enemies Miss Stacy had to be in a better position to serve than she was in the beginning, if poetic justice was to be served.

The next step was to find a logical thread of events that could lead to such a conclusion. The first problem was to get Ebba solidly involved with the matron so that firing the matron would compromise Ebba. If the old lady were falsifying the housekeeping books, Ebba would have to know she was doing so. But if the ending was to be a success for Miss Stacy, there could be no scandal; and the rich board member would have to stay on the board and be reconciled to Miss Stacy. The revelation of the matron's guilt would have to come about through something the old lady herself did, rather than from any cold accusation by Miss Stacy. If she were sufficiently afraid, the old lady might give herself away. There would have to be a strong stimulus to make her do this. She would have to do it in a way that would not get sympathy for her, but would get it for Ebba. This was the course of reasoning that produced the first draft of a course of action:

It is just before the Community Chest allotment is to be made, and a scandal would destroy the home.	BUT
The new treasurer discovers that the matron has muddled the housekeeping books and fears investigation by the city auditor.	THEREFORE
Miss Stacy resolves to get rid of the matron tactfully, by saying she is too old to do the job.	BUT
The rich board member counters that an investigation will also show that Ebba is overage and the home has no right to keep her.	THEREFORE
The board compromises by voting the job of bookkeeper to Ebba to justify her staying and to lighten the matron's work.	THEREFORE
The matron begins a policy of intimidation of Ebba, continues to falsify the books, making Ebba appear to be in collusion.	BUT
The new treasurer finds the falsified item.	AND
Ebba breaks into tears and refuses to speak.	AND
The matron walks off with the book.	AND
When the treasurer wants to show Miss Stacy what has happened, she finds the falsified page torn out.	AND
The matron says she burned it to save dear Ebba.	THEREFORE
Miss Stacy speaks privately to the rich board member, asking her to remove the matron before she ruins Ebba's reputation.	BUT
The rich board member is insulted and walks out.	BUT

She reconsiders and agrees to hear Ebba and the matron together state the situation.	BUT
The matron is afraid to have the truth told.	THEREFORE
She ties a rope across the cellar steps, sends Ebba down cellar on an errand; Ebba falls, has a brain concussion, and cannot testify.	BUT
One of the orphans discovers the matron removing the rope.	THEREFORE
The matron admits her whole guilt.	THEREFORE
Ebba is saved, the old lady is removed, and the rich board member has to be satisfied.	

A week after writing this, the playwright knew that it was too sinister, that it made the old matron a maniac; left Ebba a mere pawn, not a desirable objective; and did not reveal Miss Stacy as particularly volitional until the showdown after the matron had burned the telltale page. The character study of the aunt had turned into a melodrama. The student still wanted to keep the matron; but he had to convey the important idea that Miss Stacy was fighting like a mother for her child. He had to get Ebba alive.

Among the material which came to light while he was working on the course of action was a character named Margie, the child who caught the matron removing the rope. He had been thinking of ways to make her attractive, so that the audience would be touched by her saving Ebba. In this quest he used a statement of his aunt that the girls in the home often talked about their mothers, and that it was rather pathetic, since many of those who had mothers were illegitimate. To make this little girl attractive, the playwright invented a mother for her, a night-club singer who wanted to take Margie into the business. There was to be a pathetic scene in which Margie realized that she did not like her mother. It was some time before the playwright attached this material to Ebba herself. When he had done so, his worst problem was solved. He had a course of action that made Miss Stacy volitional, and made Ebba a desirable objective:

It is just before the Community Chest allotment is to be made, and a scandal would destroy the home. THEREFORE

The board wishes Ebba were out, as she is overage and they are not authorized to keep her. THEREFORE

The rich board member has written Ebba's mother, but received no reply. THEREFORE

Miss Stacy has paid for a business course to help Ebba get a job after high school. AND

The matron is a bad influence in the home psychologically, as well as a bad bookkeeper. BUT

She is a poor relation of the rich board member and cannot be fired. BUT

The new treasurer finds evidence of fraud in the housekeeping books. THEREFORE

Miss Stacy plans to get rid of the matron on the ground of her age, thus avoiding scandal. BUT

The board votes Ebba the job of keeping the books to justify her staying in the home. THEREFORE

Miss Stacy resolves to protect Ebba at any cost. BUT

The matron intimidates Ebba while involving her in the falsified accounts. THEREFORE

Ebba is afraid to tell Miss Stacy what is happening. BUT

Miss Stacy suspects but cannot find conclusive evidence. AND

She cannot proceed because of the fear of scandal just before the Community Chest drive. BUT

The arrival of Ebba's mother promises a solution. BUT

133

Miss Stacy realizes she will hate to part with Ebba and cannot bring herself to urge the mother to take Ebba. | THEREFORE

The rich board member has to speak to Ebba's mother. | BUT

Her snobbish manner offends the mother. | AND

The mother does not like Ebba. | AND

Ebba, thinking she is safe, tells her mother of being involved with the matron. | THEREFORE

The mother uses the story as blackmail to prevent them from making her take the girl. | BUT

The rich board member threatens a libel suit and dismisses Ebba from the home. | BUT

Miss Stacy insists on an investigation of Ebba's story and discovers that a page of the housekeeping book is missing. | THEREFORE

The matron is sent to get Ebba. | BUT

Afraid of being accused, she lays a trap to prevent Ebba from testifying. | AND

One of the orphans finds Ebba at the foot of the cellar steps unconscious. | BUT

The matron is discovered removing the evidence, the rope over which Ebba tripped. | AND

Hysterical, she confesses. | THEREFORE

Ebba is saved, the old lady has to be removed, the rich board member has to apologize, and Miss Stacy has what she wanted.

This is much more dynamic than the first draft. In the first draft the protagonist, obstacle, and objective perform only five of the key actions, the dynamic character being the matron, a maniac. In the second draft, fifteen of the main actions are performed by actors in the main character-situation. A step has been made in the direction of getting sympathy for Ebba, and the matron has been reduced to the role of a complication, as she should be.

One serious weakness remains: there is no evidence of a deep bond between Miss Stacy and Ebba. Later the playwright inserted a bit of past action that helped to solve this difficulty. There were a great many additions, of course, and some major changes. But this was the course of action upon which the student began to build his plot.

Sometimes a young writer is aided in his own work by seeing the faults of others.

Usually, as Baker points out,[7] the young writer is burning to write dialogue before he knows what to write. The many hours of ruminating on his material seem unrewarding. He likes to see the pages stack up. The actual writing of a play can be accomplished in a surprisingly short time —three weeks or a month by a writer with facility. But a play a year is the average output of professional writers. Allowing a month or two to write and a month or two to revise, there is still almost a year left to plan. Often, indeed, a plan lies fallow for several years, until the emotional and logical connections are complete. To assimilate all the elements of a play takes time. Putting these elements together properly is the most difficult part of the playwright's work. But unless the necessary time is spent on construction, the job of revision is endless, devitalizing to the script, and heartbreaking to the playwright.

Often difficulties occur because the young playwright does not know his material as well as he thinks he does. His source does not furnish him with a wealth of incident from

---

[7] Baker, *Dramatic Technique*, p. 74.

which to select his course of action; he does not know his characters well enough to invent incidents for them; or he has not a broad enough knowledge of human nature to utilize freely the specific characters of his play. Some of this knowledge can be gained through research or analysis. Some of it depends on his having had analogous experiences by which to understand the motives and relationships of his characters. Sometimes he should frankly shelve the material until he has enough knowledge and experience to write the play.

One of the most common sources of difficulty is the failure to define the main character-situation. Enough has been said to convince the young playwright that unless he will determine his protagonist, obstacle, and objective, he cannot define his goal, and hence cannot compose a course of action.

Even when a playwright knows his material as thoroughly as research and experience can inform him, he sometimes fails to see potentially causal relationships. A good illustration of this difficulty is a folk-fantasy about Paul Bunyan[8] by a man who had combed the written sources thoroughly. In the first act of the play, Paul is clearly set up as the protagonist, and King Pete of Europe is presented as the villain (obstacle). At the end of the first act, King Pete leaves three henchmen in Paul's camp to destroy the morale of the lumberjacks. When Paul discovers the conspiracy, he declares he will win his men back

---

[8] In fantasy the material is unfamiliar and unreal to the audience, and therefore belief and empathy must be achieved with even greater care than in realism.

by undertaking the greatest fight of his life. He leaves the conspirators in camp, and goes away to fight Shot Gunderson, the Iron Man of the Mountain, who has not hitherto figured in the story. In Paul's absence, the conspirators lure the men completely away from logging. The playwright forgot that Paul, as absolute czar of the camp, had the power to punish the conspirators at once; and that King Pete was really at the root of the trouble. If the story had to end with the men being lured away in Paul's absence, then the connection between King Pete and Shot Gunderson, mentioned in Act I and forgotten, should have been developed and brought to a focus, so that Paul would not have had time to punish the conspirators before settling Gunderson. Obviously, to have remembered these simple relationships would have changed the course of action toward the end of the play; would have produced a gain in credibility; would have made Paul a more intelligent protagonist; and might have been used to create suspense, of which there was a great dearth in this play.

In writing historical plays, or dramatizing novels, a playwright is often embarrassed by the difficulty of selecting from a wealth of material just the incidents that are significant to him. After rejecting "all he possibly can," he ends with a chronological series of one-act plays. This difficulty is resolved to a large extent by limiting the objective, so that the story has a definite and necessary beginning and end. When he has so limited the play, he may then transpose—in either time or space—any material he considers pertinent to his intended action, provided the material can logically be transposed. The task of the dramatizer is to remodel a chronological series of incidents into a causal system.

There is no order in which a play must be planned. Every playwright has his own approach; perhaps every play is reduced to order in a different manner. But somewhere in the process, a skeleton of story takes shape, a system of causes leading to one definite conclusion.

However, in constructing a course of action, the playwright encounters much more material than appears in a bare story outline. His knowledge of the material grows constantly, both by his deliberate effort and by assimilation and maturation. He should not discard any material until he has weighed all of it. For wider knowledge often produces changes of attitude, and thus matters which originally seemed insignificant become important, while striking material sometimes has to be suppressed in view of its irrelevance to the climax as the playwright desires to make it. A scenario, even a course of action, may change many times during the months in which the playwright is planning his play, especially if the playwright is actually weighing his material and seeking to amplify it. This is the reason that the construction of a play takes a long time. It is also the reason that the initial course of action cannot be regarded as binding upon the playwright.

It may be that the play has seemed to burst full-blown like Minerva from the brows of Jove, and that the playwright is much further along in his task of constructing than the mere outline of the story. He may have a full scenario and even some dialogue. If the play moves clearly in a definite direction, the writer will discover that it can easily be outlined in story steps that have a systematic causal relationship to each other and to the concluding event. If this relationship is not apparent, the playwright had better revise before writing further, for the play has no backbone.

EXERCISES

1. Analyze:
   Outline and criticize the course of action in *The Criminal Code, Johnny Johnson,* and *I Remember Mama.*

2. Starting with a character of your acquaintance, find or invent an objective that would place him in clearer harmony with his universe. Assume that he recognizes his need for this objective, or for a substitute which he thinks he needs. Explain what might stand in his way and let this constitute the obstacle. Then plan a course of action in which he gets the objective, another in which he fails to get it.

3. Start with the ending of a crime story. Regard the murdered individual as the objective, the murderer as the obstacle. Find a protagonist and plan a course of action.

4. Start with a news story: a prize fighter discovered that his wife, a former chorine, was being unfaithful with his manager. In the divorce court he asked the custody of their son on the ground that his wife was unfit to rear the boy. Find protagonist, objective, obstacle, and course of action.

5. Start with the plan of a gang to rear a boy as the kidnapped son of a wealthy and prominent family. Find protagonist, objective, obstacle, ending, and course of action.

6. Take any of the assignments given so far, or any material of your own that appeals to you, and (*a*) state the character-

situation clearly, (*b*) state your point of view about the material, the meaning, (*c*) find the ending that will express this meaning, (*d*) outline the important evidences of initial instability, (*e*) find a course of action by which you will reach this ending and at the same time satisfy the audience. Take at least an hour a day for two weeks for this assignment.

ASSIGNMENTS

PLAYS: Maxwell Anderson, *Valley Forge*. Washington, D. C.: Anderson House, 1934. John Van Druten, *I Remember Mama*. New York: Harcourt, Brace & Company, Inc., 1945.

ADDITIONAL READING: William Archer, *Playmaking: A Manual of Craftsmanship*, Chapter IV. New York: Dodd, Mead & Company, Inc., 1937. George Pierce Baker, *Dramatic Technique*, Chapter IV. Boston: Houghton Mifflin Company, 1919. A. Craig Baird, *Public Discussion and Debate*, Chapter I. Boston: Ginn & Company, 1937. Gustav Freytag, *The Technique of the Drama*, Chapter III. Chicago: Scott, Foresman & Company, 1904. Clayton Hamilton, *"So You're Writing a Play!"*, pp. 77-93. Boston: Little, Brown & Company, 1935. John Howard Lawson, *Theory and Technique of Playwriting*, Part III, Chapter IV. New York: G. P. Putnam's Sons, 1949. Brander Matthews, *Playwrights on Playmaking*, Chapter IV. New York: Charles Scribner's Sons, 1923. Brander Matthews, *A Study of the Drama*, pp. 175-210. Boston: Houghton Mifflin Company, 1910. Alan H. Monroe, *Principles and Types of Speech*, Chapters VIII, XVIII. Chicago: Scott, Foresman & Company, 1939. Allardyce Nicoll, *The Theory of Drama*, pp. 38-60, 71-81. New York: The Thomas Y. Crowell Company, n.d.

9

The Obligatory Scene

THE CONCEPT OF THE OBLIGATORY SCENE COMES FROM
Francisque Sarcey, arbiter of the nineteenth-century
French stage.[1] As a translation of Sarcey's term, *scène à
faire*, "obligatory scene" is somewhat unfortunate, for,
lacking the connotation of zest which the French phrase
has, it arouses red antagonism in the breasts of some playwrights who do not trouble to discover exactly what it
means. They see in it only compulsion to follow the rules
of the old-fashioned well-made play of Scribe and Augier,
and they wildly declare that art must be free, that each
age makes its own forms, that no scene in a play is obligatory. Against these feelings there is no argument.

Actually, to the playwright and the critic of the nineteenth century as of today, a *scène à faire* is a focal scene,
one toward which the playwright himself has deliberately

[1] Archer, *Playmaking: A Manual of Craftsmanship,* pp. 225-227.
Among Sarcey's many uses of the term see *Quarante Ans de Théâtre,*
Vol. VIII, p. 5 (review of Hervieu's *Les Tenailles*) and p. 28 (review
of Brieux's *Blanchette*). Paris: Bibliothèque des Annales Politiques et
Littéraires, 1900.

aroused the anticipation of the audience. In the words of John Howard Lawson,

> No play can fail to provide a point of concentration toward which the maximum expectation is aroused. The audience requires such a point of concentration in order to define its attitude toward the events. . . . Just as the climax furnishes us with a test by which we can analyze the action backwards, the obligatory scene offers us an additional check on the forward movement of the action. The obligatory scene is the immediate goal toward which the play is driving.[2]

For example, in *Elizabeth the Queen,* Elizabeth and Essex vow that nothing can come between them. In the next scene Cecil does come between them. He parts them and intercepts their correspondence. Elizabeth is made angry and miserable by receiving no letters from her lover. Essex, resentful and suspicious, returns to England for a *coup d'état.* His next meeting with his mistress and queen is one which the audience keenly anticipates. The scene is obligatory simply because the playwright considered it focal, and for two acts deliberately led the audience to desire it. But conversely, once the playwright has aroused anticipation, he may not cheat his audience. Lawson phrases this point admirably:

> The idea that the plot leads in a *foreseen* direction toward a clash of forces which is obligatory, and that the dramatist must give double consideration to the logic of events and to the logic of the spectator's expectation, is far more than a mechanical formula. It is a vital step toward understanding the dramatic process.[3]

---

[2] Lawson, *Theory and Technique of Playwriting,* p. 263.
[3] *Ibid.,* p. 53.

Actually there may be as many as four or five of these obligatory scenes in a play. These are likely to be of different kinds.[4] The most important kind structurally is the scene in which the major opposing forces come to a decisive clash.[5] This is the *scène à faire* of Sarcey and the nineteenth-century writers; it is also the focal scene of the play, which gives the play unity and meaning. In *Winterset*, Mio must actually confront Trock, Garth, and Gaunt, the three who stand in the way of his father's vindication. In *Dark of the Moon*, Barbara must strive with the preacher, who represents her own earthy soul. In *Our Town*, Emily, whose whole nature craves life, must adjust herself to man's great enemy, Death. The manner in which the scene is handled in each case rests upon the very personal decision of the playwright; but in no case may he omit the scene, since it contains the main issue of the play.

Again, if one of the main characters formulates a plan of any sort, the audience will expect to see the plan tested. When once the Friar gives Juliet the potion; when Hamlet cries, "The play's the thing!"; when Cecil and Raleigh of *Elizabeth the Queen* plot to send Essex to Ireland—the scene in which the plan is put into operation is eagerly awaited by the audience. The only way in which the scenes would not be obligatory in these cases would be to omit the material that leads the audience to expect them. But of

---

[4] Archer's categories are as follows: a scene necessitated by (1) the inherent logic of the theme, (2) the exigencies of dramatic effect, (3) the author leading up to it, (4) a change of character or will, (5) history or legend. See *Playmaking: A Manual of Craftsmanship*, p. 227 f.

[5] Cf. Matthews, *A Study of the Drama*, p. 106. Matthews seems to recognize only this kind of obligatory scene.

course the scenes that create the anticipation were introduced because the playwright wanted the audience to anticipate and enjoy the working out of the plan.

Another type of obligatory scene is one which fulfills the interest of the audience in the relationships of characters. This is true of Juliet and her nurse. The pragmatic and earthy old woman is really not compatible with the maiden who says of marriage, "It is an honour I dream not of," and who is willing to die rather than be unfaithful. The time must and does come when Juliet finds the nurse inadequate and says, "Thou and my bosom henceforth shall be twain." In *Elizabeth the Queen*, Penelope's love for Essex must find expression, and Anderson allows her a farewell kiss to complete their relationship. In *Street Scene*, Shirley's possessiveness brings her into conflict with Rose; but since Rice, and incidentally the audience, tends to respect Shirley, a reconciliation between Rose and this minor character is given. The scene is necessary in that the audience would be disappointed without it.

Another type of obligatory scene occurs because a subordinate character has aroused so much interest that the audience wants to see what happens to him. The treatment of Ado Annie and the Peddler of *Oklahoma!* was mentioned in the last chapter. Other examples are the death scenes of Neil and Tench in *Valley Forge* and the final monologue of the telephone operator in *Counsellor-at-Law*.

When the audience knows something that will affect a main character when he learns it, the anticipated discovery is an obligatory scene, such as the one in which Maurrant of *Street Scene* returns to find proof of his wife's infidelity.

Or, when information is withheld until the curiosity of the audience is piqued, the revelation of this information is requisite. In *Idiot's Delight,* for example, the question of Irene's identity comes up several times before the audience is allowed to know who she is. In this case, the exposition of past action actually becomes obligatory.[6]

Scenes are obligatory, then, not because there is any rule about them, but because the playwright himself has seen them as important and has taken some pains to make the audience anticipate them.

The many preparatory devices which the playwright uses to create anticipation[7] tend, of course, to stave off the obligatory scene. Thus, one naturally finds important obligatory scenes rather near the end of the play. Three types of obligatory scene are generally saved for the last third of the play. These are the obligatory major clash between protagonist and obstacle, the obligatory completion of relationships, and the obligatory satisfaction of interest in subordinate characters. On the other hand, the obligatory revelation of information often occurs earlier, even within the first third of the play.

Many beginners fail to distinguish and provide the obligatory scene. As an extreme example, there is an unproduced play about the old Mayor of a village, who simply wants to end his days among his friends. The first scene is devoted to his static objective. In the second scene, the Mayor's shrewish and ambitious wife, to further her own

---

[6] See Chapter XV, "Special Kinds of Plants."
[7] See Part II, "Suspense."

design of moving to a nearby town, starts a rumor that the Mayor has been stealing, and causes his friends to turn from him in the third scene. Now the reader wants a showdown between the Mayor and his despicable wife. But the last scene takes place in the village railway station, where a funeral crowd awaits the arrival of the Mayor's body. We gather that the wife has had her way about moving; but if there was a showdown, it happened offstage. And we are even cheated of paying our last respects to the Mayor, for the playwright substituted a farcical scene in which the body failed to arrive. Of course the playwright was entitled to use the station scene, if he had prepared for it. But no one is entitled to lead the audience to expect something he does not intend to give.

The same fault occurs in a farce about a man named Elmer, who sells an instrument which purports to cure all ills. Elmer incurs the wrath of one Plute Dow by fastening the instrument to the ankles of Plute's wife. Plute hales Elmer to court, but is only further exasperated when Elmer uses the machine on the Judge, putting him to sleep; and Plute leaves the courtroom swearing that he is not yet done with Elmer. The exposure of Elmer is obligatory, and the first two acts indicate that Plute Dow will expose him. The big scene of the play, to judge by several pointers, is a box party. While Elmer begins an elaborate scheme to sell his machine, an entirely new character, Little Betsy Ann, inadvertently reveals that the machine is full of sawdust. Elmer flees the concerted wrath of the village; but his relationship with Plute Dow is never finished.

It has been shown that a large part of the playwright's

skill consists in putting off the obligatory scene and increasing the tension until the scene he considers focal actually becomes obligatory, in the sense that the audience will be disappointed if it does not occur.

Many inexperienced playwrights and some experienced ones betray the fault of bringing the focal scene into the first act and simply repeating it with variations in subsequent scenes. This fault occurs in the work of even so expert a writer as Maxwell Anderson. In *Valley Forge,* Washington asks his men in the first scene if they want to continue the war, and gains their support. In the third scene he asks his officers the same question and gains their support. And in the last scene, in the midst of a skirmish, with three of the most sympathetic characters dead or dying, he again offers to give up the fight, but the men insist on going on with it. One crucial scene is played three times, with perhaps increasing intensity: Washington asks for support.

It is easy to blame the actors, the director, or the laziness or stupidity of the audience if a play does not "get across." A better attitude for a playwright to take is that if the play lacks clarity, or impact, the writer himself is at fault. If the first scenes are what the playwright wanted them to be, then he must supply any scene which these earlier scenes seem to promise. On the other hand, if he did not mean to lead to the scene which the earlier material promised, he must revise to avoid arousing false expectations. And he must be careful to make the audience want the scene he himself regards as focal. In other words, no scene is obligatory unless the playwright means it to be; but a skilled writer will create exactly the expectations he wants, and satisfy those expectations.

So far no attempt has been made to describe the processes by which anticipation is stirred, or by which the subtle moods and nuances of character are created. The chapters have dealt only with essential structural factors, the joists and beams, the basic material and design of a play. The illustrations have been diverse enough to suggest that the matters treated are as applicable to Elmer Rice as to Shakespeare, as germane to *Lysistrata* as to *Our Town*.

In the foregoing chapters the goal of the playwright has been defined as an audience experience of climax. It has been shown that in order to create this experience there must be someone (for the apprentice playwright, preferably an individual) who strongly desires some objective which the audience wishes him to achieve; and that there must be some impeding force about as strong as the protagonist. The end of the play has been seen as the achievement of the objective or the failure to achieve it, whichever most clearly expresses the playwright's attitude toward his material or the meaning he attaches to it. It has been shown that the playwright's conception of what the climax should be indicates the general nature of the course of action, and furnishes a reference point from which to evaluate all other details to be included in the play. Finally, it has been indicated that there are certain developments of story or relationship which may be termed obligatory in that the playwright particularly conditions the audience to demand them.

There are distinct advantages in this sort of attack on

the construction of a play. It gives the writer tools to analyze his own materials and purposes when he gets "stuck," and helps him to look for definite answers to his problems instead of waiting for inspiration's caprice. It also serves as a pigeonholing device in which to file new ideas as they come, so that one can always see details in relation to the whole. Moreover, it provides a clear directional structure, which means a minimum of revision and a tremendous saving of time and emotional strain during rehearsal.

Since skill in the use of tools cannot be achieved without practice, the student should regard his apprenticeship not as a period of searching for new techniques, but as a time for learning to manipulate the tested tools at his disposal. The apprentice playwright may well consider the words of a great teacher of musical composition:

> It is narrow-minded to assume that these exercises and the persistent application of "rules" will hamper genius. They need not be executed coldly and mechanically. Subjective, personal enthusiasm may course just as hotly here as in the pursuit of any other occupation; and the student is nowhere invited to check this enthusiasm—only to control and guide it. Properly applied by the student, these exercises thus only increase the power of his genius.[8]

---

[8] Percy Goetschius, *The Larger Forms of Musical Composition.* New York: G. Schirmer, Inc. Copyright 1915 by G. Schirmer, Inc. Copyright renewal assigned, 1943, to G. Schirmer, Inc. Reprinted by permission.

1. Analyze:
   a. Find the main obligatory scene of *Paris Bound* and discuss Barry's treatment of it.
   b. Point out all the obligatory scenes in *Holiday*.
2. The attractive but prudish protagonist constantly reprimands two delightful old friends of her father for taking a drink. She becomes engaged to a fine lively young man, the proprietor of a tavern. What is the obligatory scene?
3. Two women are close friends. One of them discovers that her husband is ruining the husband of the other and forcing him into bankruptcy. What is the obligatory scene?
4. One of the guests at a dinner party, a newcomer to the town, is particularly nervous. Another guest seems to recall meeting him before. Still another finds that he makes her nervous. What is the obligatory scene?
5. After a hard day at the office, Jack plans to lounge with the papers all evening. He does not know that his wife has asked her parents to dinner. What is the obligatory scene?
6. A woman in love with her husband does not know him to be a criminal. What is the obligatory scene?
7. In each of the assignments at the end of Chapter VIII, name the obligatory scene.

ASSIGNMENTS

PLAYS: Philip Barry, *Holiday*. New York: Samuel French, Inc., 1929. Philip Barry, *Paris Bound*. New York: Samuel French, Inc., 1929. Philip Barry, *Tomorrow and Tomorrow*. New York: Samuel French, Inc., 1931.

ADDITIONAL READING: William Archer, *Playmaking: A Manual of Craftsmanship,* Chapter XIII. New York: Dodd, Mead & Company, Inc., 1937. John Howard Lawson, *Theory and Technique of Playwriting,* Part IV, Chapters III, IV. New York: G. P. Putnam's Sons, 1949. Francisque Sarcey, *Quarante Ans de Théâtre,* Vol. 8, Essays on the *Théâtre Libre.* Paris: Bibliothèque des Annales Politiques et Littéraires, 1900. Percival Wilde, *The Craftsmanship of the One-Act Play,* pp. 216-218. Boston: Little, Brown & Company, 1938.

10

The First Draft of the Scenario

TEACHERS OF PLAYWRITING HAVE PRESENTED ARGUMENTS in favor of writing a scenario before beginning to write dialogue,[1] and playwrights have made various statements about whether they do or do not write the scenario. Usually the apprentice is quite sure that a written scenario is unnecessary.

It has been sufficiently emphasized in this book that the teacher cannot constrain the artist to work in a way that is uncongenial to him. One young writer will think more clearly if he jots down his thoughts as they come; another will have the whole subject clearly and in great detail in his mind, and does not need to write down his scenario. It seems reasonable, in general, to ask an apprentice to commit his thoughts to paper, partly to habituate him to the

---

[1] William Archer and George Pierce Baker argue in favor of the written scenario. Archer, *Playmaking: A Manual of Craftsmanship,* Chapter IV; and Baker, *Dramatic Technique,* Chapter IX. Baker presents some excellent examples, including the full scenario of *Kismet,* with notes on the changes made during the writing and rehearsal periods.

necessity for organization, partly in order that he and the teacher may have an objective check upon his plans and progress. Yet there will be cases in which the check can be made orally, and cases in which the student's orderly habits of thought make a written scenario seem too elementary. Certainly the student, as he develops skill and maturity, must evolve his own system of organizing the materials of his play.

Whether the scenario is written or not, as soon as the course of action becomes somewhat clear, technical problems begin to arise. Three main problems have to be solved rather early: what to do with a host of characters who pop in and out of the story, yet do not seem to have any vital connection with it; how many acts and scenes will be needed, and in what settings; whether all the important action can take place on stage, and if not, what to do with time intervals while it takes place offstage. These matters are the substance of this chapter.

If a character insists on coming into a play, the playwright should know how to put him to work, or the character will be like a wallflower at a party, with nothing to say; or he will steal the scene from the bride at the wedding, or worse, clutter the ending of the story like the old maid who talks of her crocheting while the house across the street burns down.

Before going into this matter, it would be wise for the student to make a list of all possible characters in his play, including maids, butlers, and innocent bystanders, and anyone he can think of who might happen into the story as the writing gets under way. For people, either directly or as representing some aspect of the environment, have the greatest possible influence upon character and actions in life; and they are likewise the most fertile source for enriching a play. Any such list may have from ten to a hundred characters on it, perhaps six of whom may appear at the very first glance to have definite functions—protagonist, objective, obstacle, or complicating element. What is one to do with all the rest?

There are at least ten good reasons for using auxiliary characters in a play, aside from those which have already been mentioned.

Very often a character or several characters are introduced to give exposition; that is, to let the audience know some past action or present situation which is vital to the understanding of the play. A prologue did this for Shakespeare; but in the nineteenth century it became the practice to open the play with a maid and a butler commenting on the circumstances which had to be made clear before the action began. Since that time, however, playwrights have used as many characters as they needed to perform this function, and they have been free to use any sort of character who could do it most clearly, logically, and interestingly. In *Paris Bound*, Barry introduces the estranged mother and father of Jim in a scene which has a double use, both to tell what Jim's background has been, and to reveal the pitfall into which infidelity may lead him. In *Elizabeth the Queen*, two soldiers begin the play with surmises as to why the Queen is angry, and why Essex has stayed away for two weeks; Raleigh and Penelope contribute a few facts to the exposition, notably that the lovers have quarreled, and that Raleigh would like to supplant Essex. In *The Criminal Code*, the prosecuting attorney questions the witnesses of a murder, so that one knows at once that Bob is a good boy and not entirely to blame. In *Counsellor-at-Law*, a whole office full of people reveals Simon's respected position and his relation to his wife. His boyhood is exposited by three characters. The framed alibi is told by the character for whom the alibi was framed. More will be said about exposition presently; but as an indication of how important it is, it is not unusual to find as many as four characters in a play whose main function is to provide exposition of some sort; and *Golden Boy* contains eight characters for this purpose.

Sometimes characters are needed to complete the setting —that is, create atmosphere—or to perform some necessary business. A great deal is added to the illusion of the hospital scene in *I Remember Mama* by the trained nurse at the desk and the two internes who discuss a case as they cross. Three butlers in *Holiday* give the illusion of great wealth much more effectively than a single maid could. *Street Scene* is full of characters who give atmosphere in addition to the other functions they perform in the play. In this category are the cops who carry off the criminals, the maid who serves the tea, the secretary who answers the telephone, the nurse who minds the children. They should be watched closely by the playwright, for they tend either to be automata or to run away with their scenes.

If a leading character is so subtly drawn that he is difficult for the audience to understand, sometimes a character is put into the play with characteristics opposite to those of the main character, so that the main character may be understood through his negative characteristics. Or sometimes the protagonist is made more attractive or good by contrast. The constrasting character is a foil. Odets uses the sordid marriage of Sig and Anna in *Golden Boy* to contrast with the pathetic romance of Lorna and Moody and the stormy passion of Joe and Lorna. Penelope in *Elizabeth the Queen*, whose whole heart is centered in love for Essex, is used to make Elizabeth's passion and her divided heart more fiercely tragic. In *Street Scene*, Mrs. Jones with her shallow morality is contrasted with Mrs. Maurrant, whose breach of convention comes from a deeply human need of love. An extremely skillful use of the foil is Lillian LaRue in *Counsellor-at-Law*, whose behavior is a cheap version of the behavior of Simon's extremely aristocratic wife. The foil is one of the playwright's most useful characters, whether or not he has any other functions.

The *raisonneur* was the character in the French well-made play who told the main character and the audience what attitude to take toward the events of the play. He was a descendant of the Greek chorus, and his lineal heirs still walk the stage. Barry uses the father of Jim in *Paris Bound* frankly for this purpose in a scene in Act III, when he urges Mary to remember his own sad case and not divorce Jim. Anderson uses Esdras in *Winterset* as a very definitely choral character. The Potters in *Holiday* serve as *raisonneurs* in at least one of their functions. Kaplan, Lippo, and Miss Simpkins, among others in *Street Scene*, do not so much express the author's point of view as present conflicting philosophies which characterize the neighborhood, but they are also *raisonneurs* in a way. The use of the *raisonneur* is dangerous for the beginner, as the character is likely to be a mere intellectual paper doll, without personality beyond the ideas the playwright gives him, and he is likely to stop the show while *"raisonnant."* But, used with care, the *raisonneur* can add a great deal to the beauty and meaning of the play. It is always wise to see that the *raisonneur* has some important wishes of his own—some character, that is—and some function in addition to that of expressing ideas.

In nineteenth-century plays the confidant was a stock character to whom the leading character confided his inmost thoughts for the benefit of the audience. To use such a character avoided the soliloquy, which was just then becoming passé. The confidant is still freely used, even quite frankly. Carr, Mio's buddy in *Winterset*, provides someone to whom Mio can express his intentions; so does Shadow for Trock. In *Elizabeth the Queen*, Bacon is the confidant of Essex, while Raleigh serves this function for Cecil, and Penelope serves as confidante to some extent for both Elizabeth and Essex. As with the *raisonneur*, the confidant is likely to become pretty mechanical unless the playwright finds some additional use for him and makes him interesting as a character in his own right.

It used to be thought that there must be some character in a play to absorb the tendency of the audience to laugh at scenes that seemed overheavy or sentimental. This function was called "comic relief." In a modern play this function also exists, though we try to disguise it. Anderson is a master of this sort of character. In *Elizabeth the Queen* he inserts a half-pathetic Elizabethan fool to take the edge off Elizabeth's wild temper. In *Valley Forge* there is the character Alcock, a wry individual who, just as the recital of the army's woes begins to be unbearably depressing, reveals the loss of his pants. MacManus serves this purpose in *The Criminal Code* by his naïve admiration for the system which regiments prisoners like machines. Gillespie gives relief from tension between Eve and Hay in *Tomorrow and Tomorrow*.

Sometimes "relief" does not mean comic relief, but simply an emotional outlet, a small climax of a sort, coming before the main climax, to enable the audience to discharge some of its tension before the scene that is to be built to emotional heights. Penelope in *Elizabeth the Queen* has this function in addition to her function of confidante. In the last act, just before the tensely tragic scene between Elizabeth and Essex is over, Anderson shrewdly allows Penelope to kiss Essex good-by. The audience is allowed to weep at this minor climax, while Elizabeth remains too great and tragic for tears. In *Valley Forge,* Anderson uses the character of Neil, the consumptive lad, to stimulate the audience *before* a long repetitious scene. The third scene of the play asks and answers the question, "Shall we continue the war?" This question has been asked of the enlisted men in Act I; now it is to be asked of the officers, whose answers are more reasonable, less conducive to pity than those of the men. At the beginning of this scene, Neil comes into the room. With deep reverence for Washington, Neil says, "The truth is, I'm dying . . . damn it, let me die for something! let me be on a field with a gun in my hands, and die there, not die retching my lungs and brains out." This pathetic scene brings the audience with heightened emotions to the ten-page argument which follows. Probably such a device as the "relief" character, whether comic or serious, comes into a play most often at a late stage of planning, in rehearsal, or even in a tryout performance. To use such a character skillfully, one needs a rather keen sense of the audience's power of endurance—how intensely the audience has been moved, and how much it can endure.

Sometimes characters are used for architectonic functions—making transitions, getting attention, or making the audience aware that something is to happen. Examples of transitional characters are Herman and the two girls in *Winterset*, the Stage-Manager of *Our Town*, the Western Union boy and others who come and go in *Counsellor-at-Law*, the three Labor Men and Sam in Act II of *State of the Union*, the maid in *Born Yesterday*. The Men in Serge in *Winterset* get attention and also establish a sense of impending danger. In *Hotel Universe*, Barry includes a butler who creates a feeling of urgency by announcing the time every fifteen minutes. The choral characters Sis and Sue in *The House of Connelly* also serve as pointers of the disaster that is to overcome the house.

Very often characters in this category serve more than one purpose, but it is not unusual to find characters put into a play for architectonic functions alone.

One other use of the auxiliary character may be mentioned; that is, as agent for one of the main characters. If the obstacle or the objective is an abstraction, it is often wise to introduce a character as the concrete symbol of the abstraction.[2] Such characters as Gleason and MacManus in *The Criminal Code* represent the law and prison regimentation, the chief obstacles against which Bob Graham struggles in his effort at rehabilitation. Odets uses the character of Foley in *Paradise Lost* to represent the social structure under which the Gordon family struggles to live. But it is difficult to find examples of the effective use of this device, because when a playwright becomes skilled, his characters become so lifelike that one can hardly call them symbols of anything. By stretching a point, one may regard Oswald, the objective-obstacle of *Ghosts,* as a symbol of the sins of the elder Alving. But Oswald is himself, the son of Mrs. Alving, a living individual. On the other hand, it is easy to find examples of the ineffective use of agents for main characters. To cite only one, *Mary of Scotland,* which enjoyed a long run as a starring vehicle for Helen Hayes, is a struggle between Mary and Elizabeth. Elizabeth in person at certain points of the play plots Mary's downfall; but whenever Mary comes to grips with her obstacle, she fights not Elizabeth but agents of Elizabeth, Darnley, then Throckmorton. She has many other obstacles, the Scottish lords, violent John Knox, her own simplicity. Thus the final scene with Elizabeth, intrinsically powerful though it is, does not seem any more necessary than a scene with Knox might have been. There are

---

[2] In a series of memory tests reported by H. L. Hollingworth, it was proved that an object named and seen is three to six times as effectively remembered as an object merely named or merely seen. Thus a visual symbol of an objective or obstacle is desirable because it is more emphatic than an abstraction which is heard about but not seen. *The Psychology of the Audience,* p. 64.

two general cautions with regard to the use of "agents": it is wise to make sure that the main actions of the play are performed by the main characters, or unexpected emphases may develop; and it is necessary to invest an agent with lifelike qualities of his own if he is to be more than a cold abstraction.

Although characters may be introduced for any or all of these functions, there are a few practical considerations against large casts for the beginner. First, of course, the larger the cast, the harder it is to arrange a tryout performance, even in the nonprofessional theatre. The beginner who tries to sell his plays professionally will find that a large payroll may be a deciding factor to a producer gambling on a new writer.[3] There is a consideration of more importance than this, however. Each character that is brought on the stage must become known before the audience can understand and react to him; the more characters there are in a play, the less time the playwright has to develop his main characters and situations.

On the other hand, professional playwrights actually use a larger average number of characters as they gain skill. This is partly because their plays are no longer a gamble to the producer, and partly because they have learned to select characterizing details with accuracy and economy. Perhaps more important is the fact that they learn to utilize their characters for more functions than one. For

---

[3] J. B. Priestley states, "It pays a dramatist to be modest in this fashion because it means that not only are the initial costs . . . much smaller, but that touring, repertory, and amateur rights are more in demand." *Johnson Over Jordan,* p. 128. New York and London: Harper & Brothers, 1939.

example, the crowded cast of *Street Scene* contains an Italian, Lippo, one of the neighbors. Lippo is a *raisonneur*, preaching beauty as a desideratum of life. He is also a foil to the hot-tempered, argumentative Maurrant, and he is a slight complication when Sankey enters to find him dancing with Mrs. Maurrant. At least eight of the characters in *Street Scene* serve more than one function. If a character enters the play, he must be made to "earn his keep."

One point should be reiterated in regard to the use of auxiliary characters. Not only should they be really auxiliary, but they should also be well motivated; that is, they should have some drives of their own to make them real. The trouble with the old confidant was that he existed only as an ear into which the protagonist might pour his hopes and fears. If the maid and the butler must give exposition, then they must have some interests of their own to keep them from being mere gramophones. The modern audience, having some acquaintance with psychology, is quick to detect a mechanical use of a character.

Briefly, there is no actual limit to the number of characters that may be used in a play; one may use as many as will make the play good. But in introducing characters, one must see that every character has some definite function.

The next important point to be discussed is the division of the play into acts and scenes. It has been asserted that, since an audience can sit for two hours without interruption at the movies, there is no reason that it should not watch a play without intermission. But it must be remembered that long movies are seldom as long as two hours; that the long cinema program is actually a group of presentations consisting of a more or less serious movie, a newsreel, and probably a "short" of some kind; that the attention of the movie audience is restimulated about every ninety seconds by a shift of scene or camera angle; and that attention at a movie is seldom as intense as at a good play—witness the freedom with which the spectators comment to each other at a movie, while comments during a play are relatively few.

It seems reasonable to suppose that some means may be devised for sustaining a mood throughout a whole performance. Several modern experiments have been made in this direction. Barry's *Hotel Universe*, a 1930 attempt at a nonstop play, ran only briefly. Paul Green has tried music and cinema sequences as continuity to avoid the need for a new build-up after each intermission; but the two plays in which Mr. Green made these attempts [4] are so highly emotional that they need not continuity, but some sort of relief. More recently, Katherine Cornell's *Antigone* had a substantial run. But so far, the nonstop long play on a modern theme has not managed to draw audiences. The theatre, like every other living thing, is subject to change; but it is safe to say that at present the theatre audience of this country expects intermissions and that the playwright must make a virtue of necessity and know on what basis he can provide intermissions with the most advantage to his play. [5]

---

[4] *Tread the Green Grass* and *Shroud My Body Down.*
[5] Krows, *Playwriting for Profit*, p. 139.

Although there is a tendency to use more or less than three divisions, the old three-act structure persists. In this structure, usually the exposition, the collision factor, and the statement of the objective are presented in the first act. Sometimes a complication is introduced into the first act, and sometimes some exposition is left to the later acts. The second act generally brings the action to the point of crisis, sometimes adding more complications, and frequently bringing down the curtain at an apparent impasse. The third act, of course, provides the solution or ends the story in some way.

Plays with more than three divisions usually contain two intermissions, which fall at the ends of what the playwrights call acts. That these divisions generally follow the pattern of the three-act play will be shown presently. For the moment, however, it is interesting to look at the reasons for dividing a play into more than three units,[6] whether these units are called acts or scenes.

The most fundamental reason is that a certain portion of the course of action has been accomplished, a step has been taken toward the objective. A division for this reason might be called a unit of action. Such a unit is Act I, Scene 3, of *Elizabeth the Queen,* in which the conspirators succeed in forcing Essex to go to Ireland. In Act II, Scene 2, another unit of action, Essex decides on a *coup d'état.* In Act II, Scene 3, Elizabeth arrests Essex. Such units can be found in every play. Even in *Our Town,* though its man-

---

[6] A unit is a division of a play between two curtains, or between any two devices that mark the end of a portion of a play and ask the audience to wait, however momentarily, for the next portion.

ner is somewhat different from the chronologically arranged conventional play, one finds three clear units of action in the second act: George visits his in-laws on his wedding day, George proposes to Emily, George and Emily get married. The last act of *Our Town* is clearly a unit of action. In all units of this type, a definite portion of the course of action is completed.

Another type of division of a play is based upon clarity. In a three-act play, exposition is tucked into the first act, as a rule, along with some action. In the multi-unit play, one or more divisions are often given entirely to exposition. A good example of a unit of this type is the prologue and six opening scenes of *The Criminal Code*. The prologue merely tells the reason that Bob is in prison. Five flashes follow to show how prison life brutalized him. It is not until Act I, Scene 6, that the action starts. The first unit of *Golden Boy* is sheer exposition of how Joe got his start as a boxer. The second unit of this play is also exposition of the background from which Joe came. All of the first three units of *Our Town* are, of course, expository, and designed, like all good exposition, to influence the emotions of the audience. The first unit of *Counsellor-at-Law* merely tells the audience what people think of Simon, while the second unit is also exposition, revealing Simon through his behavior.

Most plays are entirely made up of units of action and units of clarity. In a play of more than three or four divisions, units of clarity usually occur before the first intermission, while the units after the first intermission are generally units of action.

Sometimes a unit is introduced chiefly to create emotional attitudes in the audience. Anderson uses the emotional unit very skillfully. *Winterset* opens with the shadowy movements of the Men in Serge under the bridge, and the deeply bitter soliloquy of Trock against the city. There is a good bit of exposition in the first unit, but its primary effect is to grip the audience with the danger that surrounds Mio and the other participants in the tragedy. The second unit of *Elizabeth the Queen* also contains exposition, but its primary effect is to sweep the audience into sympathy with the lovers. Barry uses the opening unit of *Tomorrow and Tomorrow,* in one sense a unit of exposition, primarily to put Eve in the sympathetic light of a woman who deeply wants a child, before allowing her the less sympathetic action of taking a lover. Flavin uses the unit of emotion in *The Criminal Code* at the crisis—a flash scene in the prison yard at night, with sirens howling, to gain a breathless moment of suspense after Bob commits the murder and before he is returned finally to prison. As has been shown, the unit of emotion very frequently includes some exposition, but it is exposition chosen for its emotional effect rather than merely for credibility. The use of this type of unit is usually a mark of high skill in a playwright.

Once in a while a playwright uses a scene merely to give an illusion of time passing. Barry uses this unit frequently in *Tomorrow and Tomorrow.*[7] It is made clear in the first scene that Eve's marriage will not be complete until she has a child. In the second scene, an action unit, she meets

[7] See p. 190.

Hay, a psychiatrist, who finds her a little more than attractive. But in order that the love between Eve and Hay may not seem cheaply sensual, their intimacy is delayed by a time unit in which Eve confesses to Hay her need for a child. The second and third units of Act II are also primarily time units to bridge from the love scene with Hay to the scene in which the child falls into a psychopathic coma after an accident, and Eve calls Hay back to save him. Again a time unit is employed to bring the child's illness to a crisis. In the last unit, Eve reaches her major decision, to remain with her husband and child instead of going away with her lover. Four of the nine scenes of *Tomorrow and Tomorrow* are thus primarily time units, skillfully used to gain suspense and to deepen sympathy for the characters. But Barry has the gift of being able to write extremely attractive dialogue that somehow justifies itself even when the substance of the act is very thin. For less skillful writers, however, the time unit is a dangerous one, and can be clearly recognized by the audience as padding.

Usually, if it is necessary that the audience become aware of time passing,[8] a more economical device can be found than to give a whole unit to this purpose. A change in the light, in the foliage outside the window, in costume, will establish that time has passed. A brief narration of some sort can usually tell any minor development that affects the action. If the material is very important, probably it should be made into a unit of action or of clarity, and presented on the stage. Often the material

---

[8] See *Othello*, Act III, Scene 5, the first "temptation" scene.

within a unit can be so arranged that time *seems* to have passed. This may be done by starting the time-consuming action early in the unit, interrupting it by some important action or actions, and finishing it at the end of the unit. Time is relative. If much has happened, a great deal of time seems to have passed, while the reverse is true if little has happened.[9] The overuse of the unit of time is one of the main faults of inexperienced writers who have not yet learned to select and build the critical moments of their stories. It has been shown that the elements of a play form a causal system rather than a chronological chain. If there is more than one AND THEN connective [10] in the scenario of a beginner, it is likely that the wrong scenes have been chosen, or that more careful arrangement of the material is needed to show relationships, or that some telescoping of the material is needed.

As a means of summarizing the practices of professional writers in regard to the division of plays into units, a table has been made of the patterns of ten plays frequently referred to in this book. Only three of these have the three-act structure; the others have from five to thirteen units. It can be seen that there are generally more units before the first intermission than in the other scenes, and generally fewer units after the last intermission. But clearly no law can be made from these practices, since, aside from the three-act plays, no two have the same form.

---

[9] See *Othello*, Act II, Scene 3.
[10] See above, Chapter VIII.

THE PATTERN OF A PLAY

	Act I						Act II				Act III				
Number of units	1	2	3	4	5	6	1	2	3	4	1	2	3	4	5
Elizabeth the Queen	c	e	a				a	a	a		a				
Winterset	e	c	a				a				a				
Paris Bound	c						a				a				
Holiday	c						a				a				
Tomorrow and Tomorrow	e	a	t				a	t	t		a	t	a		
The Criminal Code	c	c	c	c	a	a	a	a			a	a	a	e	a
Golden Boy	c	c	a	a	a		a	a	a	a	t	a	a		
Street Scene	c						a				a				
Counsellor-at-Law	c	e	a	a			a	c	a		a	a			
Our Town	c	c	c				a	a	a		a				

"C" means a unit of clarity, "a" a unit of action, "e" a unit of emotion, and "t" a unit of time.

Analysis of the contents of the units indicates that it is almost a matter of universal practice to get most of the exposition done before the first intermission. Fully half the units of the combined first acts are units of clarity. The unit of emotion is used in only five of the ten plays, and the unit of time in only two, while by far the most of the units are units of action. This analysis of units recalls the old maxim, "First act clear, last act brief, and all the acts interesting." [11]

One further point should be made. The young playright who feels jealous of his freedom in proportioning his acts and scenes has a tendency to write too many very short

[11] Krows, *Playwriting for Profit*, p. 52. Krows attributes this to Dumas *fils*, who heard it from his father.

units. But there is hardly a unit in the above plays which lasts less than ten minutes, except the five short flashes by which Flavin reveals the brutalizing effect of prison in *The Criminal Code;* and these flashes all say exactly the same thing. It is impossible to build up a consistent illusion, much less any very strong emotion, if the author asks his audience to wait in blank darkness every few minutes for a scene shift, and to get oriented in a new scene at every turn.

Much has been written about bringing down the curtain "with a bang"—so much that the modern playwright tends to rebel against the practice as theatrical, and often succeeds in closing an act very quietly.[12] Before committing oneself to an opinion, it would be wise to note how established playwrights handle this matter. One practice is general, that of ending the scene before the last with something exciting, usually a crisis in the main action. *Elizabeth the Queen* has the startling arrest of Essex at the curtain before the last. The penultimate unit of *Winterset* ends with Mio turning against Miriamne and rushing out of the house and into Trock's deathtrap. In the second act of *Holiday,* Linda confesses to Ned that she is in love with Johnny, and gallantly joins the party crowd to congratulate Johnny and Julia on their engagement. The last four units of *The Criminal Code* end in strong crises. The scene before the last in *Golden Boy* drops the curtain as Joe starts on a wild joy ride after killing Chocolate Drop. The second act of *Street Scene* contains the one lurid scene of the play,

---

[12] Baker, *Dramatic Technique,* pp. 214-233; and also Archer, *Playmaking: A Manual of Craftsmanship,* Chapters XVIII and XXI.

and ends at a high point of emotion with Rose following the body of her murdered mother offstage, and Maurrant not yet caught by the police. Even *Our Town* uses its most moving scene, the wedding, to end the second act; and instead of a curtain, a surprise anticlimax, the blunt speech of the Stage-Manager, "That's all the second act, folks."

The reasons for a "strong" curtain on the scene before the last are fairly obvious. The audience is not resting during the two hours of a moving play. Even if the seats are fairly comfortable and in a good location, which they frequently are not, emotions have made tensions. By the end of the play the audience is physically tired, and needs strong stimulation to carry its emotions over even a slight intermission. The metropolitan audience will glance at watches during the last intermission, and estimate the chances of getting to bed by midnight or of keeping an after-theatre engagement. Their own personal affairs will encroach on the play as the last scene starts, unless a strong crisis compels the spectators to desire a resolution. Finally, the last scene is often too short to build anything like a climax without the full force of all that has led up to it. Unless the audience has some emotional tension at the beginning of the scene, the release of tension, or climax, cannot occur.

For the same reason, the other units of a play usually end, if not in a minor crisis, at least with an indication of something ahead to carry interest and emotion forward. It is not necessary to bring all curtains down "with a bang," but a beginner should attempt to end most of his units with something a little interest-provoking, until he has learned to build the body of a unit so solidly that he does not need to tease the audience into being interested.

A word or two about settings will conclude the discussion of scene divisions.

For the beginner, a small number of settings is desirable, for the same reason that a small cast is desirable; namely, that it minimizes the risk a producer takes in buying the show, and increases the chance of some amateur group giving the play a tryout performance. But even more important, a change of scene may be a time waster. Every time the curtain is lowered or the lights go out, however briefly, the audience has a chance to slip away from the carefully built illusion. And every time the curtain rises on a new scene, the audience must adjust itself to new visual stimuli before it can pay attention to the words of the play.

On the other hand, there are abundant examples of plays with many settings, not the least of which is Rice's *Dream Girl* with fifteen changes of locale in the first act. The playwright need not limit himself if all his settings are well motivated, functional, and practicable.

Generally the setting is a place where the chief characters can conveniently be—home, office, or favorite resort. A public place furnishes a convenient location where many characters may gather, but does not easily permit intimate scenes.[13] Sometimes an important event seems to demand

---

[13] Note how carefully Rice avoids intimate scenes in *Street Scene*, except at night, early in the morning, and just after the murder. One scene in which Rose admonishes her mother is extremely brief and hurried.

a setting in which no other action of the play could possibly take place. Before deciding to use such a setting, the playwright would be wise to ask himself if the event could not possibly occur in some more useful setting. Certainly one should not force the whole play into this one setting just because one scene must occur there. But one should select settings that furnish the greatest number of motivations for the characters to enter.

Settings may, of course, simply furnish an adequate background, either realistic or suggestive, for the action. But they may be useful in other ways as well. They may enhance the mood of the play, as do the settings of *Dark of the Moon, Porgy and Bess, Winterset,* and a dozen others that spring to mind. They may contribute to the revelation of character, situation, or milieu, as does the opening of *Elizabeth the Queen,* or the apartment of *The Voice of the Turtle,* or the basement dwelling of Esdras in *Winterset.* They may even legitimately be used to gain attention —*Thunder Rock* is set in a lighthouse, *Flight to the West* in an airplane, *Outside Looking In* in a boxcar, part of *Once in a Lifetime* in a pullman. But many problems of motivation arise as a result of straining for novelty; and in general, novelty, if not actually distracting, wears off in a few minutes, and it is the play itself which must hold the interest of the audience for two hours and a half.

Whatever setting the playwright may choose, his requirements must be practicable. This is not a serious limitation if one knows the diverse facilities of the modern stage designer. Turntables which permit the rapid shifting of small vignette settings were used to make the action almost continuous in *I Remember Mama* and *Lady in the Dark*. A set of pivoted wagons made the instantaneous scene shifts in *Dark of the Moon*. Three rooms were shown simultaneously in *The Voice of the Turtle*. A series of scrims and inner stages made the quick changes in *The Glass Menagerie*. Yet there are a few requirements which the designer does not often meet with perfect success. One must not expect convincingly realistic exterior daytime sets,[14] nor can one expect split-second shifting of large, heavy, realistic interiors except in an unusually well-equipped theatre. To know the full possibilities and limitations of the stage greatly increases the freedom of the playwright in selecting his scenes.

The playwright's description of the scene requires a word. The designer cannot begin his work without a good description of the scene. The playwright must tell him the period, what the place is used for—home, office, dock, field—the sort of people who frequent it, the time of day and year, and any peculiarities of the place that affect the actors or the action. But the playwright should remember that the designer, too, is an artist, specially trained to do whatever research is needed upon the details of the setting, and to express the quality of the play in terms of line, mass, color. The playwright should be wise enough to welcome the inspiration and skill of a fellow-artist and not fetter his creative powers by loading the description with physi-

---

[14] Krows, *Playwriting for Profit*, p. 215 f. Here Krows offers a further reason to avoid exteriors, if possible: "We never really know a person until we see him indoors." He urges that important characters be introduced to the audience in an interior setting.

cal requirements. Furthermore, although the playwright should say what doors, windows, and furniture are needed in the scene, he should not dictate where these are to be unless he has had some experience not only in design but also in directing. For the locations of openings and the major pieces of furniture determine to a large extent the areas in which particular scenes are to be played and the effects of various entrances and exits. To insist stubbornly on a particular arrangement may cramp the director, who knows better than the playwright, as a rule, the communication values of the actor in space.

Two of the problems to be discussed in this chapter have now been at least partially answered. The third remains to be undertaken, that of offstage action.

Before the scenario is complete, one must be sure that all the action can be done on stage; or, if anything must be done offstage, that it can be made effective. Such important scenes as the fall of Solness from the church steeple in *The Master Builder* and the lynching and burning of Abe in *In Abraham's Bosom* are impossible to stage. And often a scene of violence is less effective on the stage than in the imagination of the audience. The truth of this statement may be evidenced by a comparison of a scene from a beginner's play and a scene from Shaw's *Saint Joan*. The beginner's play is a study of the Mexican Penitentes. In one scene the members of this fanatic sect are required to flagellate themselves. The actors accepted the assignment with their usual hardihood. But at final rehearsals visitors asked repeatedly, "They don't really hurt themselves, do they?" Evidently the spectators lost the illusion of watching the characters in a story and could think only of the actors as people, the minute physical pain was involved. It was decided, therefore, to end the scene with the Flagellants beginning to whip themselves as they left the stage. In the other play, *Saint Joan*, the burning of Joan occurs offstage. One sees the writhing conscience of Warwick. There is a red glow, which grows, in the sky. Then the English priest comes in almost physically sick, and mentally quite overcome by having witnessed the burning. The illusion is never broken and the scene is extremely moving.

Two principles come into play here. First, empathy demands that the audience lose its personal consciousness in the happenings on stage. Whenever the audience is asked to empathize in physical pain, its attention is turned to itself and the illusion of participating with the characters is broken. Besides, beauty is a spiritual experience. Suffering is important only insofar as it leaves marks on the soul of the sufferer, or of some character in the play. In other words, the actual scene of violence that so mightily intrigues the young playwright may often be suppressed as less important and less interesting than a scene in which its effects are revealed.

On much the same principle, scenes which require elaborate stage effects are often left to the imagination of the audience. It took an extremely naïve mind to ignore the clicking of trap doors in *The Bluebird* when Bread and Water made their magic entrances, and when the graves opened to reveal beds of flowers. The raising of the apple barrel in *Dark of the Moon* lost a subsequent line or two while some of the audience realized that a trick of business had been used to cover the designer's trickery. One unit of a beginner's play ended with a posse setting fire to a house. The technicians worked long and carefully to make this a tremendous effect. But someone failed to open the ventilators above the stage, and the audience, very nearly asphyxiated, coughed all through the ensuing scene. In general, the playwright would be wise to avoid "dramatic" scenes that depend on the technician; for the audience will always concern itself with how the effect was achieved, instead of with the result upon the character.

If an action must occur offstage, one must be particularly careful to let the audience know what is going on. There are several means of doing this, at least three or four of which are generally used to make a single offstage action clear and interesting.

First, the scene may be built up in the anticipation of the audience. The murder of Runch in *The Criminal Code* is treated in this way. Galloway tells Bob that Runch must pay for squealing. Runch asks the Warden's protection. Then Runch has a hysterical scene with Bob, asking if he has been framed and crying that he knows he is to be killed. Then Galloway comes with the knife.

Two other devices are employed in getting this particular action clear and strong. The action is begun on stage, with Galloway chasing Runch into the next room. Bob then looks into the alcove, and his expression of horror tells the audience what he sees. Shortly afterward the Warden and Gleason enter and comment on the murder, and Gleason actually talks offstage to the dying man: "Who did it,

Runch?" Beginning the action on stage, and showing the reactions of characters on stage are useful means of making offstage action clear.

A report of what has happened is often a rather pale and unexciting way of conveying offstage action; but it need not always be unexciting. In *Golden Boy*, Chocolate Drop's manager comes into Joe's dressing room after a bout, examines Joe's gloves, and then flies into a passionate announcement that Chocolate Drop has died as a result of the fight.

A report of offstage action can be made exciting by producing evidence. Gail enters in *Tomorrow and Tomorrow*, carrying little Christian, who has fallen from his horse. Montoya, in *Night Over Taos*, returns from the execution of his son covered with blood. Oedipus comes from the house with bleeding eyes. It should be noted, however, that audiences are very skittish about the sight of blood on stage, and are as likely to laugh as to gasp.

Somewhat comparable to producing evidence is to conclude the offstage action on stage. In *Street Scene*, Maurrant goes upstairs to kill his wife. There is a scream and a shot. Then Sankey appears at the window screaming for help. Maurrant drags him away and there is another shot. Later, Mrs. Maurrant is carried downstairs on a stretcher, to die as Rose tries to talk to her. In *See Naples and Die*, Charles goes into the room where Nancy is held prisoner. There is a sound of a scuffle, and the two Italian guards are pitched out on their posteriors.

A few cautions should be observed in using offstage action. The playwright should make sure that the action is more effective offstage than on; then he should take care to let the audience know what is happening; and finally, he should make the incident as exciting as it should be in terms of its value to the play as a whole.

Some offstage action is of no importance in itself, yet logically involves the passage of time before the character performing the action can appear on stage again. Such is the case when a character is sent on an errand, or when he goes out to answer a doorbell, or when he has to change clothing within a unit. The audience does not need to know any more than that the character has gone, and for what purpose. However, action on stage continues. The scenes which allow time for offstage matters of this sort have been called *cover* scenes.

Strictly speaking, there should be no such thing as a cover scene. If an action must take place offstage, yet is not important enough to demand any particular emphasis, there are several ways of handling the material. The action may occur between units, with only a clear, brief exposition either before or after the event. If the offstage action can be accomplished in a brief time, such as bringing on an already prepared tea tray or answering a doorbell, a piece of business or a speech or two may be enough to cover it. If a costume must be changed, sometimes the actor on stage can carry on a conversation with the actor changing offstage. In *The Guardsman,* the actor changed his costume and makeup on stage while dragging out a conversation with his wife, to the immense delight of the audience.

But if the action must occur offstage within a unit, and must consume a good bit of time, the best plan is to arrange the material of the unit so that the unimportant action may take place offstage while important material is being presented on stage. Any other treatment will be recognized as padding, and will let the audience relax its attention. Examples of careful arrangement to avoid stopping the play with a cover scene can easily be found. In *Winterset*, when Esdras goes out to call the police, the five pages intervening until his return are used to present the main crisis of the play, Mio's realization that he would rather have Miriamne's love than his former objective of vindication and revenge. In the first act of *Paris Bound,* the bride and groom must change to street clothes. While they dress, sixteen pages of expository material are conveyed by Jim's parents. In the same play, while Jim waits for a long-distance call to come through, he and Mary have a happy love scene which sharpens the discovery, in the next scene, that Jim has been unfaithful. The utilization of time, in these instances, does not just happen; the playwright knows that he must use every moment of his two hours to accomplish something important, and he plans accordingly.

A common failing of a beginner's script is that he does not allow time for these matters. The doorbell rings and a character enters immediately. A character goes out to change his clothes, and returns in an elaborate costume half a page later. Inevitably a few rehearsals will reveal these flaws; but a skilled playwright will recognize them before his play is read by a cast.

The scenario at this stage is still incomplete, far from rigid, easily altered at need, even at the most fundamental points. As it stands, it is like a Christmas tree upon which to hang all of one's bright ideas; yet it serves to suggest that the main emphasis should be upon the shining star at the top, the climax. The first scenario is merely a device for seeing at a quick glance whether the play really has the emphases the playwright meant it to have, says what he meant it to say.

EXERCISES

1. Analyze:
   a. State the functions of all characters in *Mary of Scotland*.
   b. What are the bases of scene division in *In Abraham's Bosom?* In *Dark of the Moon?*
   c. Justify the number of settings in *The Criminal Code* and suggest how these could be made practicable.
   d. What motivates the settings of *The Criminal Code?*
   e. What makes the offstage lynching of Abe in *In Abraham's Bosom* clear and moving?
   f. Find and explain the treatment of all cover scenes in *The Voice of the Turtle*.
2. Find from six to ten auxiliary characters and state their functions in the following character-situations:
   a. A well-publicized murder case.
   b. A famous labor leader's fight with Congress.
   c. "The Fall of the House of Usher."
   d. The kidnapping of a two-days-old baby.
3. If the Cinderella story were being adapted for the stage:
   a. Select six to ten of the most important auxiliary characters, and state their functions and their relations to the story.
   b. Divide the story into acts and scenes, and state the basis of

each division, where each unit is set, what is the function of each setting, and what occurs at each curtain.

c. Tell what action would have to take place offstage and how it could be treated.

d. Tell what material could be used to cover the time between Cinderella's ordering her coach and the loss of her slipper. Find treatment for any other cover scenes in the play.

ASSIGNMENTS

PLAYS: Maxwell Anderson, *Mary of Scotland*. Garden City, New York: Doubleday, Doran & Company, Inc., 1934. Paul Green, *In Abraham's Bosom, Pulitzer Prize Plays,* Ed. Kathryn Coe and William H. Cordell. New York: Samuel French, Inc., 1931. Martin Flavin, *Broken Dishes*. New York: Samuel French, Inc., 1930.

ADDITIONAL READING: William Archer, *Playmaking: A Manual of Craftsmanship,* Chapters IV, V and VIII. New York: Dodd, Mead & Company, Inc., 1937. George Pierce Baker, *Dramatic Technique,* Chapters V, VI, and IX. Boston: Houghton Mifflin Company, 1919. Gustav Freytag, *The Technique of the Drama, pp.* 210-216, 230-245. Chicago: Scott, Foresman & Company, 1904. Clayton Hamilton, *"So You're Writing a Play!",* Chapter VI. Boston: Little, Brown & Company, 1932. Arthur Edwin Krows, *Playwriting for Profit,* Chapters IX, XV, and XXXVII. New York: Longmans, Green & Co., Inc., 1928. W. T. Price, *Analysis of Play Construction,* Chapter XXVIII. New York: W. T. Price, Publisher, 1908. Percival Wilde, *The Craftsmanship of the One-Act Play,* Chapters XXVII and XXXVI. Boston: Little, Brown & Company, 1938.

PART TWO: SUSPENSE

SUSPENSE HAS BEEN defined as a straining forward of attention.[1] It is more than this. It is a combination of hope and fear regarding an event which one foresees. If one wishes a character to accomplish something, if one sees his hope threatened, one is in a state of suspense. Real suspense in a play is like suspense in a severe illness; the patient may live, or he may not. It is like a tie in the last three minutes of a basketball game; anything might happen. One hopes the home team will win, but fears it will not. Suspense is uncertainty toward an eventuality one cares about—not only intellectual uncertainty, but hope alternating with or existing side by side with fear.

Many a young playwright, chock-full of the novel and the short story, feels that one is asking him to play tricks with his material when one asserts that suspense is essential to a drama. The answer to such a protest must be to examine his purpose in writing plays. His intention is to create for the audience the experience of climax, a release of tension in satisfaction as to the outcome of the play. But of

---

[1] Baker, *Dramatic Technique*, p. 207. But see Krows, *Playwriting for Profit*, p. 34, "Curiosity is essentially a cold emotion."

course it is impossible to release tension unless tension exists. The suspense-creating devices are the ones that build up this tension, the necessary antecedent to climax.

A second answer is to look at his materials again and discover if they are really as simple and unexciting as his glancing eye has seen them. If something happened to the protagonist, something as simple as a new neighbor coming to live next door, what enormous possibilities of happiness or unhappiness! If he paid a little more or a little less than usual for a suit of clothes, what drastic changes might occur in his whole behavior and outlook on life! Life is not so certain and simple as one needs to regard it in order to function efficiently. Under the surface every action is fraught with difficulty, danger, uncertainty. It is true that melodrama results from artificially injecting this uncertainty into a play. But by adopting the habit of looking into and under the material, by seeking not the static but the fluid, the countless possibilities of change in relationships, one will find that suspense is not so many tricks played on the audience, but the very pulse of life making itself felt as the play unfolds.[2]

It is easy to recognize suspense, and not very difficult to create it, if one understands the problem and knows his material intimately enough. One can find elements of danger and uncertainty in any person's life, in the most commonplace situations. For example, day after day, John

---

[2] Schlegel expresses this point: "The dramatic poet is, more than any other, obliged to court external favor and loud applause. But of course it is only in appearance that he thus lowers himself to his hearers; while, in reality, he is elevating them to himself." *Lectures on Dramatic Art and Criticism*, p. 38.

Brown comes home to lunch, and his wife, Mary, is a little late in serving it. John sulks a bit, but since fundamentally he loves Mary, his good humor is soon restored. These are ordinary people. There is apparently nothing in their relationship with which to create suspense. What could happen to them? Yet the most commonplace details of their housekeeping reveal the tenuousness of their tranquility.

The curtain goes up on Mrs. Brown at the telephone. She is young and pretty, wears a ruffled apron, and has a large white cat on her lap. She seems eager to be done with the conversation, but polite. Finally she tells her neighbor that it is nearly lunch time and John gets very grouchy when his lunch is late. The neighbor keeps her talking, while the cat jumps down from her lap and goes into the kitchen.

Suddenly Mrs. Brown screams and rushes to bring the cat back; he was just about to get the shrimp she was making into a salad. Again Mrs. Brown giggles that she must hang up, as John has vowed he would turn her over his knee and spank her if she was late with lunch again, and she really believes he would do it. She agrees that John does not look like a cave man, but he is very strong-minded.

John appears on the porch, and Mrs. Brown quickly hangs up, rushing to the kitchen as he enters. He is unusually hungry, and delighted to hear that the roast is just out of the oven. She suggests that he would have time to fix the lock on the screen door while she makes the gravy, and hands him the tool kit. Laughing to hide his impatience, John reminds her that he has vowed to spank her, and will do so if lunch is not on the table in ten minutes. Mary puts her arms around him and makes him say he loves her; but he gives her a quick spank as he brushes her away.

As he starts to repair the lock, he cuts his finger. Mary rushes out to administer first aid, though he declares he could bandage his own finger, and reminds her this would not have happened if lunch had been ready on time. While they argue, the gravy burns. John reaches to spank Mary, but she escapes, screaming that she still has three minutes left.

As John finishes repairing the lock, Mary brings in a salad which John nibbles and does not like. He looks at his watch, and starts to roar, when a neighbor enters to ask directions about baking a cake. She stands in the kitchen door, while Mary gives elaborate instructions. John picks up the tool kit, asks Mary to put it away after lunch, sets it beside the kitchen door. The neighbor takes the hint and leaves, tripping over the tool kit.

While John nibbles a roll, complaining that the butter is missing, Mary starts from the kitchen with a tray containing everything but the roast, which is on a platter ready to serve. She trips over the tool kit, upsetting some of the dishes. John picks her up and helps her to get the things on the table, giving her little admonitory spanks as he does so. At last he sits down and be-gins filling his plate as Mary goes to get the roast.

Suddenly there is a scream from the kitchen. The cat has run off with the roast. John dashes into the kitchen, drags out the sob-bing Mary, turns her over his knee, and spanks her.

This is a farfetched little story, overcrowded with inci-dent in order to demonstrate a point. To make a good play of it, the writer must be able to imagine nuances of feeling and relationship between this particular husband and wife. But as it stands, the story serves to show how endlessly one can find possibilities of suspense in a very stable-seeming, commonplace situation.

The devices used here are common devices for making

suspense. First, the characters are attractive, Mary because of her appearance, her eagerness to be efficient, and her love for her husband; John because Mary loves him, and because he is patient, hungry, and dominatingly masculine in his way, though not really dangerous. Each wants a desirable objective: John his dinner, and Mary to please John. The fundamental obstacle is Mary's rather amusing inefficiency. The simple story is utterly clear as to the alternatives: Mary must provide food or she will be spanked.[3] But over and above this clear skeleton, there are three devices which create suspense. They are:

1. Keeping the audience aware of the objective and its alternative by means of many and various repetitions (Pointers).
2. Bringing into play crosscurrents of action which alter the course of action of the protagonist (Complications).
3. Intensifying the desire for the objective by bringing it almost within reach and then snatching it away (Crises).

These devices are not coldly mechanical if the playwright will sincerely utilize only those pointers, complications, and crises which arise from the life of his particular characters and situations. But however thoroughly he may ransack his material, the devices with which he ultimately succeeds in creating suspense will be these three.

Sincerity means fidelity to the material *and to the pur-*

---

[3] See Wilde, "The premises must be clear and the sympathy of the audience must be won." *The Craftsmanship of the One-Act Play*, p. 192.

pose of the playwright, which is to make a climax express the exact spiritual truth he means to express. He can no more achieve this purpose without suspense-creating tools than a painter can create a meaningful design without rhythm, or an architect can make a bridge without mathematically calculated supports. Sincerity is not negative, the rejecting of tools; it is utilizing the precise tools needed to fashion specific materials into an audience experience.

ASSIGNMENTS

William Archer, *Playmaking: A Manual of Craftsmanship,* Chapter XIII. New York: Dodd, Mead & Company, Inc., 1937. Gustav Freytag, *The Technique of the Drama,* pp. 133-137. Chicago: Scott, Foresman & Company, 1904. Arthur Edwin Krows, *Playwriting for Profit,* pp. 38-42. New York: Longmans, Green & Co., Inc., 1928. John Howard Lawson, *Theory and Technique of Playwriting,* pp. 142-158, 226-228. New York: G. P. Putnam's Sons, 1949. Allardyce Nicoll, *The Theory of Drama,* pp. 119-122. New York: The Thomas Y. Crowell Company, n.d. Albert T. Poffenberger, *Psychology in Advertising,* Chapters VIII-XI. New York: McGraw-Hill Book Company, Inc., 1932. Percival Wilde, *The Craftsmanship of the One-Act Play,* Chapters XX and XXI. Boston: Little, Brown & Company, 1938.

11

Complications

PERHAPS THE MOST USEFUL DEVICE FOR CREATING SUS-
pense is complication, "the introduction of a new force
which creates a new balance of power and thus makes the
delay in reaching the main obligatory scene necessary and
progressive." [1] The definition has two elements: first, a
complication is a "new" force; and second, it accomplishes
something.

First, a complication is a "new" force; that is, outside
of the main character-situation. Tybalt, for example, is
not attempting to separate Romeo and Juliet when he en-
gages Romeo in a duel, for he does not even know that they
have met. The murder of Runch in *The Criminal Code* is
committed without reference to Bob's parole.

Yet it should be noted that both of these complications
are evolved from the circumstances surrounding the main

---

[1] Lawson, *Theory and Technique of Playwriting*, p. 232. Although
Lawson says little about the means by which complication is provided,
his shrewd criticism of the lack of complication in some contemporary
plays is illuminating.

character-situation. Tybalt is part of the feuding Capulet family; and the murder of Runch is a product of the prison monotony and suppressed violence in which Bob lives.

To understand this point of view should remove some of the feeling that complication is theatrical and artificial, and should aid the playwright in finding complications for his own work. Every individual lives in a complex world, is himself complex. The pursuit of any objective is threatened not only by the common risks of humanity—accident, plague, financial insecurity, and the injustices of God and man—but also by the personality and environment of the individual seeking the objective. To look carefully at any life is to realize that progress in a straight line is rare rather than usual, and that ordinarily the course is a devious one, fraught with both mischances and happy circumstances.

The second part of the definition is that a complication effects a change of some sort in the original course of action. The duel between Romeo and Tybalt results in Romeo's banishment, and ultimately in the death of the lovers. The murder of Runch puts Bob irrevocably on the side of the criminals, and costs him his chance of freedom.

To regard complication as a *cause* should eliminate some of the false leads in the plays of inexperienced playwrights, and should make for singleness of direction in the play as a whole. A complication does not merely stave off the main obligatory scene; in the devious way of life itself, it necessitates a change in the course of action.

The ways in which a course of action may be complicated are as various as the facets of an individual's life. One has only to "suppose" something happened, or to say "if" someone else came into the story, to open whole vistas of possibilities. To say that one cannot find or invent suitable complications is to admit that one does not adequately know the individuals about whom one is writing; or that he sees these individuals as impervious to the fluid forces of life. It may not always be necessary to use complications; but if the necessity arises, complications can be found by simply opening the doors of "if" and "suppose."

One of the simplest ways of finding complications is to consider the persons with whom the main characters of the play must or might come into contact, any of whom might alter the pursuit of the objective. The complicating character may be on the side of the protagonist or of the obstacle, or he may not be on either side. His action is often performed without reference to the main action. In *Romeo and Juliet,* for example, Paris does not wish to harm Juliet, but he complicates by forcing her to an immediate and drastic step to avoid marrying him. Mercutio is a friend of Romeo, yet his hot temper forces Romeo into the fatal duel with Tybalt. In *The Criminal Code,* the man who sends Bob the knife is trying to help him. On the other hand, in *Mary of Scotland,* Darnley, whom Mary marries, is actually an agent of her enemy, Elizabeth.

No one lives in a world by himself. The veriest hermit is subject to human contacts unless he lives on the fruits of a desert island. Whatever the present status of the protagonist, he came from a family, any member of which, dead or alive,[2] may affect the emotional drives and hence the behavior of the protagonist. If he has an income, anyone who can affect his income, either for good or for ill, can affect the pursuit of his objectives. If he has an occupation, it is inevitable that some business associate will influence or be influenced by his actions. If he is a human being, someone likes or dislikes, fears, envies, wishes to help or to harm him. Nor is it necessary that the complicating element be in direct relationship to the protagonist. The course of action may be complicated by a character impinging on the life of the obstacle or the objective or some other character.

If a character is used to complicate, the playwright should see to it that the character actually does have an effect on the pursuit of the objective. A member of the family may prod the protagonist to action, as the Warden's daughter does in *The Criminal Code* when she reveals that she is in love with Bob; or as Lady Macbeth does when she cries, "What beast was't then, that made you break this enterprise to me?" But the influence of the family may be less direct, as in *Holiday*, in which Linda gets courage to break with her family by seeing how the family ruined her brother. In *Green Grow the Lilacs* Aunt Eller's attempt to lure Laurey to the party with Curley has the effect of forcing her to go alone with the psychopathic Jud Fry, and thus in a roundabout way effects the end she intended. A business acquaintance may increase or remove opportunity, may stimulate or frustrate, as in *Counsellor-at-Law*, in

---

[2] Lona Hessel, the long-absent sister-in-law, complicates *Pillars of Society;* the Ghost of Hamlet's father and the Ghost of Peter Grimm complicate the plays in which they appear.

which a rival causes a change of Simon's plans and thus
effects a rift between Simon and his wife; or as in *Rocket
to the Moon,* in which the *affaire* between Stark and Cleo
is precipitated by Cleo's being kissed by the doctor upstairs.
A friend in *Paris Bound* reveals Jim's infidelity quite by accident, and thus brings about a temporary change in the
relationship of Jim and Mary. In any case, if a character is
brought into the play to complicate, the playwright should
make sure that the character does have some perceptible
effect on the course of action.

Just as the protagonist lives in a world of people, so he
lives also in a world of events. His milieu is not static if it
in any way resembles the real world in which human beings
think and act. This world is subject to natural laws and to
the vagaries of these laws. Summer, winter, day, night,
drought, disease, fire, famine, tornado, and accident may
come into his scheme of things to aid or thwart him. It is
a world of human affairs, where one's private concerns
operate in a larger circle of business, religion, government,
and social custom. One has to consider taxes and mores,
and the way he will vote, and the state of the stock market,
and his transportation to work, and what he will buy or
sell at what price, and where he will spend Saturday night
and eternity. He may lose a business opportunity, a loved
one, or his life because a careless workman fails to throw a
switch. He may lose his sweetheart because of religious or
political differences, or a misunderstanding. He may become a millionaire or a convict because he ran a black-
market. He lives in a particular time and place, and is
influenced by the customs and events and philosophy of

his day and his immediate milieu. A competent young woman may become a derelict because she moves in an environment that rejects her particular kind of competence, or her "foreign" manners. A poet commits suicide because he cannot make a living; yet twenty years later a publisher makes a fortune on his work. In medieval Europe, to win his lady, a young man had to have battle scars upon him; in eighteenth-century London, he had to be able to write a sonnet; in New York in 1900, he had to prove to the lady's father that he could make money. Every character lives in a world much broader than the circle of his own personal aims and problems; and the things that happen in the world outside himself have a perceptible effect on his own thoughts and behavior. As long as one is alive it is possible for something good or bad to happen to him, through the people that he meets, or through the world he lives in. Indeed, it is impossible for a human being to live untouched by these factors.

By carefully constructing the milieu of his play, the dramatist can find complications. In *The Criminal Code,* Bob wants to get out, and the Warden is doing all he can to get Bob paroled. At the same time a political campaign ties the Warden's hands to some extent; and the prisoners are planning a murder. These two facts are the main reasons for the Warden's failure. In *Winterset,* a group of residents of the ghetto dance to the music of a hurdy-gurdy, and a dumb cop breaks up the dance. By baiting the cop, Mio kills his chance of escape later, for the cop does not believe Mio when he reveals the murder of Shadow. Even an accident, drawn from the milieu of the principal characters, may complicate, as does the breaking of Joe's fingers in a boxing match in *Golden Boy.*

Characters and events are the most common devices by which plays are complicated, but there are many others that may be employed. Sometimes the complication is a spiritual factor, such as the change of personality induced by drunkenness in *Broken Dishes,* which permits the hen-pecked husband to assert himself; or the remorse of the lovers in *The Field God,* which prevents them from enjoying their marriage. Sometimes a revelation brings about the complication, as it does in *Paris Bound,* when Mary accidentally learns of Jim's infidelity and decides to leave him; or in *Hedda Gabler,* when Hedda learns that Lovborg has died an ugly death, and finds herself without incentive to live any more. A past action may complicate, as it does in *Counsellor-at-Law,* when the discovery of a single dishonest act almost disbars the counsellor and does disrupt his marriage.

Indeed, the devices that may complicate are no less varied than the threads of the fabric of human life. The more deeply one looks into life and its vicissitudes, the more clearly one sees that complication is not merely an arbitrary tool of the playwright, but also a vital means of giving to the central characters the mobility and roundness of life.

It would be easy to analyze the complications in some well-known script such as *Elizabeth the Queen* or *Pillars of Society.* But the student might still say, "But that is a play; I want to know how to complicate my material, which is from life and does not seem complicated at all."

Therefore two situations have been invented to illustrate the ways in which complications may be brought into a play. The first is the hackneyed but ever-useful boy-meets-girl plot, the other a more serious story.

COMPLICATING A FARCICAL SITUATION

Main character-situation.	Mary Brown (Protagonist), a rural schoolteacher, wants to marry John Jones (Objective), a local businessman and member of the school board. Mary's father (Obstacle), a widower, forbids the marriage because he wants Mary to keep house for him.

ACT I. *Mary's home.*

Course of action (positive—a plan of the protagonist).	Mary plans to get her father's consent by asking their neighbor, the Widow Smith, to work on Mr. Brown. Her first move is to make the Widow like John. Therefore Mary persuades John to get an increase in salary for the Widow's son, Henry, also a schoolteacher. John agrees, BUT
Complication (unexpected behavior of the objective).	John is jealous of Mary's interest in Henry and breaks a date with her.
Complication (unexpected behavior of Mary's agent).	The Widow thinks the salary increase was due to Henry's merit and praises him instead of John to Mr. Brown.
Complication (relationship).	The Widow has long resisted an inclination to marry Mr. Brown, because she had to take care of Henry.

198

Effect (Mary's agent sets up a counter plot).	The old people now see a solution to their problem in getting Mary to marry Henry. The Widow persuades her mawkish son to ask Mary for a date, and Mary, hurt by John's jealousy and sullenness, agrees.

ACT II. *A night spot, a month later.*

Complication (seasonal pressure of business).	Meanwhile John has been too busy to see Mary for an explanation and Mary has had several dates with Henry.
Complication (misunderstanding).	John has retaliated by a series of engagements with his stenographer.
Effect (action).	One evening the two couples meet in a night spot. Pretending not to care, Mary notes an engagement ring on the stenographer's finger.
Effect (emotional outburst from Mary serving as a stimulus to Henry).	Utterly defeated and miserable, Mary reveals to Henry that the Widow has arranged this situation so that Henry might become interested enough to marry her.
Effect (Henry's confession, a new complication through revelation).	Henry, a born old maid, is shocked and refuses to marry Mary. He was once indiscreet enough to give a girl a ring, which he never got back. He refuses to have any further part in Mary's intrigue and further insists that his mother stop seeing Mr. Brown so often.

ACT III. *Mary's home, the next day.*

Effect (Mary has to restate her problem).	Mary now realizes that the Widow began the situation in the hope that Henry would marry himself off her hands so that she could marry Mr. Brown. The new problem: if Henry could be persuaded to marry, the Widow would be free to marry Mr. Brown, and Mary could then marry. But who would have Henry? And John is engaged to someone else.
New course of action.	Mary tells her father she is engaged to Henry, thus forcing him to ask the Widow to marry and take care of him, and opening the way for the Widow's consent.
Effect (action).	With the path clear, the old couple elope.
Effect (action).	Mary prepares to call John, but Henry comes to confront her. He declares her responsible for his being left alone and demands that she marry him and take care of him.
Effect (a new complication; clash of personalities).	Mary in turn accuses him of taking her to places where John could see her, thereby causing John's engagement to the stenographer, a mousy little thing, just what John needs to feed his ego.
Effect (revelation).	Henry resents Mary's insult to the stenographer and reveals that the ring she wears is the one he gave her.
Effect (action).	Mary now calls the stenographer. Henry and the stenographer quarrel over the phone, with Mary interceding and John at the other end raging that this is a business

	phone and finally firing the stenographer and banging out of the office. Henry and the stenographer make up, with Mary's help.
Effect (action).	John comes to demand that Mary leave his stenographer alone, declares he will fire Mary from the school system. Mary says she intended to retire anyhow, because, with the stenographer taking care of Henry, somebody will have to take care of John.

Complications in the above scenario are made by three persons (the Widow, Henry, and the Stenographer), by a condition of the milieu (seasonal press of business), by an accident (the chance meeting of John and Mary in the night spot), by two unknown past relationships (the Widow's intentions toward Brown and Henry's relation to the stenographer), and by a clash of wills (Henry's refusal to be a pawn any longer). Each of these complications is derived from the milieu or the relationships implicit in the initial character-situation, and each has a concrete result. These complications do not by any means exhaust the possible complications of the story. Further complication might be made by the pupils or the teachers of the school where Mary and Henry work, by the stenographer, by someone reporting that Mary and Henry were seen at the night spot, by John having to go out of town on business, by a strike of the town's main factory, by a hurricane, by a war being declared. No one play will ever need more than a few of the complications from which a resourceful playwright may select.

Of course it is easier to find complications in a farce situation, where the intent is simply to create light suspense for entertainment only, than in a serious plot, where intense sincerity must be maintained. Therefore a second illustration has been provided to show how complications may be found even in a serious and, on first glance, a static situation. The character-situation must be framed very carefully before complications can be devised.

COMPLICATING A SERIOUS SITUATION

Initial stimulus.	A picturesque old man lives in a big house with a girl who may be his granddaughter. He is about seventy, she about twenty-three. They seem to have plenty of money and to be quite happy.
Author's point of view.	Yet one feels vaguely sorry for the old man. Upon analysis, the source of this pity is a vague conviction that he once had great power of some kind, which he no longer possesses.
Analysis of the objective.	The objective most likely to evoke pity in an audience would be the attempt of the old man to reaffirm his lost power.
The ending.	There are two possible endings: either the old man fails to complete his work or the completion of the work forces him to recognize his mental as well as his physical disintegration. The latter ending is the more tragic.
Further analysis of the objective.	Two factors seem important in deciding what the work is that the old man tries to do. It will have to be something that seems

right for a man of his appearance; and, since the course of action depends largely on the occupation, it will have to be one which the playwright knows rather intimately. The appearance of the old man suggests that he must have had an intellectual occupation. Possibly he was a writer. Perhaps he wants to write one last great work, the embodiment of his mature wisdom about life, death, and humanity.

Possible complications.

If he was a novelist or a poet, the completion of the work is publication. Complication might arise from the current economics of the business, from personalities in the business, from the critics, from the life of his granddaughter, from some event which would force him to change his life habits. If he was a playwright, the completion of the work is production, a process highly critical in itself and productive of all the above complications and many more. And this is an occupation with which the present writer might presumably be familiar.

Final statement of the objective.

The objective, then, might be finally stated: the old man wants to produce one more play, to transmit to posterity, especially to his granddaughter, his deep understanding of life.

The obstacle.

The content of the old man's play is the obstacle. In the first place, the philosophy of the play is that of an old man seeing life in perspective. Moreover, the form of the play is extremely unconventional.

Statement of the initial situation.

Hayden Eliot, a seventy-year-old playwright, has completed a tetralogy, his first output in ten years. His granddaughter, Judith, has read but not understood it. It is now in the hands of Roger Trent, director of some of Eliot's earlier plays. No one else knows there is a new play by Eliot; but Kraus, Eliot's former agent, still producing, has been trying for years to get something of Eliot's. Eliot himself is not too confident of the new play.

ACT I. *Eliot's home.*

Collision factor.

Kraus is paying a social call when Trent comes to report that he does not like the script but has given it to Margaret Lewis, a retired actress who formerly played Eliot's leads. Kraus insists on producing the play, sight unseen, relying on Eliot's prestige and the unconventional form of the play. He lures Trent to direct it in the hope of making enough money to build the Shakespearean theatre of which he has dreamed. Eliot sees they are both starting out in the wrong attitude.

Complication (character).

Judith, at the start of her career as an actress, is trying to impress one of her grandfather's younger friends, a critic. He is very keen and honest, and dissuades her from acting in a play that may fail at a crucial stage in her career.

Complication (character).	Trent and Kraus call Margaret and persuade her to try the part. She has a glimmer of what the play means, enough to give the others confidence.
Effect.	Trent now agrees to direct the play.

ACT II. *The stage, ten days later.*

Complication (revelation).	The designer, young and imaginative, reveals through his designs a mixture of austerity and almost clownish lack of humor in the writing.
Effect (complication— relationship).	Trent suddenly realizes he can save the show by playing up the comic elements; but Eliot insists on suppressing all comedy. They quarrel, Eliot becomes stubborn, refuses to revise since part of his meaning is clear.
Effect (complication—events).	The actors, told one thing by Trent, another by Eliot, draw their own conclusions. One, under the impression that the play means that human suffering is unimportant, walks out on a serious family situation. Another, gathering that the play means life is unimportant, kills himself.
Effect (complication—character).	Margaret comes to believe that the message of the play is a negation of morals and moral responsibility. She resigns.
Effect.	Judith now agrees to play the part; but not believing in the play, and feeling that her future is threatened, she is brusque with her grandfather, thereby forfeiting the respect of the critic she wants to impress.

ACT III. *Eliot's home, three weeks later.*

Complication (Act of God).	The old playwright, nearly brokenhearted at the rift with his granddaughter and his old friends, more than ever eager to have the play understood, and exhausted by rehearsals, suffers a heart attack and is unable to attend his opening.
Effect.	Judith persuades the critic to pan her instead of the play, and regains his respect.
Complication (character).	Trent calls just before the show to say he understands the play at last, and intends to retire as a result of it.
Effect.	Eliot now fully understands what he has written. The immense perspective on life, which makes old age endurable, is a sign of the disintegrating will in a failing body. This knowledge is of no use in solving the problems of living men immersed in the world. The ecstasy and pain of youth, the quiet of age, are all parts of a whole life, and Eliot negated his philosophy by breaking out of that quiet. He has already done irreparable damage by selling his philosophy to the cast, may do more if the play runs.
Effect.	Trent assures him it will fail.

The possibilities of complicating this material have scarcely been tapped. The backers, the unions, Judith's career, the past relationships of Eliot and Margaret, business, or even the weather in New York might have affected the course of action. The complications above have been rapidly chosen, but all are sincerely derived from the initial character-situation and are in keeping with the philosophical intent of the play. They may not be the complications which would be selected if one decided to write the play, but they serve to show that effective complications can be found even in the most apparently simple and static material.

Occasionally a playwright will object that there is no need of complication. He will cite *Our Town* and *The Cherry Orchard* as examples of good plays without complication of any sort. The only answer to this contention is that it is true. Chekov and Thornton Wilder have consummate ability to create highly volitional characters, and can move their audiences without much complication of the story. Ordinarily, however, a playwright uses from two to seven complications, or an average of four to a play, to increase suspense tensions and to prevent the story from developing too easily toward the showdown.[3]

On the other hand, an overcomplicated plot is likely to be confusing. *Mary of Scotland,* which the vibrant playing of Helen Hayes and Philip Merivale kept running for two years, had so many intrigues that it was next to impossible, without reading the play, to be sure which of the great powers the subordinate characters were working for. *Night Over Taos,* which has approximately seventeen major and minor complications, was so great a strain on the attention of the audience that it closed after eleven performances.

---

[3] Percival Wilde declares, "Lack of complication in a serious play reduces it to the proportions of journalism; lack of complication in a comic play reduces it to the proportions of a simple joke." *The Craftsmanship of the One-Act Play,* p. 190.

Not only is an overcomplicated play likely to demand an impossible amount of concentration; but the complications, which all have to be prepared and developed, consume time that might perhaps better be spent in getting the audience acquainted with the main characters of the play. A highly complex play is likely to be either too heavy or shallow and melodramatic.

If complication, then, is prepared carefully and developed to its optimum extent, it is not often necessary to find a great many complications.

The plays of beginners, however, often show two faults, aside from the fault of having no complication at all: failure to utilize potential complications and failure to prepare for the complications that are used. The first misleads, the second shocks the audience.

Paul Green's first long play, *In Abraham's Bosom*, which won the Pulitzer Prize in 1927, has the fault of not utilizing material that looks as if it should complicate. In the first scene Abe has a fight with a Negro named Bud, who has his eye on Abe's girl and threatens to get her. But Abe marries Goldie, and Bud is not heard of again. Goldie herself might complicate, but she merely endures with patience Abe's many forced migrations and privations. Toward the end of the play, one expects trouble from the fact that Goldie is working for Lon McCranie, Abe's white half-brother. But nothing comes of this, either. Undoubtedly, *In Abraham's Bosom* is a character study and may not need complication; but the play would be improved by either utilizing or eliminating the several false leads in it.

A potential complication is skillfully not used in *The Cherry Orchard* in the character of Lopakhin. This bashful young man is indicated as a possible solution for Barbara, and even promises Madame Ranevsky to marry her. But in a scene full of suspense and pathos, he finds that he cannot speak to her of love. In other words, he was not actually a potential solution at all, and the skill of Chekov lay in letting the audience surmise this before the crucial scene took place.

The second fault, that of not preparing for the complicating material, results in such incredible melodrama as Chet Armstrong's return in *Broken Dishes* or the unexpected change of character of Oklahoma in *Outside Looking In* and the frightful and not wholly defensible return of Shadow in *Winterset*. Methods of preparation will be dealt with in a later chapter. It may be said here, however, that unless a surprise on stage is made to seem more plausible than if it occurred in real life, the audience hears the creaking of plot construction.

Yet whatever may be the difficulties of complicating any particular plot, the beginner should attempt to master this highly useful dramatic device. Fine writing may fall very lamely on the ear, if it is mere padding to make the play last two hours. The most skilled acting and directing cannot keep tension in a play whose main crisis has passed in the first act. But if the writer applies to his work the maxim, "The course of true love never did run smooth," if he thoroughly explores his material in the search for complication, he will not only find plenty of devices for prolonging the play with increasing tension, but he will also discover a wealth of material to clothe his characters in the rich garments of life.

EXERCISES

1. Analyze:

    What complications are there and of what kind are they in *Anna Christie, Rocket to the Moon, Paris Bound, Elizabeth the Queen?*

2. Taking any of the assignments at the ends of Chapters 7, 8, or 9:

    a. Define the initial character-situation.

    b. Decide what the situation means to you.

    c. Determine the ending that will best express this meaning.

    d. Devise a course of action.

    e. Find as many complications as you can, consonant with the material itself and with its significance to you. Make sure that you have at least two persons and two events to complicate. Make sure that everything you consider a complication has a perceptible effect on the course of action.

ASSIGNMENTS

PLAYS: Philip Barry, *In a Garden*. New York: George H. Doran Company, 1926. Eugene O'Neill, *Anna Christie*. London: Cape, 1923. Clifford Odets, *Rocket to the Moon*. In *Six Plays of Clifford Odets*. New York: Random House, 1939.

COMPLICATIONS

ADDITIONAL READINGS: William Archer, *Playmaking: A Manual of Craftsmanship,* Chapters XI and XIV. New York: Dodd, Mead & Company, Inc., 1937. George Pierce Baker, *Dramatic Technique,* Chapter IV. Boston: Houghton Mifflin Company, 1919. John Howard Lawson, *Theory and Technique of Playwriting,* Part IV, Chapters 1 and 2. G. P. Putnam's Sons, 1949. Percival Wilde, *The Craftsmanship of the One-Act Play,* Chapter XXI. Boston: Little, Brown & Company, 1938.

12

Crisis

TO SUMMARIZE THE MANY IDEAS OF CRISIS WHICH HAVE been promulgated by others would only result in confusion. In this book, crisis means quite definitely one thing: a moment in which the underlying instability of the situation is evident, a moment of uncertainty, clash, or danger in the situation on stage, accompanied by tension in the audience. A crisis may be as gallant a moment as when Christian, after taunting Cyrano to desperation about his nose, is left alone with him to face the consequences; or it may be no more dangerous than when George Gibbs stands before his father-in-law on his wedding morning expecting an embarrassingly intimate talk about marriage. Crisis differs from climax in that crisis always implies something unfinished, while climax is the satisfaction accompanying something finished, settled, restored to equilibrium and harmony. Crisis is the high point of tension; climax is the release of tension in emotion. Crisis is the essentially dramatic moment, while climax is static, lyric.

Crisis is one of the three major means by which suspense

is created. Unlike complications and pointers, however, it is probably not something one can inject into a play by intellectual effort. It is not a trick, but a habit of thought resulting from the writer's awareness of the precarious complexity of human life.

The prologue of *The Criminal Code* ends with an example of crisis as the result of the author's underlying recognition of this complexity. In a series of conversations, the prosecuting attorney, Brady, has brought out the following facts: the victim was the son of a man with great political influence; the prosecuting attorney is seeking office and elections are near; the young murderer has a "nice personality," had a bad break, and could plead self-defense. At the end of these talks, the defense attorney, Nettlefold, pleads for clemency (crisis). Brady snaps that he will ask ten years to life. Nettlefold points out that Brady has a child of his own (crisis). Brady angrily offers to ask a maximum penalty of ten years' imprisonment. When Nettlefold urges that the boy was just unlucky (crisis), Brady retorts savagely with "an eye for an eye," the Mosaic law, and the criminal code. He is rather pleased with his own superiority as he ushers Nettlefold out. "Like taking candy from a baby," he grins. He returns to a study of the case, but can not keep his mind on the book (crisis). He looks up, thinking. Suddenly, very grim, he murmurs, "Christ!"

Obviously the crises in this scene are not merely tricks to keep the audience excited. They arise from the fact that the prosecuting attorney is something more than Mr. Flavin's intellectual mouthpiece. He is a human being, conscious of committing an injustice, full of sympathy, pardonably vain of his powers, forced by the immediate exigencies of his political career.

The skilled writer recognizes and makes use of the impact of situation and character upon character. He sees the moment of decision as a moment of exciting possibilities, not merely affecting the situation at hand, but having far-reaching consequences in the life of the person making the decision, and in other lives. It is not trickery that makes crises. It is the dramatist's mode of thought, his awareness that every decision, every action, is portentous with unforeseen consequences.

Some confusion has probably resulted from thinking of *the* crisis and *the* climax of a play. Surely there are both a main crisis and a main climax, the one when the most intense clash between the opposing forces occurs, the other when this clash is resolved. However, a play has far more than a single crisis and climax.

The number and violence of crises in a play depend, of course, on the characters and situations of the play. *Paris Bound* contains only a few crises, and these are generally quiet, as might be expected of people well-bred and accustomed to self-restraint. In *Golden Boy*, on the other hand, the characters are passionate and deeply frustrated. Naturally their reactions in general tend to violence, and over a hundred crises can be counted in this play. However, a quiet, internal or subjective crisis may be as moving as one in which the characters come to blows.

Most frequently, crisis occurs as a verbal clash between characters challenging, defying, threatening, frankly questioning, reminding, pleading, and so forth. Old Mr. Bonaparte wants his son to be a violinist; Joe asks his father's blessing on a boxing career. Essex challenges, "Could you forgive me and keep your throne?" The Warden pleads with Bob, and demands that he save himself. Maurrant's erring wife asks when he will return from a trip, and he retorts, threatening, "Just in case somebody wanted to come around callin', is that it?" In *Holiday,* Linda, in love with her sister's fiancé, accuses, "You don't love him, do you—do you, Julia?" In *Paris Bound,* Mary's father-in-law tries to taunt her with exaggerating the significance of Jim's infidelity. These are crises in terms of verbal clash. They account for fully a third of the crises in a play.

Not so frequently, yet often enough to provide plenty of examples, the clash between characters amounts to physical violence of one sort or another. Trock and Shadow finger their guns when they disagree; Fuselli's threats in *Golden Boy* carry a gangster's ruthlessness; Elizabeth, angry with fate, kicks the Fool; old Christopherson in *Anna Christie* runs at his daughter's sweetheart with a knife; Maurrant resorts to blows when old Kaplan disagrees with him; Counsellor Simon stands on the window-ledge ready for suicide. Sometimes a physical clash is a pull of characters toward rather than away from each other. From Juliet's, "Good pilgrim you do wrong your hand too much," to Bill's "This is too damn silly," in *The Voice of The Turtle,* the physical proximity of lovers has constituted a crisis. In *Rocket to the Moon,* a kiss, the climax of a series of provocations, is also a crisis, as it leaves Cleo vulnerable to the advances of Stark.

Crisis sometimes occurs when a character does not behave as he was expected to behave. In *Holiday,* the first threat to Julia's romance comes when Johnny learns that she is rich. She had expected some conventional remark from him, but Johnny is frankly delighted. This is a crisis because it reveals the underlying incompatibility of the engaged couple. A terrible crisis occurs in *Winterset* when Shadow, last seen floating down the Hudson with a bullet in his chest, returns to "get" Trock. In *The Criminal Code,* there is a striking crisis when Bob's apathy slips away as he sees Mary for the first time. In *The Voice of the Turtle* a major crisis occurs when Sally, in the most unalluring pyjamas the costumer could devise, remarks, "I have a beast in me, too." Mio reaches a serious crisis when he realizes that in finding Miriamne he has lost his taste for revenge. In the same category is the crisis which arises from Elizabeth sending Bacon out with protestations of confidence and immediately ordering spies to follow him; and from her disarming Essex and then ordering his arrest. The crisis is of the same sort in *Golden Boy* when Joe not only knocks out Chocolate Drop but also kills him.

A discovery or revelation may be a crisis. Such is the case when Mary in *Paris Bound* learns that her husband has been traveling abroad with another woman; and when she discovers who the woman was. The uncovering of a past action makes the first serious crisis for Counsellor Simon, and his own discovery of his opponent's double life makes another turning point. There is also a crisis in this play when Simon realizes that his wife has been accompanied on her trip to Europe by Darwin. In *Dark of the Moon* the revelation that Barbara has borne a witch child is the crisis that ultimately gets her to church. In *Hedda Gabler,* Brack's revelation of the sordidness of Lovborg's death shocks Hedda from her false sense of elation to the abyss of despair.

An interruption is a familiar and easy, if rather mechanical device, for creating crisis. In *Golden Boy,* Joe has made Lorna promise to break off relations with Moody; it is a crisis when he happens into the office to find her kissing Moody. In *Street Scene,* Mrs. Maurrant is dancing with a neighbor when her lover happens on the scene. In *The Criminal Code,* Galloway is warning Bob to keep out of the way, when the Warden enters. Simon's suicide leap is interrupted by the entrance of Regina. In *Paris Bound,* the entrance of visitors prevents an *affaire* developing between Mary and Richard.

Occasionally an accident will make a crisis. Of this kind are Bob's return in time to witness the escape of the murderer in *The Criminal Code;* Gail's unexpected business trip in *Tomorrow and Tomorrow;* and the turning of the frog-sticker against Jeeter in *Green Grow the Lilacs.*

The use of accident is often decried by playwrights and teachers of playwriting on the ground that the illusion of reality created by a play is tenuous at best, and that any strain upon belief is likely to break the illusion completely. However, if one is aware of the danger, one can resort to preparatory devices to make accidents acceptable. Odets makes the killing of Chocolate Drop credible by first revealing Joe as powerful enough to break the hands of the vaunted Kaplan; then by having him break his own hands.

Sankey's accidental entrance on the dance scene in *Street Scene* is prevented from being a striking accident by the fact that he is *returning* from an errand which the audience saw him start upon. Bob's accidentally witnessing the escape of the murderer in *The Criminal Code* is prepared by several means. He is in the Warden's office when the alarm sounds for the prison break; the Warden tells him to remain there; he runs out on impulse for a moment— just long enough for Galloway to kill Runch; he comes back quickly so that the Warden will not know he has disobeyed; the Warden's return is no accident, for the break was a ruse, quiet is easily restored, and the Warden would naturally return to his own office at once. Too many crises because of accidents will undoubtedly make a play seem constructed rather than caused by circumstances; but there is no reason that an accident, if necessary to the action, should not be made as credible on the stage as in life, provided that it is well prepared.

Crisis is also made by stage business, like Mama's scrubbing the hospital corridor in order to sneak into her child's room in *I Remember Mama;* and by stage effects, like the offstage sound of the riot in *The Criminal Code* or the sudden appearance of the moonlight-filled room in *In A Garden.* To use devices of this sort, however, the playwright must have a fair knowledge of the resources of the stage, or he will ask for effects so difficult or striking that they will take emphasis from the main purpose of the playwright. A case of this sort occurred in *Dark of the Moon.* The Witch-Boy challenged his rival to a contest of strength. The rival picked up a barrel full of apples and set it down again. The Witch-Boy then pointed at the barrel and it rose into the air. The audience was extremely interested in the device by which the apple barrel was made to rise from the stage floor. The miracle was evidently phoney.

Most subtle is the clash which does not become overt, such as the moment when Sankey comes upon Mrs. Maurrant dancing with her neighbor in *Street Scene*. Mrs. Maurrant stops dancing in embarrassment. Her husband has a fair notion of why she is embarrassed, but nothing is said. Implied is the clash between Jim and Mary at the end of the second act of *Paris Bound*, when Jim keeps asking Mary to go abroad with him, just after she has learned of his infidelity. Clash between Curley and Jeeter in *Green Grow the Lilacs* is imminent from the moment that Curley walks in the smokehouse door; but the scene goes along, revealing the antagonism in a series of veiled threats, until Jeeter pulls a gun. The implied crisis can exist only if the relationships of the characters involved are known to be unstable in some way before the scene starts.

These various types of crises serve to show the student that a crisis is not necessarily "Your money or your life." It is any manifestation of instability or disharmony in the relation of a character to other characters or to his environment.

More important than the number and kinds of crises in a play is the way they are strung together. The skilled director knows that the audience must always be kept emotionally a step ahead of the characters on stage. When actors laugh loudly on stage before the audience does, or the beautiful heroine sobs before the audience has felt the full pathos of the occasion, the response in the house is killed. The skilled playwright also takes advantage of this knowledge by not allowing his characters to break into blows, verbal or otherwise, immediately upon entering a scene. He develops his most intense clashes step by step, until the audience feels that nothing short of blows will serve in the situation. Two or three crises in an unrelieved series are extremely common practice; nine and ten in a series are not unusual; and O'Neill uses a series of twenty crises in one scene of *Anna Christie*.

To outline a few scenes may help the student to understand how major crises are built through a series of minor crises. In a ten-page scene from *The Criminal Code*, the Warden tries to make Bob tell who murdered Runch, but Bob has been warned by the prisoners not to squeal under pain of death. The Warden's entrance is a crisis.

1. The Warden asks who did it.
2. He threatens that Bob will be held accessory.
3. He reminds Bob that a second murder conviction brings death.
4. The Warden reminds him that his parole is due any day.
5. He threatens that Bob will have to go back to work in the jute mill.
6. He tries to cajole. Bob becomes stolid.
7. The Warden pleads with him to keep the law, not the criminals' code. Bob can not forget what he learned in prison, for he fears he will be killed, as Runch was.
8. Gleason enters and starts to use force.
9. The Warden makes one last eloquent comparison between

freedom and the brutalizing life in the jute mill (Main crisis). Bob sinks back into his old stolid brutality.

10. Brady orders him locked in the dungeon but without violence.
11. He gives a series of rapid orders, determined to save Bob regardless of his own career.
12. He calls the coroner to start the investigation.

Here is a series of twelve crises arranged in a pattern of four smaller series. The first group of four crises is in rather a friendly mood, with Bob as frank as he dares to be, but not abating his "honor." The second group is more impassioned, as the Warden realizes that his task is difficult. But under the pressure of hope, terror, kindness, and reason, Bob's mind retreats to his earlier prison state of whipped inertia. Desperate now, the Warden prevents the use of force, and rises to heights of eloquent pleading, but without result. Finally he sees that there is only one way to save the boy. The last three crises order Bob into solitary confinement for safekeeping, and start the machinery moving toward a solution. This is not one crisis, but a long scene in which again and again Bob is under enough pressure to make him tell what he knows even at the risk of death at the hands of the criminals. It is not mere argument, for, whichever way the scene goes, Bob's life is at stake, and with it the happiness of the Warden's daughter and the Warden's hope for political advancement. The scene is one crisis after another from the time the Warden stands in the door until he calls the coroner and the curtain gives relief from the strongly built tension.

Another tense major crisis ends the ten-page scene in

which Elizabeth pleads with Essex to accept love instead of death. Essex's long-awaited entrance just before his execution is a crisis.

1. Instead of flying into her arms, he chides her for taking his thoughts away from death, which he has already accepted.
2. She is thus forced to admit she loves him and cannot let him die.
3. He declares he flattered her merely because she was queen, but she quickly realizes this is a ruse to terminate the interview.
4. Under pressure, he admits he still loves her.
5. She begs him to show the ring that would gain her forgiveness.
6. He defies her; if she forgives him, he will take her throne.
7. The chimes ring the three-quarter hour, urging haste.
8. Essex asks permission to leave.
9. He demands, "Could you forgive me and keep your throne?"
10. She declares him hollow, faithless, an upstart.
11. He explains that in prison he realized he would rule badly, prefers to die.
12. She yearns, "Why could you not have loved me enough to give me your love and let me keep as I was?"
13. As he starts out, she cries, "Take my kingdom. It is yours" (Main crisis).
14. Penelope enters, urges Essex to ask forgiveness and life.
15. He kisses her good-by and exits.
16. Once more Penelope implores the Queen to send a pardon after him. But the chimes ring the hour. Elizabeth bows her stricken face in her hands, covering her ears.

The person who is looking for *the* crisis of this play will find it in the preceding scene, the arrest of Essex. But, like the example from *The Criminal Code,* this scene, the last in the play, is packed with crises, all leading to the terrible moment when Elizabeth knows her lover has been executed. Like the crises in *The Criminal Code*, these crises also fall into groups. The first series of four crises forces Essex to admit that he loves her, though he does not come to her arms. There is a lovers' recrimination in the two crises which follow; but the chimes bring them quickly to a state of tension, and seven crises come in quick order to the cry, "Take my kingdom. It is yours," and Penelope's entrance. Three more crises occur as a result of Penelope's pleading, the most intensely critical moment for Essex being the one in which Penelope's kiss might recall him to life, had he been a lesser person. Penelope's heartbroken pleading until the chimes ring again is hardly a crisis any more; it is the beginning of the brief resolution, Elizabeth's return to harmony with her world.

One more scene will round off the point that a really strong crisis is developed by making it follow a series of more and more insistent lesser crises. This is a twelve-page scene of exposition from *Golden Boy*. The manager, Tom Moody, is telling his mistress, Lorna, that he is developing a boxer named Kaplan to win the championship from the famed Chocolate Drop. Joe enters.

1. Joe tells Moody that Kaplan has broken his hand; Moody rages in despair.
2. Joe offers to take Kaplan's place in the bout that night. Moody warns him to get out.
3. Joe insists, explaining Chocolate Drop's technique.
4. Moody recounts the men Chocolate Drop has knocked out, trying to ridicule Joe. Joe persists.
5. Moody laughs when Joe says his name is Bonaparte.
6. Joe grabs Moody and gives him a good shaking.

7. Tokio, the trainer, enters and Moody tells him to get Joe out "before I brain him".

8. Tokio angrily explains that Joe is the one who broke Kaplan's hand.

9. Lorna begins asking sensible questions, to which Joe replies with an invented biography.

10. Gottlieb, the co-partner, calls, and Moody, still sore and unconvinced, but desperate, tells him he has a better man than Kaplan, "a cock-eyed wonder,"—Joe.

11. Joe says Tom will be surprised, and Moody flares, "Call me Tom again and I'll break your neck."

Again a pattern of crises appears. The first series leads to Joe's shaking Moody in frustration. Two more reveal that he has possibilities as a fighter. There is some relief in a series of minor crises as Lorna questions, but the antagonism flares again with the telephone call and Moody's last threat to Joe; and the tension breaks with a laugh at the curtain. The whole series is a masterly exposition of how Joe happened to get signed on with Moody. It tells a good bit about Joe's disposition, makes us like him, and makes us want to know more about him. There is no narration at all until the audience knows Joe and has had its curiosity piqued. This is exposition at its best.

These three scenes—the main crisis of one play, the final scene of another, and an expository opening scene—have been introduced to show how a scene is built by means of a series of crises. They show how tension at the beginning of a critical scene is made to mount to the snapping point before any release is given. These scenes indicate that a play is something like a boxing match, in which the boxers spar, give a jab or two before drawing blood, then settle down to steady fighting toward the knockout blow. Note that in each of these scenes there is a specific point at which tension, already high, becomes definitely higher. In *The Criminal Code,* this point is Gleason's entrance, the eighth crisis; in *Golden Boy,* it is Tokio's entrance, the seventh crisis; and in *Elizabeth the Queen,* there are two points, the ringing of the chimes at the seventh, and the entrance of Penelope at the fourteenth crisis. Although there is, of course, no rule requiring so many crises in a scene, with a factor that increases tension at such and such a point, it is evident that this scheme does build a scene which is really moving on the stage. A crisis is not mere clash; it is artfully prolonged and intensified clash.

It is unlikely that any dramatist plans how many crises he will have in a given scene. The Hollywood practice is to introduce something that will restimulate attention at least every one and one-half minutes; but a serious drama-tist probably has little notion how many crises he is going to write when he starts into a scene. The point is simply that, with or without knowing what will be the result in terms of numbers, the professional playwright *thinks* in terms of crisis, of opposition, inherent antagonisms, uncertain-ties in the web of relationships of his characters.

Something remains to be said about the *main* crisis of a play, that moment when all the forces of the play focus for the most vigorous clash and the showdown between the protagonist and his obstacle.

Several critics and a few playwrights have given for-mulas about where the main crisis of a play should come. A better indication of the common practice can be gained, however, by a close study of several of the plays frequently mentioned in this book. Although these plays are divided into various numbers of units, ranging from three to fourteen, in every case except one the main crisis falls in the last or the penultimate scene.[1]

More significant than the unit in which the main crisis occurs is its distance from the end of the play. Again the range in these plays is wide. The main crisis of *Counsellor-at-Law* comes within two per cent of the end of the play,[2] while the main crisis of *Anna Christie*, with its roaring last act, is twenty-three per cent from the end. But every one of the dozen plays except *Anna Christie* and *Street Scene* has its main crisis more than four-fifths of the way through the play.

Moreover, when the main crisis occurs a long time before the final curtain, the remainder of the play is seldom mere static climax; there are always two or three strong crises before the play is over. An example has already been given from the last act of *Elizabeth the Queen*. In this act there are several minor crises, a strong crisis in which the Queen forces the Fool to eat, another when she drives

---

[1] Of the three-act structures under consideration, *Holiday, Paris Bound,* and *Cock Robin* have the main crisis in the last unit; and the main crisis of *Street Scene* falls in the scene before the last. *Anna Christie* has its main crisis in the third of its four scenes; *Winterset,* in the fourth of its five units; *Green Grow the Lilacs,* in the fifth of six units; *Our Town,* in the last and *Elizabeth the Queen,* in the sixth of seven units; *Tomorrow and Tomorrow* and *Counsellor-at-Law,* in the last of nine units; *Golden Boy,* in the eleventh of twelve units; and *The Criminal Code,* in the ninth of fourteen units.

[2] Percentages are figured in number of pages. A better measure would, of course, be time.

out the players, and the final series outlined above, in which she parts from Essex. Thirty-eight pages follow the main crisis of *The Criminal Code,* and there are seven strong crises in these tense pages.[3] The last act of *Anna Christie,* which follows the main crisis, is built of two strong series of crises, one between Anna and Chris, the other between Anna and Burke, and a crisis which does not materialize between Chris and Burke. The main crisis of *Street Scene* occurs within the second act, fifty-one pages before the end of the play. After the murder scene, Rose meets her mother being carried out of the house; she has to brush off Easter who wants "to take care of her"; she meets her father after his capture; and she parts with Sam. Most comedies have the final curtain very shortly after the main crisis; but *Green Grow the Lilacs* has a last act of twenty-six pages, approximately one-fifth of the whole play. In a scene which begins with Laurey in an extremely unstable condition, a dog is heard to bark, heralding Curley's arrival; Curley arrives, pursued by a posse; Aunt Eller persuades the sheriff to let Curley stay the night.

Common practice thus tallies with the old dictum of Corneille,[4] that the main crisis should come near the end of the play; and we may add that if it must come earlier, it seems to be the general practice to save two or three important minor crises for the pages after the main crisis.

---

[3] Galloway sends the knife to Bob; Sheridan threatens to interfere in the investigation of the murder of Runch; Brady, under pressure, insists on Bob not being beaten; Brady discovers that his daughter is in love with Bob; Bob murders the Guard; he is almost caught in the prison yard; he confesses the murder.

[4] "Premier Discours," in Clark, *European Theories of the Drama.*

Now that the skilled playwrights' use of crisis has been rather thoroughly examined, further insight may perhaps be gained by looking into a few plays in which crises failed to come off. The beginner in playwriting betrays five common weaknesses so frequently that they should be scrutinized. He fails to prepare the audience for a crisis, he allows the crisis to come too quickly to a solution, he avoids the crisis entirely, he dissipates the tension in talk, or he substitutes for real crises little scenes of activity that have no bearing on the actual stakes of the scene.

First, he fails to prepare the audience properly for the crisis. He himself knows the implications and alternatives of the conflict; he can explain them to the director and cast; but the alternatives are not clear in the script. A person reading the play with a view to production may not always have the author near to explain. This fault is evident in an early play of Lynn Riggs, *Sumpn Like Wings*. We learn early in the first act that a certain disreputable Elvie Rapp is coming to live in the Baker home to help with the housework. In another part of the scene we learn that Mrs. Baker is too strict with her daughter, Willie, and that Willie has an ungovernable temper. When Willie learns that Elvie is coming there to live, she behaves in a violent manner, screaming and threatening to run away. Then, suddenly, without transition, she accepts the situation, breaking into tears. Study of this play leads one to think that this behavior is caused by Willie's sexual instability; but this trait is not clear when these two violent crises occur, and the result is that Willie seems extremely unattractive to a shocked audience.

The unskilled playwright often allows the critical scene to come to an incredibly quick solution. Instead of developing the tension through a series of crises, he plays his ace, so to speak, at once. A student's first play furnishes an illustration. Thomas Desiderio, a heretic priest at the time of the Inquisition, arrives in Milan in the midst of an argument between the Duke and a hunchbacked beggar. Thomas happens to touch this hunchback, who rises cured. Thomas, hardly aware of having worked a "miracle," is approached by Leonardo da Vinci:

> LEONARDO. I am a painter. My unworthy hands are trying to re-create the Lord's last supper. All my life I have searched for a man to pose for Christ. You are that man.
> (*For two brief speeches the beggars urge him to accept.*)
> THOMAS. You ask me to pose for Him?
> LEONARDO. You cannot refuse it.
> THOMAS. I am unworthy. I cannot.
> LEONARDO. You are more worthy than any man alive. Help me to recreate Christ (pointing to the beggars)—for them.
> THOMAS. To recreate Christ—
> BEGGARS. Yes, yes. Hail the Messiah!
> THOMAS. It is a holy task. It shall be done.
> BEGGARS. Viva! Viva!
>
> *Curtain*

This is actually a major crisis, a decision that plunges Thomas into the sin of pride and ultimately causes his ruin. But the crisis is reached and passed so quickly that no tension can possibly be built.

Another scene from the same play reveals a third fault of beginners, that of avoiding crisis in relationships that are essentially critical. The Duke's mistress is in love with

Thomas. She notices that he wears a new robe, which makes him look like a king. He is aware, and not entirely happy, that she does not approve of the robe nor of his dining with the rich. The talk turns to less personal matters, especially to Thomas's relation with the common people. The scene is worth quoting:

(Thomas stands on a scaffolding before the unfinished "Last Supper" for which he has been posing. Cecilia stands on the floor below him.)

THOMAS. And they love me with a love—

CECILIA. You are too strong, Thomas. Is there no weakness in you, no place where I—

THOMAS. Cecilia—

CECILIA. Other men felt that God called them. They answered it. But they lost their natural life. Your strength is still here, on earth, close to me.

THOMAS. Do you think I have not felt you near me, my life merged with yours, my heart beating with your heart? I looked at you today—just as I have so many times. My love for you wiped out everything else.

CECILIA. Thomas!

THOMAS. At that moment I would have given my very soul to take you in my arms, to hurt you with the fierceness of my love, to heal you with the tenderness of it.

CECILIA. And I would glory in the hurt, cry with the tenderness.

THOMAS. Oh, Cecilia, it is so hard for me to remember what I must do, that my life is not my own. I think of compromise—

CECILIA. Yes, Thomas. It is not right that you should give so much to them and so little to me who love you most.

THOMAS. It's no use, Cecilia. It must be one or the other, and I have made the choice.

CECILIA. Then let us take the compromise. They will not miss your love as I will.

THOMAS. Woman, would you come between me and God?
CECILIA. Forgive me, Thomas. I have not known love before.
THOMAS. I have hurt you. And I can do nothing to stop the pain.
CECILIA. Yes, but it is a gentle hurt. I would not have you remedy
it. It makes my faith in you greater, my belief that you will
succeed stronger.

They talk of other matters. A page later he assures her
that he does love her, and understands her right to have
spoken; but his life is in God's hands. He forgives her.

No doubt love scenes are as difficult for the young playwright as they are for the young actor. And the playwright
can take a lesson from the actor, first learning to overcome
squeamishness, to admit the activating force of physical
attraction. In this scene part of the trouble is that the
writer had not seen his characters with bodies. It was only
in rehearsal that he realized the inevitability of the Duke's
mistress falling in love with a strong handsome man, whose
spiritual qualities she also admired. It was in rehearsal also
that he realized that any development of the romance
might incur the vengeance of the Duke. This was a relationship very highly critical. To the young author it had
seemed a mere conflict of principles.

An equally important reason that this scene never
amounted to crisis is that Thomas *has decided before the
scene began* that love is not for him. Compare this inflexible and unhuman positiveness with the decision made
by Brady in the scene from *The Criminal Code* described
near the beginning of this chapter. Brady has decided to
convict the murderer; but *his conscience keeps pricking
him to alter his decision.* Similarly Thomas, had he been

alive, would have felt the much more elementary pricking of the flesh against his decision not to love Cecilia. Even if there were no struggle in Thomas, the danger from the Duke would make them aware of risk, crisis, in admitting their love. The author simply was not thinking in terms of crisis, for his characters are not of the flexible and volatile material of life.

The fourth common flaw in the crises of unskilled writers is the loss of crisis through too much talk. The love scene quoted above shows this fault to some extent. There is a better example in the play about Paul Bunyan mentioned earlier. Paul discovers that the henchmen of King Pete have poisoned his Ox and his men. He has the conspirators in his power. The audience is ready to ask what dire punishment the greatest logger of all time will mete out to the conspirators. He sends for the guilty ones, and begins:

Who put you up to this? Who is behind these ideas? Who, I say? By the blasting blistering furies of Hades and the eternal damnation, you may not do this to me and mine. Get out. (The woman, the only one of the conspirators who has appeared, leaves.) To work, my merry savages, Timber! (The men move away grumbling.) What is this dismal mumbling I hear? It is a language unknown to me; my ears are not used to it. There is some hero behind this. Hels Helson, there's some mystic dastard hero behind this. By the brimstone fumes of the sulphurous caverns of Gehenna, bring me to where the coward skulks. My men—my men—you shall see a monolithic battle of the ages. That will cheer your laggard hearts, your stomping feet, your blasting bellering yells, by the merry old, simmering old sassafras sawlog. You shall see how Paul can fight for you again. His arm has hurled the mountain from its base. It has wrested the curling faunching cataract, the thunderous hurricane. It has done battle with mighty forests, titans of men, tremendous heroes whose hero ghosts snarl in the halls of Asgard. Hels Helson! Care for my men. Care for my ox. (He stalks out.)[1]

This is fine Rabelaisian writing. But the hero might simply have arrested the conspirators, had Hels Helson ever obeyed the order to bring them on.

The fifth fault common in the manuscripts of inexperienced writers, and even occasionally in the work of writers of some experience, is the inclusion of irrelevant crises which tend to take on more emphasis than they are worth and thus distract or mislead the audience. One of Lynn Rigg's early plays, *The Lonesome West*, shows this fault. In this muddled four-strand story, presumably the main matter is the attempt of the wife, Kate, to force her husband, Bill, to move to town. The first act, thirty pages long, contains four fights, actual or threatened. The second act, twenty-seven pages long, contains two threats of killings. The third act, sixteen pages long, contains an attempted killing and a horse-whipping. None of these violent actions seems to advance or retard the achievement of Kate's objective, or indeed, of any objective. Barry's first play, *You and I*, contains an example of crisis for its own sake in the scene in which Geoffrey, a novelist, mistakes a maid for a guest. Another early play by Barry, *The*

---

[1] From *Paul and the Blue Ox*, by E. P. Conkle, p. 53 f. Copyright 1947 by Ellsworth Prouty Conkle. All rights reserved. This manuscript has undergone several revisions and is now published as *Paul and the Blue Ox* in *Five Plays*, by E. P. Conkle. Reprinted by permission of the author and Samuel French.

Youngest, is full of lively bits of irrelevant activity, somewhat critical in nature, and the play is extremely confusing for this reason.

More must be said about relevance and emphasis; but the examples cited indicate the necessity for adequate preparation, well-developed clash, intelligent cutting of superfluous talk, and care in subordinating secondary crises to primary ones.

The time has come to draw together all the threads of this long chapter. *Crisis* was defined as a moment of uncertainty, clash, or danger, deriving from the playwright's peculiar way of seeing life as highly volatile rather than as fixed. Many kinds of crisis exist, of various degrees of violence, from an unconventional remark to physical blows, from the most subtly motivated reactions to calculated interruptions and even well-planned accidents. Any juxtaposition of inharmonious elements is likely to produce crisis.

There is not merely one crisis in a play, but a great many, actually an average of about eighty, strung together mostly in series of from three to twenty, according to the amount of emphasis the playwright wishes to give the scene, or according to the strength of the opposing alternatives.

The main crisis is generally rather near the end of the play, though it may be earlier, in which case it is likely to be followed by two or three sharp crises before the final curtain. Probably the beginner should try to place his main crisis in the last or the next to the last unit of his first two or three plays, with the frank purpose of practicing this suspense device. He should not, however, consider this an inflexible rule.

It is not to be expected that the apprentice will develop skills in constructing crises before he has written several plays. Often he will fail to make alternatives clear; will rush ahead of his audience into violent clash, or lag behind his audience without realizing that clash is expected; will fall in love with his own fine words, to the detriment of the movement of the scene, or allow a secondary crisis to develop more fully than his main crisis. Good crises have much to do with the effectiveness of the play. To learn how to write them one must submit to long and faithful practice in the technique of making alternatives clear, and devising means of prolonging and intensifying scenes of conflict. One must cultivate the habit of looking for hidden conflicts in the apparently serene lives of the people one meets. One must achieve the maturity to discern and evaluate the precarious complexities of life.

EXERCISES

1. Analyze:
   a. Point out the crisis series in the last scene between Moe and Hennie in *Awake and Sing*.
   b. Analyze the crises in Act I of *The Youngest*.
   c. Find the main crisis and all major crises that follow it in *Night Over Taos*.
2. Arrange in series all crises inherent in the following stories:

a. (At least three crises) After Mary had quarreled with her mother and unsuccessfully wheedled her father, she bought the dress anyhow, even though she knew she would be punished later.

b. (At least eight crises) So now he was out of work. Eve hadn't wanted him to join the union in the first place. When the men got mad at Piper's being let out, Eve was so upset she couldn't eat her dinner, and of course that was bad for the baby. That night she had made him promise he'd leave the union, and the baby yelled all through the argument. But the strike had happened so fast that he hadn't had time to get out. Now he was out of work, or a scab. Well, so he was out of work; let Eve holler.

3. Write a scene of three pages containing three to five crises in series on the theme: Mary sits out the dance with John in the hope that he will propose to her, but he does not.

4. Write a scene of five pages with five to ten crises in series on the theme: Henry has to tell his wife that he has tuberculosis.

5. Write a scene of five to ten pages with ten or more crises in series on the theme: a woman discovers her son is a thief.

6. Write a scene of ten pages with ten or more crises in series on the theme: a girl admits to her chum that she is in love with the chum's fiancé.

   (In the last two assignments you may introduce either one character or one incident to increase the tension at some point past the middle of the scene.)

7. If you are working on a play, outline the main obligatory scene as a series of ten or more increasingly intense crises.

ASSIGNMENTS

PLAYS: Maxwell Anderson, *Night Over Taos*. New York: Samuel French, Inc., 1932. Philip Barry, *The Youngest*. New York:

Samuel French, Inc., 1925. Clifford Odets, *Awake and Sing*, in *Six Plays of Clifford Odets*. New York: Random House, 1938.

ADDITIONAL READING: William Archer, *Playmaking: A Manual of Craftsmanship*, Chapters IX and XIV. New York: Dodd, Mead & Company, Inc., 1937. Gustav Freytag, *The Technique of the Drama*, Chapter II, pp. 104-140. Chicago: Scott, Foresman & Company, 1904. John Howard Lawson, *Theory and Technique of Playwriting*, Part III, Chapters I and V; Part IV, Chapter III. New York: G. P. Putnam's Sons, 1920. Percival Wilde, *The Craftsmanship of the One-Act Play*, Chapter XXIII. Boston: Little, Brown & Company, 1938.

13

Pointers

THE THIRD AND LAST DEVICE USED DELIBERATELY TO create suspense is called a *pointer*, because it points to something ahead. In a hackneyed vaudeville skit, a girl enters and a man steps up to her with, "Haven't I met you somewhere before?" In a play, the scene might be as follows: the girl crosses the stage; the man starts violently upon seeing her, but she pointedly ignores him; on her exit, he turns, scratching his head in a puzzled manner. The vaudeville skit barely takes time to arouse attention. But the man in the second scene makes one want to know what has happened between the two characters, and what further developments are to take place in their story. The tiny scene arouses curiosity and anticipation by means of pointers.

In general a pointer is not merely a cold statement that something is to happen; rather, it is a tantalizing glimpse of what may happen, a suggestion that induces hope or fear. It is very like the lollipop one holds out to a baby and snatches away before his hands close on it.

A pointer is a contract, a promise to the audience. Obviously there is no sense in cramming a play full of pointers unless one has the intention of fulfilling the contract. To do so produces only confusion. But when one knows clearly in what direction his action is to go, what scenes and relationships he wants the audience to anticipate or dread, he can make these matters immeasurably more exciting by the use of pointers.

The ways in which one may be led to anticipate or to dread an eventuality are almost infinitely diverse. The playwright learns to recognize these more or less minute signs in life, and to utilize them in his play. There are six principal ways by which professional playwrights make their audiences look ahead with heightened emotion.

Most frequently used and perhaps the easiest to learn is a direct statement that something is going to happen. In *In a Garden*, the protagonist announces that he is going to transform his dining room into a garden. Torvald reminds Nora in *A Doll's House* that she is to dance the tarantella. Somewhat more subtle is the trick Rice used in *Street Scene* of letting characters speculate correctly on what will happen. The gossips wonder what Maurrant will do if he discovers that Mrs. Maurrant has a lover. One of them actually says Maurrant will kill Sankey. This frank speculation made early in the play creates a strong tension in the audience, which is almost crying out to stop Maurrant by the time he discovers the infidelity of his wife. A direct statement, especially if it is in the form of a speculation, is a very clear and useful pointer.

Another sort of pointer comes as a result of a clash of

characters, taking the form of a threat, promise, boast, plea, or warning. The old cry of "Vengeance!" in the melodrama was of this kind. Modern examples are less obvious. In *Street Scene,* Rose urges Maurrant to be nice to his wife, thus emphasing his harsh and dangerous disposition; he retorts with a threat to Rose about going out with married men, which makes the audience dread what he will do when he learns of Mrs. Maurrant's *affaire.* In *Golden Boy,* Lorna's promise to take Joe away from his family is a danger sign, for the audience regards the family as a stabilizing influence. In *Green Grow the Lilacs,* Curley boasts to the treacherous Jeeter that he can shoot through a knothole, and the audience dreads trouble between them and hopes Jeeter will be beaten.

A third type of pointer exists in the relationship of characters. If certain characters are highly compatible or highly antagonistic, the audience awaits their meeting with a keen sense that something will happen between them. A great many pointers of this kind are used in *Night Over Taos.* The protagonist, Montoya, is revealed as jealous, utterly ruthless, and an object of fear to all who know him. His older son has had an intrigue with Montoya's mistress, and his younger son is in love with the girl Montoya intends to marry. Evidently there is trouble ahead. Likewise in *Street Scene* it is the relationship between Maurrant, Mrs. Maurrant, and Sankey that keeps the audience dreading the murder. In *Holiday,* Linda's affinity for Johnny, and Julia's incompatibility with him, promise a readjustment between them. Pointers of this sort are of the very stuff of the play. They occur sometimes as plants, sometimes as crises. They always indicate that something more is to happen, and they excite the audience.

Hope or fear may be quickly aroused by emotional behavior on the part of the characters. Tina, in *Tread the Green Grass*, enters as if fleeing from something; curiosity is stimulated in the audience even before she speaks. In Act III of *Tomorrow and Tomorrow* little Christian enters in his night clothes, nervously peeps toward the door where his parents are, and hurries out of doors under extreme tension. One is alarmed for his possible fate. In *The Criminal Code*, Runch, the squealer, hysterically implores the protection of the Warden against the other criminals. Tension is very easily aroused in the audience by the sight of a character under emotional stress.

Any delay, evasion, or interruption on stage, whether or not it constitutes a crises, is likely to be a pointer. The scene of the Drunken Porter in *Macbeth* is an example. Each knock on the door, each hesitation of the Porter to open it, delays the crisis of MacDuff's entrance, and increases the tension toward the discovery of the murder of Duncan. The same device is used in *Counsellor-at-Law* while Mac-Fadden tells his long story about unearthing Baird's double life. Half a dozen times the Counsellor is about to get information, only to be told, "I lost track of him," "He wasn't there," "I didn't get in." By the time MacFadden brings out the pack of incriminating letters, the audience is ready to wring the story out of him by main force. This device is sure-fire in its effect upon the audience as the lollipop with which one teases the baby.

Sometimes the anticipation of the audience is aroused

by technical effects. Lights, sound, properties, and bits of business can be used as pointers. An effective device is the flashing sign of the Algiers Hotel outside Stark's office in *Rocket to the Moon,* constantly suggesting the convenience of an *affaire* between Stark and his secretary. In *Green Grow the Lilacs* a pair of pistols placed between Curley and Jeeter as they sit down to play cards is an ugly threat of trouble between them. In *Hedda Gabler* there are two startling uses of pistols to suggest Hedda's instability and to make the audience fear the use to which she will put the pistols. The telegram in *The Late Christopher Bean* and a hundred other plays promises information or a crisis of some kind. Business, like the throwing of Montoya's dagger in *Night Over Taos,* or Hedda's burning of the manuscript, can be used to lead the audience to expect some result. The mysterious light effects at the opening of *Dark of the Moon* are more than evocative of mood; they strongly promise a struggle of elemental evil forces. All these devices are of the same kind as the old-fashioned "letter" and "jewels" of the melodrama; and they are just as useful.

There is another device, very subtle and difficult, but so effective that it must be mentioned. This is the pointer made by understatement or by asserting the negative of what is to happen. A good example occurs in *Awake and Sing.* The first mention of Moe draws an angry retort from Hennie to the effect that he is too free with his hands. Later, Moe says that Hennie is standing him up in order to see him squirm. When they meet, she snubs him. Hennie reacts so violently at every mention of or contact with Moe that there could be only one explanation: she loves him. One shares Moe's grim hunger for the admission that this is true. The same sort of behavior is used in *Green Grow the Lilacs* as a part of Laurey's coquetry, to make the confession of her love awaited the more eagerly by the audience. A particularly fine example of understatement as a pointer occurs in *Tomorrow and Tomorrow*. It is clear that Hay and Eve have found each other surprisingly attractive. At the end of the first unit between them, Hay is left alone with his wise secretary, Gillespie. No one speaks. Then Hay says, "Shut up, Gillespie."

To classify all the pointers in a play would be impossible, since everything that leads the audience to look ahead is a pointer, and in a well-integrated play nearly everything contributes to this anticipatory tension. However, in practically every play of professional calibre one can find literally dozens of these devices included for the clear purpose of making the audience look ahead. The seven devices noted here are the most common, and should therefore be learned as one learns to operate the various types of drills and saws in the carpenter shop, or as the actor learns the uses of his voice.

Most of the examples noted have pointed to some incident, either in the main action or in a subordinate action. However, some pointers are often included for no other reason than to excite the audience. Extreme examples of this use of the pointer are the bloody hand at the window in *The Bat* and the sleepwalking nun in *Murder in a Nunnery*. *Paris Bound* opens with a pointer merely to arouse curiosity: Julia, the maid, is listening through the door to the wedding music downstairs. As there is no reason why Julia should not listen, or even be at the wedding, the obvious purpose of this business is to gain attention. The first scene of *Counsellor-at-Law* is filled with pointers to the entrance of Simon: the telephone keeps ringing, the telephone girl speaks to persons of importance, telegrams and letters keep arriving, Simon is delayed because of a speech before the Supreme Court, the office fills with people waiting to see him, they speak of him with admiration, there is even some gossip about his beautiful wife. The audience is excited about Simon before he appears. In the third act of *Counsellor-at-Law* there is copious use of pointers to create a sense of urgency: the telephone rings, the taxi is ordered, Simon is delayed in getting back from Washington, flowers are ordered for Cora's stateroom, Regina several times urges Simon to hurry if he wants to see Cora off. In *Winterset,* the almost invisible Men in Serge, Trock's gunmen, are no more useful in their plot function than they are in creating a sense of ever-present danger.

In other words, one perfectly legitimate use of pointers is simply to excite the audience. These pointers are rather frankly calculated, but there are times when they are very useful. The apprentice playwright should learn to distinguish when they will be effective, what kinds can be derived from his particular material, and how to get them into the structure of the play.

After noting the practice of professional playwrights in this matter of pointing ahead, it is interesting and instructive to see what happens when pointers are unskillfully used.

Most frequently in the plays of beginners not enough pointers are used. In a story of Kansas pioneers, Lon Allard's young brother-in-law, Ralph, is accidentally shot by a cattleman. Sandwiched into the seventh page of the unit in which the shooting takes place, Ralph is called, and pops out from behind a barrel where he has been playing mumble-peg. There is a poster on the barrel prohibiting the use of firearms, but no reference is made to this. Ralph and his sister discuss for a few speeches his returning East. A few more speeches contain an argument between Ralph and a neighbor about the pronunciation of mumble-peg. Then Ralph settles down behind the barrel, out of sight and out of mind. After this there is a remark to the effect that Clay Hatton, a two-gun killer, is in town, but may never show up. A long scene follows in which Lon tries to sell his winter wheat seed to his farmer neighbors. This is a main scene, motivating one of the main crises of the play. At the end of the negotiations, Clay Hatton enters, gets nasty at once, and threatens the farmers. Lon stands up to him. Hatton expresses his contempt for Lon:

HATTON. Oh, so you're what they put in for Mayor. Was them fancy posters your idea?

LON. They were. And we expect them to be respected.

HATTON. "Gun-totin' is strictly against the law." Well, here's how much respect I got for them posters. (He empties his pistol into the poster.) All five in the square. Any arguments? (Ralph topples from behind the barrel.)

Just a few minor changes would have doubled the excitement and the resultant horror of the shooting. First, if the material about Ralph's being behind the barrel had been closer to the shooting scene, the audience would have remembered it. Instead, the ten intervening pages included one of the main scenes of the play. Second, instead of or along with the talk about mumble-peg, it would have been in character to mention the poster on the barrel and the fact that Ralph was resting not only in the shade of the barrel but under the protection of the law. The poster might have been mentioned again by the marshal who crossed the yard on his way to the spring. There is no reason that Myrt should not have appeared just before the shooting to try to save Ralph, or that Hatton should not have made some quarrel about the futility of posters to stop a cattleman from carrying a gun.

Almost any scene will supply appropriate pointers if the material is combed discerningly.

A second fault of young playwrights is that they do not manage to make the pointer important enough to gain its effect. An example of this fault occurs in the scene just analyzed. The statement that Clay Hatton was in town but might not show up was imbedded in more important material, and the director was left with the task of making it seem significant. He failed. The pointer was lost. Other examples of lost pointers occur in Act I of *The Youngest*. The long-awaited leading lady at last appears. Amid the excitement someone mentions that the Fourth of July celebration is to be in honor of the Winslow family. As the remark is apropos of nothing, the subject is quickly changed. The celebration occurs at the end of the third act and is one of the high points of the play. It deserves a better build-up. In the next moment another pointer is lost. Alan and Augusta, headed for a swim, remark as they exit that they had better stay in Richard's good graces because of something Alan knows about Grandfather's will. No one replies to this although it is supposed to be the pointer to the main crisis of the play. At the end of Act I, a bet is made, which begins the main action of the play; but the bet is treated so trivially that it does not impress the audience, and the rest of the play seems to be headed nowhere. Probably this fault has something in common with the fault of the young actor; it takes long practice to realize that the stage is not a three-ring circus, and that an audience can catch only one thing at a time. If anything is to be important, both writer and actor must find a means of getting attention for it, and holding it long enough in the eyes of the audience to be sure it has been noticed. A pointer which is not clean cut might as well not be in the script.

Another fault, that of overpointing, is the result of the playwright's being unable to judge how much must be done to insure the audience's catching it. The effect of overpointing is to make the audience weary of the scene before it has begun.[1] *Gypsy* is the story of a woman who would be faithful to her husband if she were not married to him. The play opens with a love scene between Ellen and Cleve, her lover. He kisses her, but she half-breaks her engagement with him in order to be faithful to her husband, David. She fears that she is falling in love with Cleve. She agrees to have the engagement with him. When David ar-

---

[1] Percival Wilde suggests that the law of diminishing returns becomes operative so that suspense, overprolonged, becomes irritation or laughter. *The Craftsmanship of the One-Act Play*, p. 198.

rives, she tells him she is going out with Cleve. She changes her mind about what dress she will wear. In Act II, after Ellen has had an abortion, David wonders why she is not in love with Cleve. Cleve is mistaken by the janitor for Ellen's husband, and David exits angrily, leaving them to whatever decision they may make. They still want each other. Ellen says she will have to tell David. Her mother urges her not to leave David. Ellen starts to pack, stops to read, telephones Cleve she will be over after dinner. Two acts of "Will she or won't she?" bring one to the point of not caring whether Ellen leaves David for Cleve or not, and of thinking David a great fool for not walking out.

To correct the fault of overpointing, the playwright simply needs to realize that certain human relationships are very quickly perceived, the love relationship most of all.

One more fault commonly found in the work of apprentices is that of pointing to something which does not happen. This is often the result of hasty revision; the playwright cut some portion of the play or decided not to use some material that came to his mind in the process of writing, and then failed to detect the echoes of his abandoned purpose in the finished script. Possibly this accounts for the flaw in the first act of *The Youngest*. Mark teases his sister-in-law Augusta for being irritable although she has been married only two years. Later, Oliver teases Alan for being scrappy after two years of marriage. One gathers from these two remarks that a marital difficulty will develop between Alan and Augusta; but nothing of the sort happens. *Lady of the Rose,* an early play of Martin Flavin, deals with a play about a mysterious lady. During the rehearsals lights go on and off, everyone is nervous, people predict the failure of the play, and the leading lady faints and has to be carried off. Surely, one thinks, the mysterious Lady of the Rose will prevent the performance in some hideous way. But nothing happens, and the play is a great success. The false pointers in this play seem to have been placed there deliberately to create suspense; but they are not quite legitimate. False pointers, whether they are intentional or not, will be recognized by the cast in rehearsal, if not by the director as he reads the script; and they should be rigorously eliminated unless there is some very strong reason for including them, as in a "Who dun it?"

The playwright generally begins to use pointers well as he learns the mind of the audience. It is only by putting himself in the audience's place that he can tell just how many pointers of what kind will arouse the desired degree of anticipation, and how much each pointer must or may be developed to achieve its maximum effect.

In conclusion, if something is going to happen, the audience's interest in the event is stimulated by anticipation. A pointer is the device by which this stimulation is accomplished. It is a way of emphasizing goals, both immediate and ultimate, and of increasing tension at crises. It makes an audience wait actively—that is, with hope or fear—for an event.

Much of the actual pointing in a play is probably done in the process of writing the dialogue; but at least some of the pointers for the main scenes should be planned along with the scenario. Pointers are not hard to find if one searches the material and understands the value of the device. The student should try to include at least one of all the various kinds of pointers in his practice scenarios. He should be sure that he has at least a few for their emotional effect, as well as the ones which point to scenes and incidents. He should make certain that his pointers actually do lead to the material for which they were included, and that they stand out clearly enough to be perceived. And he should see that there is nothing that might point without his intending it to do so.

EXERCISES

1. Analyze:
    a. Find and classify all the pointers in *Counsellor-at-Law*, Act I.
    b. What is the function of Anne's father in *Hotel Universe*?
    c. List all pointers to Antrobus's first entrance in *The Skin of Our Teeth*. What pointers are there to the flood? To the war?
    d. What pointers are used in the last scene of *Jacobowsky and the Colonel*? For what purpose?
2. Invent half a dozen pointers for each of the following crises:
    a. A man confronts his wife with the evidence of her infidelity.
    b. A dweller in a New York tenement house murders his downstairs neighbor.
    c. A young poet watches his sweetheart die.
    d. Four high school students are killed on their way home from a dance.
    e. John asks Mary to marry him.

ASSIGNMENTS

PLAYS: Philip Barry, *Hotel Universe*. New York: Samuel French, Inc., 1930. Franz Werfel and S. N. Behrman, *Jacobowsky and the Colonel*, translated by Gustave O. Arlt. New York: The Viking Press, Inc., 1944. Thornton Wilder, *The Skin of Our Teeth*. New York and London: Harper & Brothers, 1942.

ADDITIONAL READING: William Archer, *Playmaking: A Manual of Craftsmanship*, Chapters X and XVII. New York: Dodd, Mead & Company, Inc., 1937. George Pierce Baker, *Dramatic Technique*, pp. 207-215. Boston: Houghton Mifflin Company, 1919. John Howard Lawson, *Theory and Technique of Playwriting*, Part IV, Chapter III. New York: G. P. Putnam's Sons, 1949. Percival Wilde, *The Craftsmanship of the One-Act Play*, Chapters XVIII, XIX, and XXI. Boston: Little, Brown & Company, 1938.

PART THREE: PREPARATION

I⟨T IS AT⟩ this point that the young playwright is likely to become a little disgusted with "rules." He has a skeleton of a play, a technically correct scenario, which falls far short of his first bright expectations. He has perhaps begun to depend on technique to solve his difficulties, and lost his inspiration, his imaginative way of looking at the material, in the process. He is tired of working for so long on one idea, when other ideas keep popping into his mind. This is perhaps the time to scrap the old scenario for one which seems more exciting. The techniques which the student has learned so far will enable him to turn out a bare scenario every two weeks. There is, however, a reason that good playwrights take a year or more over the construction of a play.

Up to this point, the playwright has been thinking in rather broad terms of action and result. He has been planning the fundamental logic of his play. Now he must begin to think in more subtle terms. A great deal of care is needed to build a powerful illusion that will involve the emotions of the audience. In the two hours of a play, the audience must know more about the characters than it learns of most acquaintances in a year. It must have a more definite attitude toward them than it does towards its own family and friends. It must see meanings and find values in apparently unimportant actions which in life might have escaped notice.

In the rough planning that has been done, the clay has been fashioned in the image of its maker; now it must begin to breathe the breath of life.

14

Planting

IT IS IMPOSSIBLE TO SAY THAT ONE ASPECT OF A PLAY IS more important than another. The arguments, beginning with Aristotle, that plot is more important than character, or character than plot, are arguments about words. A good play proceeds from real, believable characters; and the most full and understandable revelation of character is through action. Plot is character in action, character seeking the means of asserting itself, of keeping its entity in the universe. The playwright's task is to see that his characters and actions are believable and moving. This task is accomplished largely by what is known in common theatre language as "planting." [1]

Whether planting is all done in the scenario or comes into the play in the process of writing is not particularly important. The important thing is that there must be devices of some sort to enable the audience to draw its own

---

[1] The term *plant* is not entirely satisfactory. It has been selected, however, because no other term was found to distinguish this very definite type of preparatory material from such other forms of preparation as the establishment of clarity, the choice of setting, the use of pointers, etc. Cf. Wilde, *The Craftsmanship of the One-Act Play*, p. 161.

inferences. There should be no need to take the word of the author or of another character; the audience should believe, like, or dislike on the basis of plain evidence.

Since the creative mind is not a machine working neatly backwards from the ending, as this book has done, but flies at all parts of the task at once, there are probably already a good many plants in the scenario upon which the student is presumably working. But there is still much to be done. A simple experiment will prove that the play is not yet ready to be written. If the student will make his scenario as complete as possible on the basis of the chapters already studied, and if he will give the scenario to somebody to read who has not heard a great deal about the characters or the story, he will find that the reader does not get excited. He may appreciate the possibilities of the play, he may admit that the writer has seen where his climax is to be. But the fact is that the reader is merely interested, not moved.

This is not solely because there is no dialogue. The facts back of the dialogue, the details that still need to go into the plan of the play, are basically responsible for the dialogue being effective or not. The scenario is cold until the job of planting has been done. There remains the task of tightening everything, of making the merely logical and plausible seem inevitable, of enriching character and situation so that they command belief and sympathy, and of undermining prejudices and enhancing values that are already sympathetic to the audience.

Planting is a form of preparation designed to increase the credibility and the emotional effect of material that is to be used later. A plant differs from a pointer in that the pointer urges the audience to look ahead toward something that is to follow, whereas the audience tends to look backward toward the plant from the later scene in which its use becomes apparent.

There are two general means by which credibility is increased: by enriching the milieu and the relationships of the character, or by putting him in more situations than are strictly needed to make him seem capable of the actions in which he is involved. Obviously a stage character who is surrounded by easily recognizable persons, objects, and happenings, and who reacts in an understanding way to his surroundings is more easily credible than one whose mind and behavior the audience knows only in relation to the main objective of the play. For the life of a person with powerful desires is not simple, but complex and various.

Counsellor Simon is a great example of a character built up largely in terms of his milieu and relationships. We know the attitudes of various people toward him—his telephone girl, the burlesque actress for whom he handled a breach-of-promise suit, an old neighbor of his ghetto boyhood, his partner, his secretary, his office boy. By making all these people real in themselves, Rice makes Simon extremely real and attractive.

Credibility is also increased by tying up the focal situation of the play with the larger world situation and by increasing the number of details within the focal situation. Odets extends *Awake and Sing* beyond the walls of the Berger flat into the whole structure of American life, not only by countless references to specific places and practices of the average little man in the Bronx and Brooklyn, but also by providing the characters with jobs that connect them to the world outside, a world that is responsible for their personal frustrations. Moe has lost a leg in World War I; Ralph works in a textile house; Morty runs a ladies' clothing establishment; Hennie is a stenographer; Jacob is a barber. Werfel uses the same technique in *Jacobowsky and the Colonel*. He lets us see not only Jacobowsky and Colonel Stjerbinsky and Marianne, but also the French petty officials and the innkeeper and the aristocratic old lady from Arras and the avaricious chauffeur of the Rothschilds. And to Jacobowsky's personal story, Werfel adds that he was president of two symphony orchestras in Vienna and had business relations with the house of Rothschild in Paris. Kingsley in *The Patriots* adds credibility to the first scene between Washington and Jefferson by details gained in careful research: the argument over the establishment of the treasury, Jefferson's account of the court of Louis XIV, the Paris corset that was too small for Mr. Adams's daughter, Humphrey's use of "sire" and the president's predilection for fishing.

Thornton Wilder, whose characters are universal mankind, uses a great deal of familiar detail to gain credibility. Mr. George Antrobus of 315 Cedar Street, Excelsior, New Jersey, is Adam and prehistoric man, with the ability to work and to invent, the love of home, the essentially social spirit, and the indomitable optimism—qualities that have carried him down the ages, and that make a mere anthropological concept seem familiar to the uninitiated. The Ice Age pushes Montreal cathedral into Vermont; the flood interrupts a convention at Atlantic City; the war ends, and people come up out of shelters and start over again; the remote is always made understandable in terms of the familiar. In *Our Town* the characters are built by means of extremely minute detail, and are given stature by frequent reference to their typicalness; that is, by extending their relationships in time and space. The Stage-Manager points out that the Gibbses and the Webbs are America. At Emily's wedding he says, "I've married two hundred couples in my day. Do I believe in it? I don't know, I suppose I do. The cottage, the gocart, the Sunday-afternoon drives in the Ford—the first rheumatism—the grandchildren—the second rheumatism—the deathbed—the reading of the will —Once in a thousand times it's interesting." [2] This is a typical *Our Town* device to make George and Emily represent America or even universal humanity.

Werfel's practice in *Jacobowsky and the Colonel* illustrates the second method of increasing credibility, that of making a character react to a great many situations in order to bring out facets of his character. Jacobowsky has an unusually rich character. He is described as "a heavy-set man of middle age with a rosy round face and fine eyes with long lashes. He is dressed in scrupulous neatness in a somewhat old-fashioned...cutaway. His manner...is courteous...His speech is well considered, stylistically perfect, sometimes to the point of formalism...Only occasionally a trace of nervousness...makes it apparent that his self-discipline is the result of his battle with fate." [3] This

[2] All material from *Our Town* used by permission of the publishers, Coward-McCann, Inc.

[3] Reprinted from *Jacobowsky and the Colonel*, by Franz Werfel, by permission of the publishers, The Viking Press, Inc.

is for the reader. The audience learns more about him. Evidently he is *sociable*, because he goes out in an air raid to bring *marrons glacés* to help the ladies pass the trying night, and because he selects in the shelter a place next to an old lady and promptly begins to chat with her, telling her some of his past life. He has a *fatalistic* attitude toward life; on his first entrance during the air raid someone teases him for thinking himself indestructible, and he replies with a mathematical calculation on his chances of getting hit. He is both fatalistic and *sentimental* when, forced to flee, he has to leave behind not only his valuable antique furniture, but also his cherished Persian rugs that are to him a symbol of home. Again he reveals his fatalism when Stjerbinsky challenges him to a duel and he accepts, asking Stjerbinsky first to show him how the pistol works. He is *shrewd financially* in his purchase of the automobile, and later when Stjerbinsky taunts him with securing his money belt as a last precaution before going to sleep. He is *impractical* in mechanical and physical ways, not being able to shoot, swim, nor drive a car. Yet he is highly *resourceful* in providing food and gasoline for the escape, and endearingly *attentive to the needs of others*, providing cognac for the Colonel and even chocolates for Marianne's little dog. He yells with *fright* and *rage* when his car will not go, and sweats with *nervousness* when the Germans question him. He shows his *pride* when he does not take offense at Stjerbinsky's arrogance, and when he refuses to shake hands with Stjerbinsky. He reveals *patience* as Stjerbinsky again and again forgets his name, as they start their desperate flight by going first into the jaws of the Germans to get the

Colonel's sweetheart, as he addresses the dead Kamnitzer in the *Père Clairon*, "You were impatient." He is *hot tempered, gallant, tactful, optimistic, happy*, and deeply *humorous*, to end the list of his qualities without further elaborating the incidents which plant them. Naturally these incidents are not used solely to characterize Jacobowsky; they characterize also the persons with whom he has the scenes; and many, if not most, of the incidents advance the action. But the point to be made is that here is great richness of detail, carefully selected, to make of Jacobowsky not a mythical wandering Jew nor a picturesque Cyrano, but a highly understandable and lovable human being.

Plants are used not only to deepen credibility, but also to create emotional attitudes. They help the playwright to remove prejudices and to enhance sympathies that already exist.

Sometimes the dramatist finds himself impelled to write of matters that cut across common prejudices or require the audience to sympathize with something toward which it is ordinarily hostile. The canny playwright will take care not to antagonize his audience, but to find some aspect of the material which he can count on the audience liking, and to present this before risking aspects that may be badly received.

The Voice of the Turtle contains a good example of this practice. Van Druten carefully contrasts Sally with Olive, a lady of definitely easy virtue. Sally is shocked and repentant at her own love life, which is represented as meager. She is determined never to have another *affaire*. She is practically trapped by a severe rainstorm and the crowded conditions of New York hotels into lending her day bed to a soldier on leave. Only after we are convinced that Sally is at heart a nice home-town girl does Van Druten allow her to bring out of her own bureau drawer her ex-lover's pyjamas, an act which is in itself an evidence of her naïveté.

In *Tomorrow and Tomorrow*, Barry gives a touching scene in which Gail falls asleep while Eve tries to account for her not having a child; and he places Eve and Hay in three scenes in which they do not make love before allowing Eve to go with Hay "under the laurel."

Odets opens *Waiting for Lefty* with a patriotic speech which will disarm persons to whom the *bourgeoisie* are not hell-black obstructionists, and will evoke ironical antagonism from good communists. Next, a cab-driver who declares he is not a communist but just a hard-working guy relives a scene in which his wife was all but forced to a life of shame in order to provide their children with bread. Next Odets presents the suffering of a young couple who cannot marry because the boss gets all the profits. In the next episode a union member exposes a spy hired by the bosses to break up the union. By this time the audience is convinced that the hard-working cab-drivers are being played for suckers by the capitalists, and it is now safe to use frank propaganda. A young actor, failing to get a job from a rich producer, is given a dollar by the producer's secretary and told, "It will buy ten loaves of bread, or nine loaves of bread and a copy of the *Communist Manifesto*." In the episode that follows, racial discrimination drives a young Jewish doctor to support socialized medicine and to talk of going to Russia. Finally the speaker who calls on the men to strike recalls that people who have helped him out of tight spots have called him "comrade"; and this speaker also uses socialistic phraseology, "Stormbirds of the working class. Workers of the world." Evidently this talk would not have been accepted by American audiences without strong emotional planting to condition the response.

Not only must the prejudice and inertia of the audience be overcome, but even a normally attractive and sympathetic matter must be made doubly attractive to insure a strong climax. One example of this practice will serve to show that it exists. It is hard to say why Emily Webb of *Our Town* pulls heartstrings as she does. But examining the first act of the play, one discovers quite a few emotional plants: Mrs. Webb declares that she would rather have her children healthy than bright, and Emily replies, not smugly but as appreciating an objective fact, "I'm both. I'm the brightest girl in school for my age." Her amiability is contrasted with the whining of Rebecca Gibbs. She gives up fun with her chum, "I can't, Lois. I've got to go home and help my mother. I promised." She suffers the family nagging about her walk, and is affectionately impertinent to her father on the subject. George admires her persistence in getting her lessons, but she is not bookish; she replies, "I don't really mind it. It passes the time." The scene in which she asks her mother if she is good-looking, and Mrs. Webb tells her she is pretty enough for all normal purposes, leaves her frustrated and more attractive. She helps George with his les-

sons while the moonlight goes on being "just terrible."
When at the end of the act her father asks, "Haven't any
troubles on your mind, have you, Emily?" she replies,
"*Troubles,* papa! *No!*" These eight separate bits are introduced in their "artless" way to make Emily not only
attractive but adorable by the time George gets around
to proposing to her. A less skilled writer might have de-
pended more on the personality of Martha Scott, the
actress who created the role.

Emotional planting is shrewd practice, but it is not
cheap trickery. It is frank appraisal of one's material in
terms of its probable acceptableness; it is intelligent use
of the material to convey the message the playwright
wants to convey.

Plants are introduced to induce belief and to create attitudes regarding characters, important actions, minor
incidents, and even single speeches.

Many of the plants in a play are introduced to make
characters understandable, and to make the audience
either like or dislike them. Elmer Rice is particularly skillful in this respect. Among the many devices by which
the audience is made to sympathize with Mrs. Maurrant
of *Street Scene* is the incident which introduces her to the
play. Willie Maurrant calls up to his mother for money.
She protests that he has already had money to spend that
day, but gives him a dime. Thus one sees her at once not
as vicious but as weak-willed, morally fragile. The character of Cora in *Counsellor-at-Law* is made known to the
audience in a series of plants. She asks the telephone girl
(whose salary is about thirty dollars a week) to take a

message for her from Bergdorf-Goodman; she borrows a cigarette and light from Regina, the secretary; she uses a lipstick in just the way Lillian LaRue, the adventuress, uses hers. These tiny incidents are much more revealing plants than the somewhat farfetched scene in which Cora snubs Simon's plebeian mother. The sum of the devices is an audience response of shocked antipathy for Cora. *The Left Bank* contains a memorable plant of character. John and Claire, American *émigrés* in Paris, wake up with hang-overs. John goes to take a bath, leaving Claire in her dressing gown to entertain a man whom both of them know as a rounder. Claire calmly goes about straightening the room, while he tries to seduce her. The audience responds by loathing John and feeling warm admiration for Claire.

Certainly the scenario contains many of the plants which make the basic actions credible and moving. All the steps in the course of action serve as plants; yet each of these basic steps reveals the need of its own preparation. It was surely after Anderson conceived the striking scene in which Elizabeth arrests Essex that he realized the need of taking the edge off the shock for the audience. He therefore inserted a scene between Elizabeth and Essex's friend, Bacon, wherein Elizabeth pretended to have utter confidence in Bacon, and dismissed him with protestations of friendship; but no sooner had he gone than she sent for her spies to follow him. Thus one was not wholly unprepared for her perfidy to Essex. Rice prepares for the murder of Mrs. Maurrant in a number of ways, two of them outstandingly good. Kaplan, the old intellectual Jew, declaims against the yellow journals for carrying too many stories of crime; and later Maurrant starts a fist fight with the helpless old man because of a difference in political views. The first of these plants merely puts into the audience's mind the concept of murder; the second shows that Maurrant is capable of blind violence. The scene in which Jeeter purchases a frog-sticker in *Green Grow the Lilacs* was introduced to absorb some of the shock of the accidental murder of Jeeter in the shivaree scene. The murder of Runch for squealing in *The Criminal Code* furnishes an insistent reason for Bob's not telling what he knows about the murder.

It is unnecessary to labor further the use of plants in the main action, except to point out, first, that plants for action usually have some characterizing value; and second, that they almost invariably have some value in absorbing shock, or otherwise creating emotional attitudes in the audience.

A careful playwright will not only plant for his major actions, but will make each minor incident, each bit of preparation itself, more credible and moving by the use of plants. For example, in *Counsellor-at-Law*, the audience's general disapprobation of Cora is brought to a focus in a speech of Harry Becker, a Communist, in which he calls Simon a traitor to his class with his "kept parasite of a wife ...and her two pampered brats." This scene is prepared not only by all of Cora's behavior up to this point, but also by a scene in which the children snub everyone in the office where Becker is waiting to see the Counsellor, and by the fact that Becker has been in trouble because of his violent behavior. The major preparation of Jim's infidelity in *Paris Bound* is an ugly scene in which Noel, drunk, implores Jim to love her. This scene is prepared in turn by gossip indicating that she has been desperately in love with Jim, by Mary's statement that she asked Noel to be in the wedding party simply to stop the gossip, and by many reports that Noel is drunk and behaving badly. The major action in *Hotel Universe* is the revelation that all the experiences that an individual has ever had are eternally present in his personality. This revelation is prepared by a particularly grim scene in which two characters start by making believe, as they did in childhood, and end by being unable to distinguish between fantasy and reality. This scene is further prepared by the almost wholly comic scene beginning, "Nine-thirty A.M. The great Norman Rose enters his office." Tom does a satirical impersonation of Norman, and has to be forcibly stopped when the scene begins to be serious. And this again is prepared by various emotional devices, such as the statement that the house "on the edge of the world" where the characters meet was an old hotel that failed because time was peculiar there. It is this care with which not only the main actions, but even the plants themselves, are prepared that gives a play deep roots in causality. The playwright avoids asking the audience to take his word about anything; he shows them the evidence; he shows them the causes of the causes. There can be no question of their credibility.

Occasionally a speech is made more moving by preparation. A good example occurs in Mio's last speech to Miriamne in *Winterset,* "I love you and will love you after I die." These words are moving only because we know why they are sacred to Mio. They are the last words his father said to Mio before being executed. In *Tomorrow and Tomorrow*, Eve agrees to Hay's suggestion that she name her son Christian; thus we are prepared for a maladjustment in the child by hearing him called Christian. In the same scene with Hay, Eve speaks of singing *Frère Jacques* to her baby. Later, during the child's illness, Eve sings this song, and it is clear that she is reaching far back into his babyhood to bring him out of his psychoneurotic coma.

These illustrations show that whenever material is important, the playwright carefully prepares his audience to understand it and to feel toward it the way he wants them to feel.

Planting is done by means of several common devices, and innumerable special devices arising from the specific material of a given play. The devices about to be described are basic tools, used frequently by every dramatist. The young playwright should be able to use them all at will, and he should add devices of his own as circumstances permit.

The most common device for planting is a speech or a group of speeches. In *Golden Boy*, the gift of the violin is made logical by a speech of Joe's to Lorna that he is about to celebrate his twenty-first birthday; it is made moving by Mr. Bonaparte telling his ambition for Joe to become a musician. In *Street Scene*, Kaplan tells his disgust at the crime stories in the newspapers, thus planting for the double murder. In *Tomorrow and Tomorrow*, Eve tells Gail that she wants a child, a speech that plants emotionally for her taking a lover. Speeches are used in large numbers as plants.

The basic crises of a play are plants as well as pointers for subsequent actions. In *Winterset*, Mio almost gets arrested for being flippant to a policeman. This crisis plants for the policeman not taking Mio seriously when he accuses Trock of the murder of Shadow. In *Tomorrow and Tomorrow*, Gail's falling asleep while Eve yearns for a child plants for the revelation of Gail's sterility and for Eve's liaison with Hay. In *Elizabeth the Queen*, Essex's brush with Raleigh over the silver armor plants for Raleigh's taking part in the conspiracy. Thus a crisis can plant.

A simple piece of business is often useful in planting. The way the criminal, Galloway, watches Miss Brady in *The Criminal Code* prepares the audience to learn that Miss Brady was drugged. In *In Abraham's Bosom*, the beating of Abe by his half-brother is the plant which accounts for Abe's killing Lon at the end of the play. Hay's bringing Eve a sprig of laurel, and her lingering over it as Gail kisses her good-by, plants the emotional conflict that will affect her child in *Tomorrow and Tomorrow*. Cora's use of her lipstick plants her as akin to the demimondaine, Lillian LaRue, in *Counsellor-at-Law*.

Suggestion plants the suicide of Jacob in *Awake and Sing*, while seeming merely to characterize him as a disappointed old man. When Bessie drives Jacob out of the room, he tries to make a little joke by saying, "Bessie, some day you'll talk to me so fresh... I'll leave the house for good." When Jacob and Morty and Moe speak of the many suicides in the paper, Jacob's response is, "If someone said five-ten years ago I couldn't make for myself a living, I wouldn't believe—" When Bessie complains that she gets nothing for the trouble of raising her children, Jacob replies, "when you'll lay in a grave, no more trouble." He gives his will to Morty for safekeeping, in case of fire or robbery. Morty declares he has good years ahead. Jacob replies, "Behind." There are quite a good many suggestions of this kind, not strong enough to be pointers, yet enough to make it clear what Moe means when the janitor and Bessie say Jacob slipped off the roof, and Moe retorts, "Slipped?" When suggestion is used to plant, the writer must not be so subtle that the audience fails to understand the accumulated suggestions.

In discussing the uses of auxiliary characters, it was shown that a character may be introduced solely or primarily to plant. Such a character is Schlosser, the janitor in *Awake and Sing*. This pathetic and rather humorous character enters in Act I to complain of the dog. Two advantages are gained by this brief scene in which he is involved: it plants for Jacob's taking the dog on the roof the night of the suicide; and it avoids diverting interest to the janitor when he reports the suicide. The confidant and the *raisonneur* are also often used to plant; and it has been shown that characters are often introduced for the sole purpose of conveying past action. More will be said on this point in the next chapter.

It has been shown that the setting itself has some value for conveying exposition. Costumes have the same value. In *Counsellor-at-Law* both Lillian LaRue and Mrs. Chapman are quickly characterized by the clothes they wear.

Mrs. Becker's shawl tells a good bit about her background. Of course period costumes are good planting devices. President Washington in *The Patriots* is characterized by his removing his wig and putting on an old hat to go fishing. Properties also plant. In *In A Garden*, a Chinese shawl is brought to Lissa by Bliss, with whom she once fancied herself in love. Following some plain surmises about the affair, Lissa's wrapping herself in the shawl quickly reveals that the surmises were true and plants for the subsequent love scene. The sprig of laurel in *Tomorrow and Tomorrow* characterizes the love of Eve and Hay as spiritual rather than sensual. In *White Wings*, another Barry play, an oil can characterizes the heroine as the apostle of the machine age and prepares for the entrance of the automobile later. Luggage either plants or points to arrivals and departures, and characterizes its owner. Particularly arresting is the hat-box in *Night Must Fall*.

A relationship between characters sometimes has the effect of a plant. In *The Left Bank*, the behavior of John and Susie, headed for an *affaire*, emphasizes the decency and restraint between Claire and Susie's husband. In *Mary of Scotland*, Mary's love for Bothwell doubles the pathos of the scene in which she takes Darnley for her husband. Planting by means of character relationships is an excellent device, but it must be used carefully to avoid overemphasis.

All these basic devices are useful. The beginner should deliberately practice using them, in order to gain a variety of means of increasing credibility and empathy.

The amount of space devoted to a particular plant is

determined by the importance of the material to be planted. If this material is extremely important, it may be emphasized by developing the plant into a minor incident or even a full scene. Many examples have already been given, from a mere incident, Cora's use of her lipstick, to the impassioned scene in *Paris Bound* in which Noel pleads for Jim's love. The extent to which a fairly important matter may be planted can well be illustrated by following through just one of the devices which prepares for the revelation of Lieutenant Cutting's treason in *Valley Forge*. As Cutting enters, a dog follows him. Cutting does not know whose it is, and the men warn the dog not to eat their food as it is poisonous. Two pages later there is a reference within a speech to the effect that the dog will probably die of eating the soldiers' food. Three pages later, Lafayette discovers that the dog belongs to General Howe, and there is some question of how it got to Valley Forge. Washington writes a note and secures a man to return the dog to Howe, in a scene of one and a half pages. There is another reference to the dog on the next page. Four pages later a quarrel between Cutting and Tench begins with a number of references to the dog. At last Spad improvises a leash by which he leads the dog out. Several single references and two rather brief scenes thus call attention to the British general's dog that followed Lieutenant Cutting back to Valley Forge, and prepare for the revelation that Cutting has been in touch with the British. In *Paris Bound* there are about four strong references to Noel's disgraceful behavior, and then a scene of about seven pages between Noel and Jim, to plant for Jim's infidelity, which is the core of the play. The problem of elaborating a plant is one of emphasis, depending on the importance of the material to be planted.

The beginner has great difficulty in learning just how much planting is enough. He tends to overplant the unimportant and easily understood, and to plant important matters insufficiently. The inexperienced playwright also uses ambiguous plants, or plants which are in themselves not quite credible, or which have no real value for the total play. Worst of all, the beginner sometimes explains an event after it has happened, instead of planting before the event. These faults disappear as the playwright learns the mind of his audience.

One of the common faults is overplanting material which is easily understood, an error not confined to the plays of beginners. In *Mary of Scotland*, Anderson built up the terrific antagonism of John Knox against Mary to such an extent that Knox seems more dangerous than Elizabeth. Yet one does not see the effect of Knox against Mary except in a narrated passage. In *Counsellor-at-Law*, Rice made the same mistake in a twelve-page scene in which Cora's children snub the clients and the office force. Their query about Simon's partner, "Is he a Jew, too?" and Dorothy's appointment with the hairdresser would be enough to motivate Becker's denunciation, for which the scene plants.

Underplanting is more common than overplanting in beginners' plays. An extreme, yet typical, example occurs in the student's play already mentioned about Thomas Desiderio. The main crisis of this play is a challenge to

Thomas to change stones to bread. Before he appears, Thomas is characterized as a man of God. The Inquisitor has claimed that Thomas raised a fog which caused the Inquisitor to lose a battle. A soldier has claimed that when he lost his eyesight during the battle, Thomas cured him. On Thomas's first entrance a touch of his garment miraculously heals a hunchback. Thomas preaches to the Duke and the people. Leonardo da Vinci asks him to pose for the figure of Christ in "The Last Supper." In the next scene Thomas tells Cecilia that the people love him. Later he is called away to restore a child to life. Yet at the actual crisis of turning the stones to bread, there is no suspense. A good bit of planting has been done. Unfortunately, however, every detail introduced to convince the audience that Thomas is capable of miracles sets up resistance; one after another, the audience refutes the allegations of restored eyesight, miraculous fog, hump removed. There is not a single plant to make the audience like Thomas as the people are said to do. Skepticism persists because Thomas is not even a live human being, much less a great priest. Plants are needed to inspire love and confidence, if the audience is to share his hope of working miracles and his conflict of pride and humility. The flaw in this play is the flaw of many young writers; they select half a dozen or so "logical" plants, and neglect the mass of intimate detail that induces belief by creating affection for the character.

Anderson follows the precedent of *Romeo and Juliet* in allowing Mio and Miriamne of *Winterset* to fall in love at the end of one dance, a reaction open to question. But both Shakespeare and Anderson gain credibility by first introducing the characters as highly lovable; for in any case it is not hard to believe that two charming young people will fall in love. Too much insistence cannot be placed on the value of emotional plants to induce belief as well as sympathy.

Often the plants themselves are not quite credible. Shakespeare himself was not above this error. The irrational jealousy of the king in *The Winter's Tale* and the senile insistence of Lear upon the flattery of his daughters are flaws that are not forgiven modern playwrights. Anderson writes of a pathological case of jealousy in *White Desert*, in which a husband finds himself maddened with jealousy because his wife confesses to "impure thoughts," and she repays his jealousy by being unfaithful in order to assert her fredeom. If one is to accept these motives, one needs a good bit of logical and emotional planting of the character of husband and wife. Barry has an example of incredible planting in an early play, *The Youngest*. The crux of this play is that Richard, the underdog, is the real owner of the family property. In the first act, Richard is nagged for smoking, for sharpening pencils, for keeping pets; Mark blows smoke in his face; his room is taken for a coming guest; the family threaten to cut his allowance. He is so much the underdog by the end of the act that he seems little better than a fool, and one cannot sympathize with him. The situation is incredible because of the triviality of the plants of the family's disagreeableness, and because of the absence of plants motivating Richard to endure, or giving him the capacity to resist.

Particularly undramatic is the beginner's fault of explaining an event after it has happened.[4] A play whose whole structure is built up in this way is Riggs's *Sumpn Like Wings*, his second long play. The first act ends with Willie impulsively running off with Boy. In Act II, Scene 1, Willie comes home with a baby, not Boy's, after a brief career as a prostitute. At the end of Act II she goes away again with Boy, this time to marry him. At the beginning of Act III the audience must be told that she has left Boy and is returning to town. In Act III, Scene 2, we also learn that the baby has died. Practically everything of importance happens between the acts and has to be narrated to the audience. Late explanations, of course, are not always bad; Ibsen uses past action as a point of crisis, and carefully prepares the audience for revelations. But an unskilled writer fails to prepare, and explains the events after they have happened.

Good planting is not accomplished overnight. It is the result of exhaustive study of the material for what needs to be planted and for means of planting. It is the fruit of careful selection in terms of the response desired from the audience. The melodrama is trivial because it rests upon highly emotional, barely credible planting; the "well-made" play seems mechanical because it depends largely on logical planting and the most obvious devices for awakening the emotions of the audience. A play of great depth will

---

[4] This is not the same sort of incident as when surprise (always carefully prepared) is used deliberately. A clear and rather thorough discussion of the uses and pitfalls of surprise can be found in Alan R. Thompson, *The Anatomy of Drama*, pp. 134-141. Berkeley and Los Angeles: University of California Press, 1942. See also Clark, *A Study of the Modern Drama*, pp. 154 f., and 181.

be rich in causes, each cause carefully built into the play by more minute causes, and the whole rooted in the most intimate life and desire of the characters.

EXERCISES

1. Analyze:
   a. Find and criticize all plants that make Claire attractive in *The Left Bank.*
   b. List all plants for the Players' scene in Act III of *Elizabeth the Queen.*
   c. How are Abe's moves from place to place planted in *In Abraham's Bosom?*
   d. In *The Criminal Code,* how is Bob's murdering the Guard planted?
2. Find five to ten plants for the following situations:
   a. A sensitive, rather fragile-looking boy knocks out the school bully. (Make the event credible and pleasing to the audience.)
   b. An old roué dies. (Make him attractive by overcoming prejudices; make his death pathetic.)
   c. A girl marries a man she does not love. (Make the event credible, the girl heroic, and the man pathetic.)
   d. A neurotic patient kills the doctor. (Make the patient pathetic and attractive; make the doctor's death ironical.)
   e. A schoolteacher resigns her lifelong job at the age of forty-eight. (Make the event credible; make her pathetic.)

279

ASSIGNMENTS

PLAYS: Martin Flavin, *Children of the Moon*. Elmer Rice, *The Left Bank*.

ADDITIONAL READING: William Archer, *Playmaking: A Manual of Craftsmanship*, Chapters XV-XVII. New York: Dodd, Mead & Company, Inc., 1937. George Pierce Baker, *Dramatic Technique*, Chapters VI and VII. Boston: Houghton Mifflin Company, 1919. Gustav Freytag, *The Technique of the Drama*, Introduction and pp. 114-120. Chicago: Scott, Foresman & Company, 1904. Clayton Hamilton, *"So You're Writing a Play!"*, Chapter VIII. Boston: Little, Brown & Company, 1932. John Howard Lawson, *Theory and Technique of Playwriting*, Part III, Chapter V. New York: G. P. Putnam's Sons, 1920. Albert T. Poffenberger, *Psychology in Advertising*, Chapters XVII and XXI. New York: McGraw-Hill Book Company, Inc., 1932. Percival Wilde, *The Craftsmanship of the One-Act Play*, Chapters XIV-XVI, XVIII, and XIX. Boston: Little, Brown & Company, 1938.

15

Special Kinds of Plants

WRITERS ON PLAYWRITING HAVE DWELT AT DISPROPOR-
tionate length on three special kinds of plants—the use of
past action (usually called exposition), the motivation of
entrances and exits, and the means of securing attention
at the openings of units. These matters are not unimportant, for everything that does not positively contribute to
the play loses time, and therefore detracts; but they are
matters which the playwright learns easily and does well
by the time he has written three or four plays. Therefore,
a few words about each of these kinds of plants will suffice.

Past action is action which has happened before the
events of the play, or between the units, and which must
be narrated to the audience in some manner if the play is
to be fully comprehensible. Such an action is Nora's forg-
ing the check in *A Doll's House,* or the murder for which
Mio's father was executed in *Winterset.* Past action has the
same uses as any other sort of plant.

Shakespeare frankly told his audience the necessary past
action in a prologue or a soliloquy, or sometimes in a dia-

logue between two minor characters. The nineteenth century, striving to be "natural," conveyed past action by letting the maid and the butler tell each other about it in the opening scene of the play. The modern playwright strains his ingenuity to avoid letting the audience realize that it is getting exposition.

As narration rather than action, past action seems to involve a particular strain on the attention of the audience. St. John Ervine [1] calls it "expired events," and cautions against the use of too much past action. In solving the problems of past action over many years, playwrights have evolved four general practices, which may save the young writer some energy and much uncertainty in planning the past action of his play.

First, the modern playwright pares his past action to the absolute minimum needed to plant the particular aspect of the play he wants to plant. The actual amount needed, of course, depends on the play. In *Elizabeth the Queen*, there is no past action as such, except that Elizabeth and Essex have quarreled. The scant details about Essex's success in the Spanish War are given as part of the current quarrel between the lovers. The mere fact that Ireland has never been subjugated is enough to motivate the conspiracy. In *Winterset*, on the other hand, it is necessary to know the whole story of the murder for which Romagna was executed. The audience must understand Garth's connection with it; something about Trock's past; a bit, at least, about Judge Gaunt; and a good bit about

---

[1] St. John Ervine, *How To Write A Play*, p. 28. New York: The Macmillan Company, 1928.

Mio's past. In introducing past action into a play, it is good policy to ask two questions: Exactly what does this information prepare for? Are all these details necessary? Unless the writer can point to a definite use for every bit of past action he has included, he may be sure he has too much past action; and he should be more severe with himself on this score than he needs to be with other kinds of plants.

Second, the modern playwright generally introduces past action with many pointers so that the audience will be waiting eagerly for the information before it is given. A suggestion of the way in which this is done is found in the second scene of *Winterset*:

Miriamne says she has noticed that both her father and her brother are afraid.

Garth denies this.

She then says she has found a letter, which he in alarm says he has burned.

She says that the letter connects Garth with the Estrella gang (a crisis).

Garth admits he knows that Romagna did not commit the murder, but denies that he knows anything more.

Pressed further, he admits he witnessed the murder but was not called to testify.

Again he says he knows nothing about it.

Yet Miriamne can see that he is painfully afraid.

Trock comes in and threatens Garth (crisis).

Trock is uneasy because the Judge who convicted Romagna has gone mad and disappeared, the police of three cities are seeking him, and he may talk.

On Trock's exit, Garth breaks into a panic, and tells Esdras and Miriamne that Trock committed the murder (climax).

Not a great deal of information is conveyed here: Trock committed a murder which Garth witnessed; another man was convicted and executed; the Judge, who might give the story away, has disappeared. These three facts are important, the core of the play. Anderson uses fourteen pages to plant them, with an extremely large number of pointers before each fact is conveyed. The audience is never asked to give cold attention; its attention is quickened by suspense until it demands information, which is then given as a climax.

Third, the modern playwright motivates the telling of past action. He does not allow a character to tell something to another character who already knows it, or to whom he would not logically tell it. But, on the other hand, as a rule, he does not have to go far to find motivations. The mere presence of neighbors reveals Mrs. Maurrant's *affaire* in *Street Scene*. In *Ghosts,* Mrs. Alving's pastor and old friend provides her with a confidant. Frequently the relationship of two persons elicits information. For example, Miriamne worries about her brother and compels a partial confession; afterward, when Trock has gone and Garth is desperately frightened, he turns to his father and his sister to break down and complete the confession. In *Paris Bound,* one learns how near Jim and Noel were to an *affaire* when Noel pleads for Jim's love. In *Holiday,* Julia tells her sister how she happened to meet Johnny. Sometimes, as in *An Enemy of the People,* a stranger is brought into the scene for the express purpose of hearing a bit of past action that the audience must hear. Past action may be conveyed as a reminiscence, a confession, a rumor. It may be a quarreling recrimination like that which explains Elizabeth's conduct of the Spanish War and Essex's popularity in *Elizabeth the Queen*. It may be a warning, such as Laura gives in *Children of the Moon*, to prevent Jane from marrying because of insanity in the family. It may be a compliment such as Bothwell pays to Mary in *Mary of Scotland*, revealing that her girlhood was spent in France. It may be a direct question and answer such as Mr. Seton uses with his daughter's fiancé in *Holiday*; or an accusation like that of the prosecuting attorney in the opening of *The Criminal Code*. There are as many ways of motivating the telling of past action as there are of getting real people to talk of their past lives. The only caution is that in a realistic play there must be a person to talk to, and a circumstance conducive to the telling.

Fourth, once a playwright has gained skill in selecting, motivating, and pointing past action, he becomes more concerned with clarity than with novel devices for conveying the material. He has reduced the facts to a necessary minimum; these few facts he wants to be extremely sure that the audience gets. Garth says in plain language: I witnessed the murder; Romagna didn't do it; Trock is the murderer. Noel frankly wishes that she and Jim had had an *affaire*. MacFadden in *Counsellor-at-Law* tells Simon of the discovery of the false alibi, Simon tells his partner, and there is a whole scene between Simon and the man for whom the alibi was framed. In *The Criminal Code* the circumstances of the murder are so important that a whole unit is given to questioning the witnesses. In *The Patriots*, sympathy for Jefferson is so important that a flashback is used to show how much he loved his wife. Past action that is very complex or very bulky may be introduced as a unit of clarity. Many contemporary playwrights, falling back on the concept that the theatre is and should be theatrical, use the soliloquy, the prologue, the narrator, or any device they please from the past, the cinema, or the radio in the interest of clarity. Of course the device chosen should be appropriate to the general style of the play, but, above all, it must present the past action clearly.

In summary, past action, if long and complex, should be put into a unit by itself and presented as action. But if it is simple and brief enough to be narrated, it should be cut to the fewest, most vital facts, introduced by pointers, clearly presented, and motivated in as natural a manner as the nature of the play demands.

A careful study of any professional play reveals that the entrances and exits of characters serve the purposes not only of the plot but also of the characters themselves. Elmer Rice opens the last act of *Street Scene* with the police collecting evidence about the murder. Two characters cross the stage gloating over the lurid accounts of the murder in the papers. Mr. Rice presumably wanted to say that the morbid curiosity of the passerby is cruel and vulgar, in contrast to the intensity of human suffering that accompanies crime. He might have used anyone who happened down the street to make this comment; instead, he used two nursemaids who wanted to see the house. Mr. Rice had one reason for bringing these girls on stage; they as individuals had quite another. The individual's reason for entering is what is meant by motivation. In a good play it is easy to find these motivations; in a poor play the actor or the director invents them, sometimes to the detriment of the play. The matter is not tremendously important; it is merely one more detail that aids in producing the illusion of life, and maintains solid continuity in the building of empathy.

Motivations of entrances and exits are provided in a variety of ways. It has been shown that a setting is often chosen because it is a convenient place for characters to enter. It is here that the main characters have to carry on the main actions of the play. In the dagger scene, Macbeth crosses the courtyard or corridor of his castle to murder Duncan, whose room is on the other side. Essex comes to Elizabeth's palace to make his peace with her. Mio comes to the ghetto under the bridge looking for Garth, who lives nearby. Jim and Mary of *Paris Bound* come through the upstairs sitting room on their way to change their wedding clothes. Gleason of *The Criminal Code* goes to the dungeon where he is murdered in order to give Bob his food. In *Counsellor-at-Law*, Cora comes to her husband's office about a friend's lawsuit.

Very often the occasion will motivate entrances. A meeting, a party, or the hackneyed but still useful device of mealtime commonly motivates the presence of as many members of the business firm, or friends, or family as are needed in the scene.

In addition to these basic motivations, there are countless pretexts for entrances. Someone enters to borrow something or to bring a message, or to pay a friendly visit. A thinly motivated pretext may be covered by pointers to the effect that so-and-so is coming or has an appointment; or the character may be called in. Pretexts should be as plausible as possible. The effect of a poor pretext can be seen in *East Lynne*. Archibald and Isabel have just arrived from their wedding trip. Because they must be got off the stage somehow, Archibald invites Isabel to view the grounds, instead of the much more logical pretext of taking her to her room after her travels. A pretext of this calibre is more distracting than no motivation at all.

Often the only motivation needed for an exit is the fact that the character has finished what he came to accomplish, and may depart as anyone would under the circumstances.

It is not worth while to labor this point. It should simply be pointed out that professional playwrights do motivate entrances and exits with scrupulous care. The apprentice will do so too, the first time a cast overwhelms him with questions, "Why do I come in here?" If the playwright has not the answers, either the actor cannot enter in character, or the combined ingenuity of cast and director may distort the play.

A third special kind of plant is that which is used at the opening of a unit to insure the attention of the audience. When the curtain goes up; programs rattle and conversations are finished hurriedly while one's neighbor removes his overcoat. The late comers two rows ahead find their seats. The setting takes its moment of attention, then the costumes, movements, and voices of the actors. Then the audience settles down to grasp the play. A shrewd playwright takes these things into account and allows half a minute or more for them, using no important material until he is sure that attention is riveted on the stage.

Some of the common devices used by playwrights to get attention deserve a word.

A pause upon an empty stage opens the second act of *Holiday*. Sometimes a pause is emphasized by the pacing of a character, as when Cora waits for Simon in Act II, Scene 2, of *Counsellor-at-Law* or when Moody paces in *Golden Boy*.

An entrance is a useful device to get attention, as movement catches the eye at once. The entrance of a butler and later of a second butler and finally of Johnny himself starts the first act of *Holiday*.

Business helps to start some scenes. In *Mary of Scotland* two soldiers are gambling as the curtain opens. The Men in Serge slink away as Trock enters in *Winterset*. A good opening with business starts the second act of *The Truth about Blayds,* when the grandson of the dead poet, after his grandfather's funeral, lights a cigarette in silence and blows smoke at the tyrannical old man's portrait.

A few speeches are part of most attention-getting devices. *Winterset*, Act I, Scene 2, furnishes a convenient example. Garth and Miriamne speak of Garth's violin until the auditorium is quiet. The second scene of *Tomorrow and Tomorrow* opens with the maid letting in Hay and Gillespie, and some remarks about Eve's whereabouts. One could multiply examples of this very common and useful device.

Stage effects often aid in getting attention. The ringing of a doorbell or telephone is a hackneyed opening. *Dark of the Moon* opens with music and an elaborate scene of fog drifting over the top of a mountain and alternately hiding and revealing the moon. Offstage shots open the last act of *Valley Forge* and the third act of *Hedda Gabler*. An off-stage automobile whizzes by to open one scene of *See Naples and Die*. *The Glass Menagerie* opens with a nostalgic scene near the levee in St. Louis, with a suggestion of the Mississippi in the distance and the "St. Louis Blues" ground out of a juke box behind the changing colored lights of a dance-hall window.

These devices are only the more common ones used at some time in nearly every play. The possibilities of invention are, of course, unlimited.

The average beginner ignores the need for securing attention before opening the story, or at most uses only three or four speeches; but the attention-getting devices of experienced playwrights may run from half a page to a page and a half, and sometimes more. The extent to which the attention-getting material is elaborated depends on several factors. If the house has a good system of letting the audience know it is time to be seated; if the setting is a more or less conventional interior; if the material of the opening scene is easy to understand; or the carry over from the last curtain particularly strong, perhaps very little time needs to be spent in getting attention. On the other hand, if the play is complex, or the setting particularly elaborate, or if the playwright wants to establish a mood at the beginning, his attention-getting device will be proportionately long and elaborate. Usually two or three of the common devices are combined to fill up the half minute or so which the audience needs to get adjusted. The whole opening of the first act of *Holiday*, to take a conventional example, is as follows: Julia is seated at the desk for a moment writing letters, when a butler enters, asks about her trip, is politely answered, announces Johnny. A second butler enters and announces Johnny, who enters. The butlers continue to empty ashtrays and straighten the Sunday papers, while Johnny and Julia exchange commonplaces, wishing to be left alone. At last Julia dismisses the butlers. Then she and Johnny warmly embrace and the play begins.

Rice commonly uses a page and a half to three pages for scene openings, while Odets in *Golden Boy* uses very bare openings, because he either opens with something violent like the quarrel already in progress in the first scene, or because the end of the preceding scene was so exciting that the audience remained keyed for what followed.

As a rule, an elaborate attention-getting device serves more functions than the mere getting of attention. It often contains some plants, which are invariably repeated later; sometimes a pointer or two; and usually some device for setting the atmosphere of the play. If time must be spent in getting attention, an economical playwright will make this time count for as much as he can toward the final climax.

These three kinds of plants are treated exhaustively in the chapters recommended in the bibliography, and need not be further elaborated here. Once the student begins to notice them in the plays he reads and sees, he is able fairly easily to invent devices that will be applicable to his own plays. His tendency will be to overelaborate his motivations of past action and of entrances and exits, and to make the openings of his units a little longer than they need be. But a little experience will teach him proportion. And in any case, as the play goes into rehearsal, it is always better to have too many answers than not enough, easier to cut than to expand.

EXERCISES

1. Analyze:
   a. What facts of past action are told in *The Voice of the Turtle*? What motivates the telling? What does the information plant for?
   b. List the motivations of all entrances and exits in Act I of *The Youngest*, *The Glass Menagerie*, and *Awake and Sing*.
   c. Compare the attention-getting devices of *Golden Boy* with those of *The Left Bank*.

2. Tell what past action is needed and give two ways of treating it in the following situations:
   a. A childless wife kidnaps a two-days-old infant and is sent to the penitentiary. Make the act plausible, the penalty moving.
   b. An elderly widow agrees to marry an elderly divorcé. Make the marriage tragic.
   c. A father consents to the marriage of his daughter to a man in whom he lacks confidence. Motivate the consent.

3. Find motivations for bringing to a White House tea: (*a*) a diplomat's wife, (*b*) a stenographer, (*c*) a high school girl, (*d*) a pianist, (*e*) a caterer, (*f*) a coal miner.

4. Find motivations to get off the stage: (*a*) a girl from her own

room (the telephone is in the room), (*b*) a host from his own dinner party, (*c*) a mother from her child's deathbed.
5. Plan attention-getting devices for scenes opening as follows:
   a. A man and wife quarrel over housekeeping expenses.
   b. A man makes love to a native woman in an exotic setting.
   c. A movie actress in costume on the set listens to the director explain what she is to do.
   d. A tramp investigates a housebreaking project.

ASSIGNMENTS

PLAYS: E. Conkle, *Prologue to Glory*. New York: Samuel French, Inc., 1938. Paul Green, *The Enchanted Maze*. New York: Samuel French, Inc., 1939. George Kaiser, *From Morn to Midnight*, translated by Ashley Dukes. London: Henderson's, 1920.

ADDITIONAL READING: William Archer, *Playmaking: A Manual of Craftsmanship*, Chapter VII. New York: Dodd, Mead & Company, Inc., 1937. George Pierce Baker, *Dramatic Technique*, pp. 144-148, 178-191, 287-294. Boston: Houghton Mifflin Company, 1919. John Howard Lawson, *Theory and Technique of Playwriting*, Part IV, Chapter II. New York: G. P. Putnam's Sons, 1949. Brander Matthews, *A Study of the Drama*, pp. 179-190. Boston: Houghton Mifflin Company, 1910. Albert T. Poffenberger, *Psychology in Advertising*, Chapters VIII-XI. New York: McGraw-Hill Book Company, Inc., 1932. W. T. Price, *Analysis of Play Construction*, Chapter XXX. New York: W. T. Price, Publisher, 1908. Percival Wilde, *The Craftsmanship of the One-Act Play*, Chapter XII. Boston: Little, Brown & Company, 1938.

PART FOUR: THE PLAY AS A WHOLE

ARISTOTLE has said that a play should have a beginning, a middle, and an end. This statement, on the surface meaninglessly simple, is a far more accurate description of the pattern of a play than any division into acts and scenes, if one understands that the pattern is actually the externalized content of the play; or, it is the material so arranged as to bring out its values most distinctly.

When a play or any other work of art is perfect, it is impossible to change any portion of it without disturbing the significance of the whole. The Venus de Milo, in the proportions and balanced strength of her body, presents the tranquil, functional grace of woman. The Varga girl, differently proportioned and always in a strained posture, but in her way, no doubt, also beautiful, has quite a different significance. But there is no way of conveying the significance of the material save through its form. Thus, to understand Aristotle's statement, one must consider beginning, middle, and end as form-content, rather than as mere formal divisions of a play.

It has been shown that the early units of a play are largely concerned with clarity or preparation. These units include a great deal of planting, the crises surrounding the collision, and the statement of the objective. First impressions of characters, little incidents that will later result in action, and all sorts of intellectual and emotional preparations are developed fully and clearly, so that the rest of the play will be easy to follow, and the emotional trend of the audience need not be interrupted by explanations.

With a growth of skill, the playwright has a tendency to elaborate not only the attention-getting devices at the beginning of the play, but also the whole play, and particularly the preparatory material in the beginning. Often the beginning is the longest part of a play. When this is the case, sometimes the audience gets the impression that nothing is happening. Surely it is not the playwright's intention to convey, "This part is boring." He wants to say, "You must pay attention to this, for it is going to be important." Therefore he tries to keep the audience willing to listen by making the beginning *seem* important. He conveys the beginning as well as the middle and the end in terms of crisis as much as possible. He uses a great many pointers in revealing something of the future use of the material. Sometimes even before he has completed the preparation he introduces a complication or even a bit of the main action to keep the emotions of the audience stimulated.

Thus the beginning is not an arbitrary portion of the play in terms of pages or minutes; it is a portion of the innermost significance of the play.

In the same way, the middle is not ncessarily the second act; it is the part which carries on the action. It contains the complications and crises that bring about the ending. The length of the middle will depend on the complexity of the action and the amount of suspense needed to make the climax release as much tension as the playwright thinks appropriate to the material of the play. Clearly one cannot say, "Preparation ends and action begins here." The action may begin at any point, even the opening curtain; and it usually carries past the main crisis to within a few pages of the final curtain. A large portion of the average play is action; but *Street Scene,* which established a record run in its day, is only one-third action.

The ending of a play may be considered as everything that follows the main crisis. It includes all actions and crises which lead toward the solution. There may be a new complication in the ending which helps to resolve the disharmony; occasionally there is even some planting still to be done; on the other hand, some minor stories may end before the main crisis. But in general what happens after the main crisis may be called the ending.

It has been shown that the ending is usually less than twenty per cent of the play. A few more details will round out the picture of the ending. If the main crisis is a long way from the end of the play, usually the playwright does not solve it at once, but leaves it forcibly stated, to be solved later. He also leaves something of importance to follow the main crisis—from one to six major crises. An example of this has already been given from *Elizabeth the Queen,* in which the main crisis occurs at the end of the penultimate scene unit. The thirty-page third act contains a group of sharp crises culminating in the long and moving series of crises in which Elizabeth offers Essex the kingdom, not a page from the final curtain. It would be difficult, if not impossible, to find a very moving play which does not save a final crisis for a spot within four pages of the end of the play.

Thus it is impossible to lay down laws for the form of a play, although there are practices to be recommended in relation to the content, and some indications can be given of the general point at which these practices are effective. The beginning means the preparatory material, whether it occurs in the first or the seventh scene; the middle is the root action of the play and all the complicating factors which create tensions, even though some of these may occur at the opening curtain; the ending is the action which directly leads to the final establishment of harmony and release of tension. The matter of proportion cannot be simply a matter of form.

16

Emphasis and Economy

IN CONTEMPLATING A PERFECT OBJECT, IT SEEMS TRIVIAL to point out the excellence of any particular part of the object, for the experience of beauty occurs as a result of the integrated perfection of all the parts. But a flaw in an almost perfect object steals attention to itself, altering or destroying the significance of the whole. An uneducated person viewing for the first time the Venus de Milo sees only her one defect. Instead of saying "How beautiful she is!" he says, "What a pity she has no arms." He becomes a critic. He makes a rule, "All representations of beautiful women should be anatomically complete."

In a good play as in a fine piece of sculpture there is an apparently unstudied perfection of relationship between the parts, and an emphasis or significance that seems to arise from the inmost nature of the design. Emphasis is the result of careful proportioning, of using each detail for its value to the whole. One cannot point out the ingredients of perfection; but one can see imperfections rather easily. Thus the material of this chapter may be approached more profitably from the negative than from the positive angle. One may learn something about good playwriting through a study of imperfect plays.

Certain practices occur so frequently in the plays of beginners and so infrequently in the plays of professional writers that these practices may well be regarded as faults. They have to do with clarity, credibility, integration, and action. They may be corrected in the scenario before the dialogue has been written.

Much has been said of clarity in the main situation; too much can never be said. If the playwright has not made up his mind as to the meaning and relationships of his basic materials, if the main character-situation and ending do not convey this meaning, there is no basis for evaluating any of the details of the play.

Chief among the faults of beginners are failure to distinguish the objective clearly and failure to create strong empathies for the characters. Examples have been given of sound professional practice in regard to these matters. Now an attempt will be made to show how unsatisfying a play is that neglects them.

The first fault is easily illustrated in Paul Green's *The Enchanted Maze*. In the first scene the most important matter seems to be Pratt's concern with the relationship of capital and labor. In the second scene the main problem seems to be Parker's concern over the expulsion of his friend from college. Later Parker avers that what he wants is self-confidence, an objective which he attempts to accomplish in two ways: first, by asserting his sexual prowess, then by delivering a valedictory speech damning the trustees who give the most money to the college. At the end of the valedictory the most capitalistic of the trustees offers Parker a job in his factory, which Parker accepts. Thus the ending does not help one to understand what Parker was driving at. One is confused first as to whom the play is about, and then as to what it is about. The same fault is to be found in *Rocket to the Moon*. Most of the play seems to be about Stark's relation to Cleo and to his wife. But at the end of the play one discovers that Cleo has been fumbling toward a decision of her own, which, by its emphatic position, now seems to have been the main objective of the play. It is almost impossible to achieve a very strong climax unless the audience knows all along what the protagonist is trying to accomplish.

Perhaps the most common fault of the inexperienced writer is that of assuming the audience is as interested as he is in his *dramatis personae,* and in neglecting to create clear empathies. Examples of this fault abound in plays that close in a week or that move from agent to agent; and they are plentiful in the plays of beginners. In one beginner's first play, the protagonist was described as "an unusually beautiful and charming girl" in a harsh and illiterate family. The audience first sees her with her hair in crude curlers, using the wash basin and mirror in a leisurely fashion, while the rest of the family, who have to get to work, stand around and wait. The other members of the family comment on her selfishness and vanity, and she uses vulgar language like "Shut up!" to them. At seventeen she has not learned to read and sees no point in learning. She knows she is "better" than her extremely unattractive family and boasts that she will not remain with them. By the end of the first act she has made up her mind to "get" the young medical student, their boarder, for her husband. Physical beauty this girl may have, if a beautiful actress is cast in the part. But the playwright has given no evidence of her charm when the first act curtain falls. The same fault appears in a play adapted from *Lawrence of Arabia*. In the first scene of this play, two officers argue about Lawrence, the one declaring him fantastic, the other half-admiring him. Lawrence has made a straightforward report of conditions in Arabia, and stands behind his report, in defiance of the brass hats. He knows more about Arabia than the higher officers; he has a plan for liberating Arabia from the Turks; he desires Arabian independence. But he has no personality apart from the Arabian question. Therefore, instead of "wishing with" him by the end of the first scene, one finds oneself asking why an Englishman concerns himself so ardently in the affairs of a nation so different from his own, and so difficult to understand. There is no answer to this question in the play. It is always a mistake simply to assert that a character is interesting or attractive. The audience will draw its own conclusions and respond with like or dislike on the basis of the behavior of the characters. If a character is to seem attractive, he must behave attractively in specific instances.

Another fault that destroys clarity is that of allowing a subordinate character to have too much emphasis. In *Potter's Field* the affections of the audience are engaged in behalf of two lovers, Milly and Sterling. But a sinister chain-gang Negro called Reverend Henry, who complicates the story, is so shocking in his unrelieved villainy that he "steals the show" from the true obstacle, Milly's husband. Almost equally destructive of clarity is the treatment of John Knox in *Mary of Scotland* and the use of Darnley and Throgmorton as proxies of Elizabeth in the same play. These faults of clarity prevent a play from going in one direction. The audience, influenced by one emphasis after another, does not perceive clearly the meaning of the whole.

A second group of practices which generally seem faulty results in either the characters or the situations being incredible.

Characters tend to be incredible either because they lack intelligible motivation or because they do not react in a lifelike way to the other characters.

When motivation is weak in a beginner's play, it is usually because the playwright has not defined the objective with sufficient clarity, or because the objective is either not quite credible or not very attractive. In *Gypsy*, an early play of Anderson, the protagonist keeps asserting that she must be free of her husband because she loves him. In *Welded*, an O'Neill play of the same era, the two main characters cry out that they hate each other because they love each other, and vice versa. The motive may have been comprehensible in the 1920's, but to individuals who find happiness in love or who hope to find it, the motive is not quite credible. In a student's play, a young American in Hawaii is having a mild romance with a native girl. The mother of the girl kills one of the girl's suitors and then attempts to persuade the protagonist to move the corpse

for her. To the average young American the mere suggestion of complicity in a murder would put an end to a
purely frivolous relationship with the girl. But in this play
a local *bona roba* makes a heroic speech, at the end of
which the boy agrees to help. One feels that American
chivalry is being strained beyond its limits, and the whole
play suffers in consequence. The audience must understand the motives of the characters.

Sometimes incredibility is the result of the characters
not behaving in a human-seeming way to each other. In
the play about the Kansas wheat fields already quoted,
Lon's fiancée comes out from the East to marry him. Lon
is so busy bringing law and order that he does not notice
for some time that she has arrived. When he does realize
it, the shy greeting between them seems cold. After they
are married, Lon expresses something like real feeling when
he learns that she is to have a child. The audience is supposed to understand that Lon loves his wife; but he tames
Kansas with little reference to her. It is hard to believe that
a man's wife could have so little influence on his actions. In
the story of Thomas Desiderio, most of the characters are
weak in their relationships. The Duke never seems to fear
that Thomas will take his mistress. Thomas never seems
tempted to take her, although she is beautiful and in love
with him, and although he says he has been tempted. Because the characters in these plays do not seem to have
adequate reasons for their behavior nor to behave toward
each other as one expects human beings to behave, the
plays themselves seem incredible.

Other plays seem incredible because of some element of

the situation. Four kinds of errors appear rather often in the plays of apprentices.

One of the most common sources of incredibility is the practice of card-stacking, of piling difficulty on difficulty to make the unhappy ending "inevitable." A student's play again furnishes an example. The protagonist has repudiated her spotted past, bought a hotel, and is attempting to "go straight." But her rival takes all her business, the church women scorn her, and the young girl whose virtue she defends like a lioness falls in love. To prevent the marriage the protagonist adopts the astonishing method of seducing the young man herself. Then Polly, the girl, turns against her, and finally the townspeople lynch her. With all these grim happenings, the protagonist has a wild temper, and not enough sense or tenacity of purpose to pursue any of her objectives. Everything is against her. She has not a chance.

Mio, in *Winterset*, also faces overwhelming odds. But Mio has several things in his favor. He has reckless determination to accomplish a single clear objective. He has no guilt, while his rival has a prison record and is in the last stages of consumption to boot. Judge Gaunt is a constant threat to Trock, since, in his lunatic wanderings, he may reveal Trock's guilt in the Romagna murder case. Shadow's return gives Mio an active chance to get out of Trock's clutches, and Mio would have succeeded in this, had he not been flippant to the policeman. He has one more flicker of a chance when he leaves Esdras's house, and another when Esdras tries to get the police. This is not card-stacking. Mio is given chances, and credible ones.

Unprepared accident and surprise sometimes appear incredible on the stage,[1] although they happen often enough in real life. An extreme example of how badly a play may suffer from the use of unprepared accident and surprise is a student's play about a girl who was in love with a priest. The girl has been brought up from infancy by the priest and is acting as his housekeeper, a premise that is hardly credible. He is to be removed from the remote Arizona desert parish to a church in Mexico City. The girl has vowed to make the priest love her and take her with him. The night before his departure, they are left alone and he suggests a little wine to signalize their parting. In the scene that follows she confesses her love. The shocked priest rebuffs her. Then, with no previous indication of lethal intentions, she announces that she has poisoned the wine and that they both have just twelve hours to live. The priest now agrees to take her with him, and they stagger out as the curtain falls on Act II. But in the third act there is another surprise. The girl has come back; the poison did not work. Shock after shock makes this play impossible to believe. An early play of Martin Flavin has the same error of using unprepared surprise. In *Broken Dishes*, a woman dominates her husband and her daughters by constantly re-

---

[1] See Clark, *A Study of the Modern Drama*, p. 154. "Little surprises and unforeseen events, however, are legitimate; the long-lost relative, the discovery of a forgotten letter, may be used with impunity —if anyone should dare to employ such relics of 'Sardoodledum' in this sophisticated age—were unquestionably dramatic in their day—as they often are in ours. The point is that these surprises are pleasant and legitimate so long as they do not interfere with the more serious business of plot or characterization." See also, on the values of surprise, Thompson, *The Anatomy of Drama*, pp. 134-141.

308

minding them that she could have married Chet Armstrong instead of her henpecked and impecunious husband. Badgered by her snobbery, one day the family assert their belief that Chet Armstrong is a fabrication deliberately concocted to dominate them. They deny that he exists. At this moment, very patly, Chet Armstrong enters. Even in farce one resents the coincidence. A skillful playwright exercises great care to make accidents and surprises credible. *Golden Boy*, for example, is rather full of accidents, yet there is much to make the accidents credible. Joe breaks his hands during a prize fight, an accident credible not merely because prize fighters' hands do sometimes get broken, but also because Joe broke Kaplan's hands in the first scene; and because Mr. Bonaparte fears that Joe will injure his hands and be unable to play the violin. Joe is killed by an automobile accident, a matter prepared by Joe's passion for loud, fast cars, and by Fuselli's concern over this dangerous taste. Accident and surprise are not taboo in the theatre; but they require special care in preparation, and they should be used with due caution by the beginner.

Startling stage devices may strain belief.[2] In *From Morn to Midnight* the tortured protagonist wanders in a snowy field, and finds his own thought externalized when the boughs of a tree become the arms of a skeleton before his disillusioned eyes. Even this appropriate expressionistic device did not wholly avoid calling attention to itself instead of to the protagonist's state of mind. Whenever attention is thus misdirected, the audience has an instant in

---

[2] See Chapter X.

which it may realize that the play is merely a play, and there is a release of tension at a moment when the author did not want release, instead of the climaxes he planned.

In this connection, much admonition has been given against mixing styles; that is, including expressionistic, fantastic, cinematic, and realistic details in the same play. Yet the mixture of styles has been successful in many plays —*The Green Pastures, The Beggar on Horseback, The Skin of Our Teeth, Lady in the Dark, Dream Girl*—and no basic psychological principle is violated by the mixture; for there is no definable line between objective reality and the truth as one believes it to be. One is accustomed to metaphor and the imaginative use of words in everyday conversation; one has had vicarious experiences which are sometimes as exciting as the real ones one remembers; one has pretended something convincingly enough to convince oneself. "Under the piano," to quote Philip Barry,[3] is any time or place one says it is. The mixture of styles is, however, often unsuccessful because the playwright forgets that shock destroys illusion. One may use devices of any kind to serve his purpose; but a device which calls attention to itself is likely to obstruct the purpose. The playwright can absorb undesirable shock in two ways. He can use his devices so consistently that they can be recognized as purposeful and meaningful; and he can use the devices early enough that the audience will become accustomed to them before an important moment. A good stage device is one that expresses the playwright's meaning better than the mental image which words could evoke; it is unobtru-

---

[3] *Hotel Universe.* New York: Samuel French, Inc., 1930.

sive, practicable, and appropriate to the material of the play; and usually it has been prepared so that it does not shock the audience.

A too facile solution is another flaw that impairs credibility. One simply does not believe the so-called solution of *Saturday's Children*. Bobbie loves Rims, her husband, as much as ever; but the marriage has been disappointing, and she refuses to go home with him. When the landlady throws Rims out at a reasonable hour, he climbs in the window of Bobbie's room and puts a lock on the door. The solution seems to be that Bobbie and Rims will continue to love each other as long as they have the illusion that their love is illicit. In *Allison's House*, the reform of a deep-dyed conservative seems to be brought about chiefly by the emotional effect of the New Year's Eve bells. *Prologue to Glory* has an equally shabby ending. Lincoln is without motivation at the death of Ann Rutledge; yet he must be shown with his face toward the future which the audience knows he had. The playwright therefore introduced a minor character to remind Lincoln that Ann would have wanted him to continue his career. This sort of ending smacks of the *deus ex machina,* and the machine creaks. It is the result of the playwright giving up at the moment when he had only one more task to accomplish; or of his failing to go back and prepare for the ending he believed to be satisfactory.

It must be admitted that some excellent plays capture the audience in spite of incredible situations. *Winterset* is an outstanding example of a play written with such passion that the audience hardly questions the logic of it.

Probably anything can be made credible if the playwright will only take the trouble to make it so by seeing that all causes are clear, and that anything difficult to believe is supported by emotional as well as logical preparation. The art of melodrama, like that of the demagogue, consists of inflaming the emotions and drugging the intellect to make implausible matters acceptable. But there is no reason that the honest dramatist should not, like the honest orator, avail himself of any devices that will help to get his message across.

Even when clarity and credibility have been achieved, the apprentice may find it difficult to integrate his materials to secure just the emphasis he wishes. Integration in a work of art as in a machine or any other kind of organization means the smooth functioning of all the parts as a whole. If one part is defective, the machine cannot run, the organization runs with friction, and the play runs at cross purposes until the nonfunctioning element is either eliminated or brought into line.

Any writer whose imagination is lively and who enjoys his work is more than likely to include some material that he cannot put to work for the good of the play. Beginners' plays commonly suffer from the inclusion of non-functioning auxiliary characters, of material which seems to complicate but does not, and of pointers that point nowhere. All these matters have been dealt with elsewhere,[4] but must be mentioned among the practices which frequently blur the emphasis in the plays of beginners. The playwright finds it very difficult to detect this material

---

[4] Chapters 10, 11, 13.

himself, and should take advantage of the opinion of a reader. If anything seems irrelevant, the playwright must find a way to make the script as coherent to others as to himself. Sometimes the refractory material can be tied into the play by giving it a function. On the other hand, some of it is really irrelevant, and should be altered or cut.

In any event, it is time wasted to write dialogue until the integration is minutely complete, for good writing does not make a play,[5] unless it builds the audience's emotions consistently in one direction through a varied but unified set of stimuli. The insistence on this point may seem drastic to the beginner, eager to count pages; but a professional playwright spends more time on the scenario, either on paper or in his head, than upon the actual writing of the dialogue.

Fourth and most serious of the faults of emphasis are those related to the action. The playwright conceives in dynamic rather than in intellectual or lyric terms. The late George Pierce Baker has left some confusion on this point by his unfortunate concept of "illustrative action."

> Dramatically speaking, then, the illustrative action is not merely something which illustrates an idea or character, but it must be an illustration mirroring emotion of the persons in the play or creating it in the observer.[6]

Baker's illustrative action is static, merely mirroring emotion as a lyric poem does. But surely it has been sufficiently shown that the basis of a play is desire, instability,

---

[5] See Hamilton, *"So You're Writing a Play!"*, pp. 216-218.
[6] Baker, *Dramatic Technique*, pp. 85 f.

suspense; and that a dramatic scene is one which builds tensions in the audience by driving a character toward an objective or snatching him away from it.

The beginner sometimes has trouble with the action of his play. He finds it difficult to think of much for his characters to do; or he includes a number of lively activities which keep the audience awake but vainly trying to grasp the connection; or, in trying to project an idea, he makes his characters mere megaphones of the intellectual arguments.

The cause of scant action may be that the playwright has not done his initial analysis properly. Obscurity as to the objective will, of course, leave the protagonist with nothing much to try for. An obscure or feeble obstacle will mean that he does not have to try very hard. Often it is one or the other of these factors that prevents a play from being dynamic. Generally, there is also a dearth of complications.

It has already been shown that a great deal of action is not absolutely necessary. Van Druten, Noel Coward, and S. N. Behrman can write on the most simple and even hackneyed themes with charm. Elmer Rice can write a tremendous piece like *Street Scene* with only one important action. Thornton Wilder writes of the most common occurrences of human life. But these writers are superlative theatre craftsmen as well as talented artists. The beginner, however, would be wise to emphasize the fundamental actions of his plays, the pursuit of a *strongly desirable objective* by a *protagonist* who has *chances* to succeed against a *powerful antagonist* and whose *course of action* is made somewhat devious by a number of *complications*. Later, having mastered the bases of dramatic action, he may succeed in making less dynamic matters exciting.[7]

Many inexperienced writers and some with experience think that a play can be made lively if it is "gagged up" with smart speeches and minor activities to keep the attention of the audience stimulated, whether or not the gags are pertinent to the play. But activity is not synonymous with dramatic action. The student may read for himself *The Youngest,* a play so full of entrances and exits that one forgets the main thread of the story. The third act of *The Voice of The Turtle* also contains a number of activities centering around the discovery of Bill's hat, a discovery which could not seriously affect Bill's relation with Sally. On the other hand, the making of an omelet, and a good bit of business in the kitchen of Sally's flat is extremely pertinent; it not only provides interest-stimulating activity, but it characterizes Bill and Sally and makes the objective, marriage, clear and desirable. It is not mere activity; it functions. The play had its long run in spite of the bad third act.

The best way of bringing into line a play full of slightly related incidents is, first, to see that the protagonist wants his objective enough to make his desire pervade the entire

---

[7] See Clark, *A Study of the Modern Drama,* p. 62. "... The dramatist who aims only at the delineation of character is practically sure to fail, as people do not and will not go to the theatre for that sort of thing. It is not a matter of theory but of cold fact that audiences will not, as a rule, sit for two or three hours in a theatre in order to follow the dramatist who dissects character and does nothing else." Reprinted by permission of Appleton-Century-Crofts, Inc.

play,[8] a method used by the shrewd adaptors of *Life With Father*. If the main action is adequately planted, pointed, complicated, and developed, there will be little time for mere activity. Next, one should examine his reasons for including each incident not used to advance the action. If he can honestly find no clear use for the material, he should delete it. On the other hand, if he can find a use, he should see that the material is not developed more than its importance warrants, and he should clarify its relation to the whole. The relevance of every detail should be as clear to the audience as to the playwright.

The last of the common faults in the action is the use of argument for action. The young playwright, for some reason, loves argument on abstract subjects. He may as well face the fact that theatre audiences as a rule do not, and that they must be made to accept argument by the most powerful devices of the playwright.[9] But audiences can be made to think, if the playwright translates his logic into terms of human desire; if he will reveal the evidence and let the audience draw its own conclusions; if the audience has first been made to care about the characters arguing;

---

[8] For a discussion of unity through the protagonist, see Aristotle, *Poetics* VIII, and Lawson, *Theory and Technique of Playwriting,* p. 176.

[9] Barrett H. Clark writes of Ibsen's "fierce individualism" and his concern with social and ethical problems: "he was first and last a dramatist ... True, he was interested in ethical problems, and he recognized the tremendous forces at work upon modern society, but these he perceived to be dramatic themes, susceptible of effective treatment in plays; he was not so much interested in converting his audience as he was in moving them by arousing their emotions. It is as an artist, not as a thinker, that he takes rank as the greatest dramatist of modern times." *A Study of the Modern Drama,* p. 4. Reprinted by permission of Appleton-Century-Crofts, Inc.

if it is assured that the outcome of the argument is of extreme importance to the protagonist not only because he thinks in a certain way, but because he must live in a certain way;[10] if each step of the argument, each wavering of a character's opinion, is a crisis with potentially disastrous effects on the personality. It is also desirable to make the argument as brief as possible, while taking care to be both lucid and faithful to the characters speaking. And it is useful to introduce suitable emotional and relief devices to keep attention. For a play is not an oration, either in its form or in its conditions of presentation. And theatre audiences want not principles, not abstractions, not preachments, but evidence; and they will deal with evidence fairly. The particular advantage which the stage has over the platform for propaganda is that the stage translates slogans and ideas into evidence; it convinces by evoking pity and love and terror for human beings.

The same principle applies to the mystery play, which has for its goal the answer to an intellectual puzzle. Many a mystery play has failed because, while the author is busy "planting suspicion" so that everyone in the play might be capable of the murder, he does not manage to make the audience care what happens to any of the characters. Whatever the play, its appeal is through the emotions, and its material the universally communicable desires of human beings.

Emphasis is a very subtle and difficult matter. It should be approached first from the positive side, with all the devices of clarity, suspense, and preparation. However, when

[10] See Schlegel, *Lectures on Dramatic Art and Criticism*, p. 30.

317

the playwright has done all he can from this angle, he may as well glance at his work to see if anything blurs the impression he wished to create. In this last examination, the things to look for are these common errors in clarity, credibility, integration, or action.

One more point remains to be discussed before closing the subject of emphasis. When scenes follow each other to advance the story with mathematical precision, or when a scene differs sharply in mood from the one which precedes it, or when similar scenes follow each other, some means must be found to blend or to isolate the scenes and to conceal the skeleton. Transition is the material used between major scenes to blend or to isolate them. It also serves as a relief device, restimulating the attention of the audience.

The amount of transition will vary from a few speeches or a piece of business to several pages, depending on the scenes which must be blended or isolated, and particularly on the scene which follows the transition. Transition may be longer between two highly emotional or intellectual scenes than between scenes that are easily understood or amusing.

Numerous devices are used to make transitions. Since, in one way, transition is an attention-getting device, all the devices mentioned for getting attention may be employed, and there are a few others. A character may speak offstage before he enters; or he may enter slightly before he is to be used, and speak a few words to the character about to make his exit. Even when it is impossible for the characters of one scene to meet those that speak in the next, a servant or some other neutral character or characters may enter the set for a moment to establish continuity between the two important scenes. It is generally bad practice to allow all characters to leave the stage at once, for this practice gives the audience a chance to contemplate the empty set, which it has already seen, and to recall that it is witnessing not life, but a play.

In a beginner's play, a gay party scene with about twenty-five people on stage was followed by a quiet, intimate family scene with only four characters. The young writer provided only a stage direction between these scenes: "The guests all get their wraps and leave." Naturally the play stopped during this time-consuming process, until the director showed the young playwright how to utilize the time for some very pleasing developments of the relationships of the characters, and some pointing and planting of the scene to come.

The practice of a professional playwright is illustrated by the following transition from *Holiday*. In a six-page scene, Julia's father warns her to be cautious in marrying Johnny. In the seven-page scene which follows, he questions Johnny about his background and prospects. The transition is three pages: Johnny is announced; Linda determines to give an announcement party; Julia reminds her father that she wants to marry Johnny; Johnny enters; there are greetings; and Julia and Ned exit on a pretext. The transition serves several ends: it conceals the skeleton of scene upon scene with some leisurely and lifelike decorations; it allows the audience to relax before the comic scene which follows; and it contains at least two pointers.

Of course such inserted material must not be allowed to

assume more importance than it is worth, nor must it fail to perform its chief function, that of leading the audience into the scene which follows. It may contain pointers or plants or even a little crisis and climax of its own, following the rule that whatever is used may be used to the limit of its capabilities, provided that it does not "steal the show," like a bad actor, from more important matters. The student can easily learn the variety and utility of such scenes from a study of the transitions of good plays.

As with all the other processes of playwriting, there is no particular time when transitions should be selected. Probably a number of them will present themselves as the scenario grows; others will not appear until a late stage of rehearsals. The important thing is that the playwright should be aware that he has this useful minor finishing tool at his disposal.

Much has already been said in passing about economy, though no attempt has been made as yet to say what economy in a play is. A few new points added to those which have already been made will help to frame a definition.

Outside the practical consideration of getting the play produced, economy in the selection of auxiliary characters and settings consists chiefly in making these characters and settings functional. The same is true of all sorts of poorly integrated and weakly utilized scenes and incidents. Everything that is not definitely useful should be cut; but everything that performs a function may be used, provided that the function is clear.

It has been shown that to allow a main crisis to occur too early in a play, so that there is nothing left for subsequent scenes but to repeat the same crisis with perhaps more intensity, is bad economy, the result of inadequate preparation and lack of complication. But repetition of an idea, interestingly varied, especially if it be the main idea of the play or the main objective of an important character, not only may be, but often must be done. There is an old rule that requires everything of importance to be said at least three times.[11]

More to the point in framing a definition of economy is a consideration of diffuseness in a play. Directors speak of "talky" plays, and cut scenes to render them less talky. But professional playwrights generally write much longer plays than beginners, the additional length being largely in the preparatory portions of the play, in the well-developed critical scenes, and in the increased number of devices used for emotional effect. Thus, a long, leisurely opening, with a long attention-getting and mood-setting device, is likely to be evidence of skill. The only place where diffuseness seems to be a fault is in winding up the play after the main crisis.

If economy does not mean conciseness, limitation of everything not necessary to the play, what does it mean?

An answer can perhaps be found in the young writer's inability to imagine a crisis fully enough, to prolong it

---

[11] Barrett H. Clark quotes the Spanish dramatist, Jacinto Benevente: "Everything that is of importance to the proper understanding of the play must be repeated at least three times during the course of the action. The first time half of the audience will understand it. The second time the other half will understand it. Only at the third repetition may we be sure that everybody understands it, except, of course, deaf persons and certain critics." *A Study of the Modern Drama*, p. 8. Reprinted by permission of Appleton-Century-Crofts, Inc.

by means of suspense devices through a series of smaller crises until it becomes highly exciting. The unskilled writer's average scene length is about three pages, and he rarely builds his main scenes to more than five or six pages. This means that his plays include many scrappy scenes of from one-half to one and one-half pages. The professional writer writes an average scene length of six and one-half pages, with a range of from one to eighteen or twenty pages a scene; and his major scenes are often built to about ten pages. Moreover, the material between main scenes, the transitions, in the plays of professional writers are from half a page to about three and one-half pages, showing an increased appreciation of the value of transition, and a sense of the amount needed for various purposes. The average length of the transitions in professionally written plays is about one-fifth of the average scene length of the play, while the transition of the beginner ranges from a speech or two to half a page, or about one-eighth of his average scene length; and sometimes the transition is hardly distinguishable from the major scenes. In other words, at every point the professional playwright develops his material more fully than the beginner.

Thus talkiness is not a matter merely of the number of words, but rather of what the words are used for. In the words of Krows:

> When the plot is well built there is never any lack of subject matter for the characters to talk about. More important than what the characters are to talk about is what they are to talk toward.[12]

---

[12] Krows, *Playwriting for Profit*, p. 326.

A consideration of these four points—general extravagance in structure, repetition, diffuseness, and insufficient development—suggests a definition of economy that has a slightly unorthodox emphasis. It permits three butlers to do the work of one. It is a definition that concerns function rather than quantity.

Economy must be thought of primarily as the adequate development of everything that aids in moving the emotions of the audience toward the main climax, and the suppression of only those details that cannot be made to serve this end. Economy is usually supposed to set limits. For the beginner it is more important to learn to develop his material to the fullest. The scenario should contain an approximation of the number of pages needed for the development of each scene, as an estimate of its importance. In this way one may hope to strike a happy balance between too much and not enough.

EXERCISES

1. Analyze:
    a. Compare the credibleness of the ending of *Abe Lincoln in Illinois* with that of the ending of *Prologue to Glory*.
    b. Discuss the devices used to maintain emotional continuity in *Shroud My Body Down*.
    c. Compare the transitions of Act I of *Holiday* with those of Act I of *The Youngest*.
2. Write transitions of approximately the right length between the following scenes, and estimate the length of the scenes:

a. A woman's cook walks out.
   The woman has to soothe her tired and irascible husband.
b. A woman promises her invalid son expensive treatments in order to raise his morale.
   The landlord demands three months' back rent.
c. A backbiter runs down the heroine to the hero.
   The hero proposes.
d. Mary accepts John's proposal.
   John tells Mary's hostile family.
e. Two spies confer.
   Two innocent characters have a love scene.

ASSIGNMENTS

PLAYS: Paul Green, *Shroud My Body Down*. Iowa City: Clio Press, 1935. Robert Sherwood, *Abe Lincoln in Illinois*. New York: Dramatists Play Service, 1939.

ADDITIONAL READING: William Archer, *Playmaking: A Manual of Craftsmanship*, Chapters XIV, XV. New York: Dodd, Mead & Company, Inc., 1937. Aristotle, *Poetics*, VIII, translated by Ingram Bywater, Modern Readers Series. New York: The Macmillan Company, 1930. George Pierce Baker, *Dramatic Technique*, Chapters V, VI. Boston: Houghton Mifflin Company, 1919. Arthur Edwin Krows, *Playwriting for Profit*, Chapter XXXII. New York: Longmans, Green & Co., Inc., 1928. John Howard Lawson, *Theory and Technique of Playwriting*, Part III, Chapter IV. New York: G. P. Putnam's Sons, 1949. W. T. Price, *Analysis of Play Construction*, Chapters XVI, XVIII, and XIX. New York: W. T. Price, Publisher, 1908.

17

Climax

EVERYTHING HAS NOW BEEN DONE TO CONSTRUCT THE main climax of the play, the moving moment when the protagonist achieves or fails to achieve harmony with his universe, and when the audience rises "with a transfiguration upon the spirit." The protagonist has been made an attractive individual, moved by an intense need to react against intolerable conditions, driven to seek adjustment with those conditions, impeded by complications, rising to struggle again, never losing sight of his goal. And now the last moment of crisis is over, the goal is grasped, and the pervading harmony signifies the deep unity at the core of existence. Lysistrata has won her battle, Romeo and Juliet lie at peace together in death.

All through the play, however, there have been glimpses of stability, moments when, however transiently, some sort of balance existed. These moments are somewhat like the alternate making and breaking of contact in the broken filament of a lamp. If the broken ends of wire touch, there is light; if they are shaken apart, none. In either case, there is a momentary stability, light or no light, even though it is certain that the lamp is broken.

In a play there may be twenty or more points at which the audience is permitted the satisfaction of seeing something done, or of hearing strong sentiments strongly expressed. Passionate wishing yields momentarily to triumph or despair. These moments do not always completely release the tension; sometimes they are designed as a slight relief to enable tension to be further increased; but at least they are moments of temporary definiteness, which may be thought of as minor climaxes.

Whether a climax is the achievement of the main objective or merely a highly satisfying subordinate moment, it always occurs as the satisfaction of the audience's hope or fear. Unless the playwright can make the audience hope and fear, no amount of fine writing will give this satisfaction. To this end the scenario has been constructed, first with clarity as to the alternatives, then with a wise use of suspense and other preparatory devices.

Most climaxes in a play are dynamic: that is, the result of action. A few are lyrical, merely the expression of an emotional state.

The main climax is always dynamic, the result of the protagonist's achievement or failure to achieve his objective. But some of the minor climaxes are of this kind also. Cecil and Raleigh plot against Essex; Elizabeth implores and commands Essex not to go to Ireland; his pride is inflamed by the conspirators until at last he walks into their trap. The audience has feared this event for two scenes; now it occurs. It is a moment of stability in the fact that the conspirators have succeeded in the first step of their plan.

A variation of the dynamic climax occurs when the event exceeds or falls short of the audience's expectations. An event of this kind acts as a shock and sometimes releases tension in laughter. One such climax occurs in *Valley Forge*. Lieutenant Cutting, a traitor and a disagreeable personality, is gagged and bound by the loyal soldiers for forbidding them to forage. He is left kicking. Alcock enters. Instead of complying with Cutting's demand to be released, Alcock robs him of his boots. A serious variety of this sort of climax is the moment when Elizabeth, after completely disarming Essex, asserts her power by arresting him. Her will to rule momentarily triumphs over her will to love.

Another sort of dynamic climax is an entrance or exit that has been made important. The entrance of Essex in *Elizabeth the Queen* is a climax. Suit after suit of silver armor is carried across the stage, to the increasing irritation of Raleigh, who asks a couple of times where it came from. On the heels of the last armor-bearer Essex enters—the donor of the armor. A climactic exit occurs in *Paris Bound* when, after a whole first act concerned with plans and resolutions for a happy marriage, Jim and Mary leave for their honeymoon.

Repetition of an action may make a climax, either tragic or comic. In *Counsellor-at-Law*, Weinberg's wooing of Regina ends, after several attempts, by Weinberg breaking into tears of frustration. In *Johnny Johnson*, the curtain line of Act III, Scene 1, makes a climax through repetition.

Dr. Mahodan has been forgetting Johnny's name all through the psychological examination. At last he is so horribly confused himself that he closes the examination with, "I think you'll make a very interesting patient, Mr. —Mr.—Mahodan."

Another type of dynamic climax is a decision or a decisive action. The statement of the objective is of this sort, especially if the collision factor has been built up in terms of crisis. In *Counsellor-at-Law,* Simon is threatened with disbarment by a rival lawyer. It is a climax when Simon sends MacFadden out to "get something" on the rival. It is a climax when Essex tears up Elizabeth's order to disband his troops and return to England, and when Tom Wingfield agrees to bring home a gentleman caller.

Finally, if the audience knows or fears something to be true, or if it hopes or fears some character will discover a fact, the revelation or discovery is a climax. This is regularly the climax of a mystery play, but it sometimes occurs in other plays. When Mio realizes that his father actually is innocent, the moment is a climax. It is also a climax when Joe Bonaparte looks at his broken hands and realizes that he can never again play the violin. "He laughs loudly and long with deep satisfaction" at this moment of the resolution of his conflict.

All the varieties of climax mentioned so far have been derived from action. There are often, however, moments in a play which are climactic simply because they intensely express a momentary emotional state. These may properly be called lyrical climaxes. These moments may be expressed in the dialogue, in stage business, even in stage effects.

They are seldom very long, even when they occur at the very end of the play.

Examples of the lyrical climax expressed in dialogue are easy to find. Mio epitomizes a moment of love and terror in the third act of *Winterset:*

> Now all you silent powers
> that make the sleet and dark, and never yet
> have spoken, give us a sign . . . let fall
> some mercy with the rain. We are two lovers
> here in your night, and we wish to live.

In *Street Scene,* Sam Kaplan cries out against the ugly and sinister environment which threatens to crush him, "The whole world is nothing but a blood-stained arena . . . life isn't worth it." Perhaps one should consider any moment a climax which sums up a true and moving situation in a passionate speech, provided that the audience has felt the situation strongly enough to justify the speech.

More frequently the purely lyrical climax is expressed in business rather than in words. An example occurs in *Paradise Lost.* The audience realizes that Ben has been killed, but his parents do not yet know it. After they have left the room, Julie, the invalid brother, embraces the statue of Ben. Another example is the breaking of Essex's sword when Elizabeth arrests him. Jacobowsky uses business to make a climax when, after reluctantly parting with Marianne and sending her off in the car, he finds her hatbox containing indispensable papers, and sets out happily on foot after her. These are all peaks of emotional expression in terms of business rather than speech.

Occasionally stage effects are used to express or to heighten emotional moments. Sound and cinema are used to make a battle scene climactic in *Johnny Johnson*; an automobile is brought on stage as a culmination of pointers in *White Wings*; the cheering of crowds as Lincoln boards the train in *Abe Lincoln in Illinois* helps to make the moment a climax. A combination of music and thrilling light effects is used to make Hordis's ride to Valhalla a climax in *The Vikings*.

It is interesting to note how many climaxes of each kind are found in a play, and how they are distributed. An analysis of the climaxes in *Elizabeth the Queen* may not be typical but it is suggestive:

CLIMAXES IN *ELIZABETH THE QUEEN*

Act and Scene	Climax	Class	Device Used
I-1 22½ pp.	1. Entrance of Essex after the silver armor.	Dynamic	Entrance
	2. Essex expresses to Bacon his love for Elizabeth.	Lyric	Speech
I-2 17 pp.	3. After quarrel sudden laughter on "Sir Walter, the silver-plated."	Dynamic	Failure of expectation
	4. Kiss on establishment of rapport.	Dynamic	Accomplishment of hoped action
	5. Second kiss, "I would rather have you mocking and defying."	Dynamic	Accomplishment of hoped action

330

Act and Scene	Climax	Class	Device Used
	6. After quarrel over the war, "Now what can come between us . . . nothing . . . never again." They kiss.	Lyric	Speech and business
I-3 21 pp.	7.* Essex walks into the trap.	Dynamic	Accomplishment of feared action
	8. Elizabeth gives Essex the ring.	Dynamic	Accomplishment of hoped action
II-1 22 pp.	1. The Fool kisses Penelope.	Dynamic	Accomplishment of feared action
	2. Bacon goes over to Cecil's side.	Dynamic	Accomplishment of hoped action
	3.* Elizabeth declares she will break Essex.	Dynamic	Decision
	4.* Elizabeth sends spies after Bacon.	Dynamic	Excess of expectation
II-2 8 pp.	5. Essex releases the courier.	Dynamic	Failure of feared action
	6.* Essex destroys Elizabeth's letter.	Dynamic	Decisive action
II-3 41 pp.	7. Elizabeth orders the Fool and Penelope whipped.	Dynamic	Accomplishment of feared action
	8.* Elizabeth discovers her courtiers have been suborned.	Dynamic	Discovery
	9. Elizabeth forgives Essex.	Dynamic	Accomplishment of hoped action

331

Act and Scene	Climax	Class	Device Used
	10. They kiss after settling his status.	Dynamic	Accomplishment of hoped action
	11.* Armin reports the palace is hers.	Dynamic	Failure of feared action
	12.* Elizabeth orders Essex arrested.	Dynamic	Failure of expectation
	13. Essex breaks his sword.	Lyric	Business
III 30 pp.	1. Elizabeth wipes the Fool's mouth, "I am the queen, though."	Lyric	Business
	2. Elizabeth admits Cecil has won, "The snake in the grass endures."	Lyric	Speech
	3.* Essex enters.	Dynamic	Accomplishment of hoped action
	4.* Essex admits he loves her.	Dynamic	Accomplishment of hoped action
	5.* Elizabeth cries "Take my kingdom."	Dynamic	Accomplishment of hoped action
	6.* Essex kisses Penelope good-by.	Dynamic	Accomplishment of hoped action
	7. Elizabeth buries her face in her hands as chimes announce Essex's death.	Lyric	Business, Effects

* Climaxes marked with asterisk are crises as well as climaxes.

Elizabeth the Queen has one hundred crises and twenty-eight climaxes, or one hundred moments when affairs stand in sharp conflict or uncertainty, and twenty-eight moments of temporary stability. A little arithmetic reveals another interesting fact. In the sixty-page first act there are eight instants of climax, or one every seven and one-half pages; in Act II, seventy-one pages, there are thirteen climaxes, or one every five and one-half pages; in the thirty-page third act there are seven climaxes, or one every four and one-half pages. This is significant. Regardless of the actual distribution of climaxes within the act, the number of moments of rest actually increases as crisis-tension increases. However, these rest moments are like the pauses a mountain climber takes; his rest periods may become more frequent as he becomes more and more tired, but he does not slip back. He pauses for a moment and goes on. Thus, of the thirteen climaxes in Act II, the six which are starred are hardly more than arrested crises, in which the playwright, climbing the heights, stops for an instant to gauge how far he has gone; to say, "What a dizzying climb; let us go further." And in Act III, the last four climaxes before the final climax are all crises as well as climaxes.

This analysis may serve to clear up the confusion that has prevented accurate definition of crisis and climax. There are moments in a play when all is unstable, and moments of stability more or less permanent. The former are crises, the latter climaxes. But the two become indistinguishable when a crisis receives emphatic emotional expression, as in Elizabeth's supreme cry, "Take my kingdom; it is yours," or when, after the pleas and yearnings of characters and audience, Essex enters, a doubtful factor, into the scene that is to decide his fate.

Another important point is clearly suggested by an analysis of the climaxes in this play. Of the twenty-eight climaxes, twenty-two are directly part of the action, while only six are lyrical. Moreover, only two of the purely lyrical climaxes are expressed in speech alone, while two others are done entirely without words. This is a strong indication that a climax does not come about as a result of fine writing as much as through sound construction, the solid building up and satisfaction of expectation, hope, and fear.[1] Thus, when climax fails to "come off," the fault is likely to be found not in the scene itself so much as in some of the preparatory scenes. There has been no tension, no emotional involvement with the characters. Thus the climax is improved by improving the scenario.

Yet it may not be amiss to consider for a moment the writing of the climax, for even with a good scenario the climax succeeds in moving the audience only by striking a happy balance between too much and not enough. As with other matters of proportion and emphasis, it is difficult to say just what makes a climax right, but a flaw is easy to detect. Thus examples of the undeveloped and of the over-

---

[1] Schlegel shows the relation of language to structure: "A dramatic work may always be regarded from a double point of view—how far it is *poetical*, and how far it is *theatrical*. The two are by no means inseparable. Let not, however, the expression *poetical* be misunderstood: I am not now speaking of the versification and the ornaments of language; these, when not ornamented by some higher excellence, are the least effective on the stage; but I speak of poetry in the spirit and design of a piece; and this may exist in as high a degree when the drama is written in prose as in verse . . . To be poetical it is necessary that a composition be a mirror of ideas, that is, thoughts and feelings which in their character are necessary and eternally true, and soar above this earthly life, and also that it should exhibit them embodied before us." *Lectures on Dramatic Art and Criticism,* pp. 36 f.

written climax may serve to show the importance of writing just enough at the climax.

The first example is from *The Youngest*. In this play, Nancy has won a bet that she could make Richard dominate his family. In the process he has gained a fortune, but as the last scene draws to a close, Richard bitterly resents Nancy's interference in his life, and the prospect of their marriage is extremely remote. However, in the last few speeches, Nancy declares that she is ashamed of herself, and Richard asks her to marry. She accepts, and he kisses her "as an equal"—a surprising note—as the curtain falls. If anything like credibility and empathy had been established for the young couple, this ending would have been intolerably perfunctory.

Yet the opposite pitfall is also to be avoided, that of overwriting the climax.[2] When an audience is carried through a play to a high point of tension, very little is needed to release the tension, and that little must be intensely sincere, or the moment of release may be ridiculous rather than satisfying. Anyone who has received condolences for a bereavement knows how inadequate, how close to insincerity, and, occasionally, how farcical and even irritating the kind remarks can sound. Moments of deep emotion usually vent themselves in few words.

The following examples reveal the fault of saying too much at the climax. The first is one of the main crises, with its climax, of a young writer's first play. The other is the final scene of another writer's second long play.

The boy-poet, Chatterton, has palmed off some medieval

[2] On this point see Freytag, *The Technique of the Drama*, p. 139.

forgeries upon the great litterateur, Horace Walpole. The poems have been so highly praised by Walpole that Chatterton is emboldened to go to London to seek the patronage of the great man. Meanwhile Walpole has discovered the forgeries, and now spends half an hour baiting the boy in revenge for his wounded pride. He laughs at Chatterton, "I took it seriously! Oh, Heaven! What a lark!" Two affected ladies of Walpole's coterie peep in.

TOM. Damn you all.

WALPOLE. You're spoiling the mood. Take care.

TOM. You're afraid of me, Walpole, that's it. That's it. God! God, it's good to feel strong and defiant and so sure you're right. I'm glad I'm here. I'm glad because it shows me that I'm dirty and hungry, and I'm clean inside. I'm clean and young—and you, Horace Walpole, are dead. I challenge you to look at your own corpse.

(WALPOLE *tries to lift a violet to his mouth, but it doesn't get there.*)

I thought it was Bristol cast me out. Only it wasn't just Bristol, don't you see? It wasn't just Bristol that made me tremble when I walked on the wharves at night, listen (sic) to the wind in the rigging, and the wail of black slaves in the holds. It wasn't just loveless Bristol that made me mad with impatience and bursting with hate. It was you, Walpole, you and your whole stuffed society—born with a title, nourished on scandal, and waiting to be told you've been dead for centuries. You coddle yourselves with your smug antiques. But when an ancient poet awakes from eternity and shouts, "I live!"—then instead of snatching him up to work for you and drain himself of the beauty he must give, you turn away. You pretend you heard nothing. You tremble at the new patterns I bring. You tremble for the sanctity of your own stifling featherbeds.

I say to you now, Horace Walpole, fourth Earl of Oxford, that

you are a dusty marionette, and your final string has snapped!
I shan't forget my memories this time, sir. I bow to you, corpse.
You've lived too long.

(*Exit* CHATTERTON. *There is a shocked silence.* WALPOLE *is
hardly visible in his big chair. The sun has turned pale yellow.* MISS BREEN *is about to open her mouth to fill the
wordless minute, but is checked by* MRS. GILBERT, *who, in
final desperation, says to* MISS BREEN)

MRS. GILBERT. Minnie!

Curtain

In the second illustration, old Gretchel Prieco has murdered one of the admirers of her daughter Falicia, to keep
her from marrying him. She has locked the body into a
closet until a time when she could get help to bury it in
the swamp. Meanwhile, Falicia comes home married to another boy. Gretchel turns over the key of the closet to the
father of the murdered boy.

ALFONSO. Why you give me this?
GRETCHEL. Open the closet.
ALFONSO. Why?
GRETCHEL. You'll see why.
FALICIA. Why don't you say something to me, mama? You say
something, please.
GRETCHEL. (*Sadly*). All right, Falicia. I'll say somethin' to ya.
FALICIA. What?
GRETCHEL. Play the piano. My piece.
FALICIA. (*Surprised*). Sure, I play for you, mama.
(ALFONSO *starts to open the closet.*)
GRETCHEL. Alfonso, wait. I'm goin' to look at the sunset. Wait
till it's dark, will ya? Then open the door.
ALFONSO. Sure, you say so, O.K. But I don't see why I do this.
Seem crazy.

CONRADO (*Gretchel's husband*). She like you, I think, Alfonso. By golly she never let me open that door.

(GRETCHEL *leans wearily against the door and looks out.*)

GRETCHEL. Yes, just like it always is. Clouds and color still paintin' the water. But now I can't hardly see nothin' like that. Only cans, old tires, garbage and junk—the stuff below. I should a seen 'em before—that's all I should a seen. That's all that's there. But I been foolin' myself and wastin' my life on seein' somethin' that wasn't there. I see now. There's no colors—no clouds —there's nothin' pretty, nothin' good—nothin' but the smell and the junk. Why didn't I look? I wouldn't a spent my nights pressin' my legs on cold cement floors. I could a had a doctor to keep me from feelin' sore. I wouldn't be wearin' this stinkin' dress. I'd a had another one, maybe. Maybe two. And I wouldn't feel dead inside of me, like I do now. But I wasn't wise. I seen things wrong. So now, what I look at—how I feel—think— they're the real thing. No more clouds—no colors—nothin'.

(*She slumps down on the box in the doorway and looks at the river silently for several seconds before speaking. Finally:*)

Yes. Tomorrow and always. It's the stuff below.

(FALICIA *begins to play "The Pilgrim's Chorus."* GORDON —Falicia's husband—leans against the piano and smiles down at her. The two children in the bedroom cry loudly, but no one seems to hear them.* CONRADO *is seated at the sofa interested in a magazine.* ALFONSO *stands in front of the closet fidgeting with the key. The sunset is dimming into blackness as*

The Curtain Falls

Gretchel does not explain anything; she just sinks right down to the abyss and stays there, saying over and over, "Isn't it awful!" And like most weepers, she weeps alone. Chatterton quickly climbs a pedestal and waves banners.

No real harmony is achieved by these speeches. In both examples the playwright has intervened between the character and the situation. He has expressed his own passion and pity and sense of frustrated justice, not the sentiments of the characters.

Fine passionate speeches seldom come from a person overwhelmed by his own life's tragedy, or whipped to a bitter realization that an idol has fallen. Words come only after the grief has abated; and the audience knows this. Othello has already wept over Desdemona, stabbed Iago, been disarmed and found another weapon, and is to be handed over to justice, when he finds his voice:

He reminds them he has been their commander.

Soft you. A word or two before you go. I have done the state some service, and they know it. No more of that.

He worries about his sullied reputation.

I pray you in your letters when you shall these unlucky deeds relate, speak of me as I am; nothing extenuate, nor aught set down in malice.

He tries to explain his crime.

Then must you speak of one that loved not wisely, but too well, of one not easily jealous, but, being wrought, perplexed in the extreme;

He laments his crime.

Of one whose hand, like the base Judean, threw away a pearl richer than all his tribe;

He cannot recognize himself weeping.

Of one whose subdued eyes, albeit unused to the melting mood, drop tears as fast as the Arabian trees their medicinal gums. Set you down this;

He cannot bear his weakness.

And say besides, that in Aleppo once

He remembers his old vigorous anger.	When a malignant and a turbaned Turk beat a Venetian and traduced the state, I took by the throat the circumcised dog
And turns it against himself.	And smote him—thus.

There is very little of the heroic here, allowing for three figures of speech and the difference between blank verse and common prose. Othello is worried about the stain on his name being put into the record. He explains his deed to officers of the state who have arrested him. He is sorry, and weeps at having killed his wife, but quickly pulls himself together. Suddenly remembering his past power, rectitude, and vigorous wrath, he kills himself. The heroics are contained only in the last line of the speech. He does not declaim as Chatterton does, nor moan lengthily like old Gretchel. What he says briefly expresses, not Shakespeare's pity, but the soldier's inability to face the loss of his love and his honor.

Some writers affect a quiet ending. They use anticlimax deliberately to avoid the heroic curtain. There can be no objection to this, if the ending adds something to the play, as it does in *Street Scene*. By sending a middle-aged couple to rent the apartment vacated by the Maurrants, Rice subtly makes a new crisis which emphasizes the meaning of the play. Anderson uses a quiet ending in *Winterset* after the death of Mio and Miriamne. Old Esdras, the philosopher and poet, breaks into his great speech of courageous resignation:

Mio, my son—know this where you lie,
This is the glory of earthborn men and women,
Not to cringe, never to yield, but standing,
Take defeat implacable and defiant
Die unsubmitting . . . on this star
Man can stand up, and look up blind, and say:
In all these turning lights I find no clue,
Only a masterless night, and in my blood
No certain answer, yet is my mind my own,
Yet is my heart a cry toward something dim
In distance, which is higher than I am
And makes me emperor of the endless dark
Even in seeking.

This is the language the blood might speak in a moment of grief. It is not realistic, but it is true. It serves the same purpose as the two brief speeches of Old Montague and Old Capulet at the end of *Romeo and Juliet*, that of bringing the audience gradually back to a recognition of itself in the sufferings of the characters on stage, and so returning to its own concerns without shock. The quiet ending is not always so felicitous; but if it is used sincerely, if it accomplishes something, there is no reason that it should not be used. For it is the dramatist's right, as well as his duty, to place the period at the end of his play, to interpret the vital connection between the bit of human desire he has presented and that great universal humanity which his figures reveal.

This book has dealt with technique, the use of tools by which the playwright constructs his scenario, as the first step in the process of translating his personal experience of beauty into an audience experience of climax. Probably

341

no one play requires the use of all the tools that have been studied; but every play that succeeds before an audience makes use of about three-fourths of them in one combination or another. If the play be rooted in human desire, the playwright may ignore any of the practices recommended here, provided that he uses enough of the others to serve the general ends of clarity, suspense, preparation, and climax. In other words, technique must be regarded as highly flexible, the resourceful use of tools, not rigid adherence to rules.

ASSIGNMENTS

PLAYS: Clifford Odets, *Waiting for Lefty,* in *Six Plays by Clifford Odets.* New York: Random House, 1939. Elmer Rice, *Dream Girl.* New York: Coward-McCann, 1946.

ADDITIONAL READING: William Archer, *Playmaking: A Manual of Craftsmanship,* pp. 321-330. New York: Dodd, Mead & Company, Inc., 1937. Aristotle, *Poetics,* XIV, translated by Ingram Bywater. New York: The Macmillan Company, 1930. George Pierce Baker, *Dramatic Technique,* pp. 215-233. Boston: Houghton Mifflin Company, 1919. John Howard Lawson, *Theory and Technique of Playwriting,* Part IV, Chapter V. New York: G. P. Putnam's Sons, 1949. Percival Wilde, *The Craftsmanship of the One-Act Play,* Chapters XXIII-XXVI. Boston: Little, Brown & Company, 1938.

18

Finishing the Play

THE CONSTRUCTION OF A SCENARIO CANNOT BE HURRIED. It is a process that involves not only conscious planning but also unconscious maturation. The scenario grows and changes while the dialogue is being written and even afterward; and it has its severest tests while the written manuscript is being molded into a stage play. This final chapter is a composite record of the experiences of about fifteen student playwrights as they assisted in the process of putting their plays upon the stage.

One of the first discoveries of the apprentice playwright is that there is little advantage beyond his own satisfaction in yielding to the hot impulse to write before he has a good scenario. A few points may be cleared up as he writes, but the many problems that he believes will settle themselves in the dialogue remain problems. His first draft is too short, or too long, full of irrelevancies, lacking in emotional preparation, lacking in suspense. As he reads the play aloud, the listeners find values he did not suspect, and miss points he thought he had made clear. His "inspiration" smashes against constructive criticism.

His most difficult task now faces him—revision. He has used up the enthusiasm that drove him to complete the first draft. Can cold judgment now furnish a better script? He returns to the scenario, inserting new material as a result of suggestions, but sometimes without real conviction. The whole thing seems wooden, mechanical. What he wanted to say was—and here he begins to formulate afresh the purpose with which he undertook the play, the meaning he intended to get across, the emotion he meant to evoke. Something like his original feeling of confidence returns as he works his way through the scenario, testing each detail in terms of the fundamental purpose of the play. He has felt and planned, felt and written; now he can be objective; he can think of how the audience will be likely to listen and respond.

Perhaps he will discard some of the suggestions he received, because they indicate that he has been misunderstood, and he will see ways of making his meaning clearer and more exciting. Perhaps as he returns to the scenario he will see some character in a new and truer light. He must suffer his story to take the new direction which the vitalized character gives it, or he must provide further or different causes for the actions he has previously decided upon. The scenario must be improved again. There is no time at which a scenario becomes sacred. It is always a guide, not a goad.

At last with a revised scenario that is once more completely (for the moment) satisfying, he will write again;

and perhaps again. And in the course of time, the play, or another play, will be ready to put into rehearsal.

His second major shock is at casting.[1] His heroine of the black hair and flashing eyes is not to be found among the available actors. The only girl whose personality could possibly fit the part looks quite different from what the playwright had imagined. He is not satisfied with some of the other castings. He realizes that his script will have to convey its meaning through the spirit rather than through appearances.

He receives another shock as the actors begin to ask questions, questions very trivial to the author, but to the actor all-important. He begins to supply details that he had thought could be omitted from the script, and to try to make his play foolproof. About the third rehearsal he realizes that some of his "best speeches" only sound long-winded, and he blames the actor, although the director assures him that the actor is very intelligent. At last he is persuaded to cut.[2] These alterations go into the prompt-book, which will be almost the last revision of the play.

---

[1] Alan R. Thompson offers a grim picture of the way in which a script can be ruined by any of the agencies of production, *The Anatomy of the Drama*, pp. 105-107. It seems wiser, however, to assume intelligence and sincerity on the part of the persons engaged in production, and to regard them as collaborators. The playwright's obligation is to make the script so clear and moving that the collaborators cannot be misled.

[2] St. John Ervine shows how the actors help in cutting, and in arranging the words to make the speeches easy to learn and to say. *How To Write A Play*, pp. 106-107. See also Hamilton, *"So You're Writing a Play!"*, p. 239. Hamilton urges the use of pantomime instead of words whenever possible, and quotes Sir J. M. Barrie, "The best moments always happen when nobody is saying anything."

One of his major shocks occurs when the director begins to block business. Now the whole play seems to get out of hand. The smooth flow of the lines is broken by movement. The rhythm of writing becomes the rhythm of speech, and only the basic ebb and flow of desire, evident in the scenario, is evident in the performance. A scene he had thought of as near a fireplace is played on the other side of the stage, because the director has some notion of saving the fireplace for another scene. Indeed, it is now evident that the director sees things in the play that the playwright did not know were there, and does not want there. And the rehearsal is very long, frequently interrupted, concerned with everything but the writing. Afterward there is an argument with the director. The playwright recovers his hope that the director understands the play, and he himself begins to understand what has been going on on the stage. But he feels that the play has ceased to be his alone. He begins to learn one important fact about a play—that it is and must be a collaboration.

Later, when business moves smoothly and the actors have got their lines, the playwright relaxes and actually enjoys some of the rehearsals. But his anguish comes again when one of the actors fails repeatedly to memorize a favorite speech and the director points out that this is not because the actor is stupid, but because the speech actually is hard to learn; it has the same cue or content, or starts with the same words, as some other speech in the actor's part. Again one of the "best speeches" has to be revised to prevent the actor from going blank in performance. The playwright feels that he is being blamed for everything.

Always the director is demanding a new scene. At the last possible moment the playwright sees the reason for this and the way of handling it. He hastens to his typewriter and provides the scene, which, too, must be revised —"tampered with"—by the director. Yet he feels grateful to the actors for taking the new scene without complaint a day or so before dress rehearsal. He is surprised to discover that the actors and even the director actually hope the show will get across and are not against him. The play does not seem to be so badly miscast, now that he has got used to the actors.

He is shocked at dress rehearsal by the invariably inadequate staging. An actor finds he cannot make his costume change quickly enough, or drink the tea the playwright has prescribed; and the playwright has to pad the cover scene, uncomfortably aware of his technical error. He finds that he cannot hear the actors over the sound effects which he has insisted upon, and which are never sufficiently realistic. The light effects only half approximate his subtle requirements. The frantic costumer reports that there is not a negligee in town as seductive as the one demanded, and if there were, the amateur actress would not dare to wear it. As most of his profanity has been cut already, he rails bitterly for a moment at the prudery of amateurs who refuse to face life. He begins to think defiantly of the professional stage. And all the time he is learning to accept and deal with more and more collaborators.

Dress rehearsal is a great crisis; he would like just to fold the show, now that he has seen it. He would like to see another actor in the lead—the brunette he wrote originally. He is still upset about that scene by the fireplace. He wants to take over the prompter's job himself and resents being told the prompter is more efficient than he.

At last the audience gathers. The playwright goes backstage to give the actors final suggestions, only to discover that he is *de trop*. Everyone seems competent, too competent; even the director seems cold toward him. He returns to the front of the house. As the curtain rises, he remembers something he meant to tell an actor; it is too late. A minor error in the opening scene ruins the rest of the act for him. The playwright stands behind each actor and pushes all evening. During intermissions and especially at scene changes he wishes he had crammed the whole play into one set. As the final curtain comes down, he hardly hears the applause. But everyone gets together afterward, and the actors are very happy, and the playwright feels that the play could not have been too much of a failure.

The next night he is able to trust the actors with their share of the collaboration, and to begin his study of his last and most powerful collaborator, the audience. He learns to interpret the pitch and rate of voices before the play and during intermissions, the amount of random movement during the performance, the nature of the laughter and applause. He is quite proud of every observation he can make about "the house," and wants to return again and again to the fascinating pursuit of interpreting the behavior of the audience. He begins to yearn for the power to make them laugh and cry and be silent. His secret, biting wish is to transport them with a mighty climax. He knows at last why he wants to write plays.

Bibliography

REFERENCE BOOKS

Archer, William. *Playmaking: A Manual of Craftsmanship.* New York: Dodd, Mead & Company, Inc., 1937.

Aristotle. *Poetics,* translated by Ingram Bywater, Modern Readers Series. New York: The Macmillan Company, 1930.

Baird, A. Craig. *Public Discussion and Debate.* Boston: Ginn & Company, 1937.

Baker, George Pierce. *Dramatic Technique.* Boston and New York: Houghton Mifflin Company, 1919.

Bonney, Merl E. *Techniques of Appeal and of Social Control.* Menasha, Wisconsin: George Banta Publishing Company, 1934.

Bosanquet, Bernard. *A History of Aesthetics.* Excerpts in E. F. Carritt, *Philosophies of Beauty.* New York and London: Oxford University Press, 1919.

Bradley, Andrew Cecil. *Oxford Lectures on Poetry.* Excerpts in E. F. Carritt, *Philosophies of Beauty.* New York and London: Oxford University Press, 1919.

Brunetière, Ferdinand. "La loi du théâtre," translated in Barrett H. Clark, *European Theories of the Drama.* New York: Crown Publishers, 1947.

Carritt, E. F. *Philosophies of Beauty.* New York and London: Oxford University Press, 1919.

Clark, Barrett H. *European Theories of the Drama.* New York: Crown Publishers, 1947.

Clark, Barrett H. *A Study of the Modern Drama.* New York: D. Appleton-Century Company, Inc., 1938.

Corneille, Pierre. "Premier discour de l'utilité et des parties du poème dramatique," translated in Barrett H. Clark, *European Theories of the Drama.* New York: Crown Publishers, 1947.

Croce, Benedetto. *A Breviary of Aesthetics.* Excerpts in E. F. Carritt, *Philosophies of Beauty.* New York and London: Oxford University Press, 1919.

Dewey, John. *Experience and Nature.* Excerpts in E. F. Carritt, *Philosophies of Beauty.* New York and London: Oxford University Press, 1919.

Dolman, John. *The Art of Play Production.* New York and London: Harper & Brothers, 1928.

Ervine, St. John. *How to Write a Play.* New York: The Macmillan Company, 1928.

Freytag, Gustav. *The Technique of the Drama,* translated by Elias J. MacEwan. Chicago: Scott, Foresman & Company, 1904.

Goetschius, Percy. *The Homophonic Forms of Musical Composition.* New York: G. Schirmer, Inc., 1924.

Goetschius, Percy. *The Larger Forms of Musical Composition.* Copyright, 1915, by G. Schirmer, Inc. Copyright renewal assigned, 1943, to G. Schirmer, Inc.

Goetschius, Percy. *The Theory and Practice of Tone Relations.* New York: G. Schirmer, Inc., 1916.

Hamilton, Clayton. *"So You're Writing a Play!"* Boston: Little, Brown & Company, 1935.

Hegel, George Wilhelm Friedrich. *The Philosophy of Fine Art,* translated by F. P. B. Osmaston. London: George Bell and Sons, Ltd., 1920. 4 Vols.

Hollingworth, H. L. *The Psychology of the Audience.* New York: American Book Company, 1935.

Hopkins, Arthur. *"How's Your Second Act?"* New York: Samuel French, Inc., 1931.

Ibsen, Henrik. *From Ibsen's Workshop, Collected Works,* Vol. XII, Ed. William Archer. New York: Charles Scribner's Sons, 1908-1927.

Jones, Henry Arthur. "Introduction to Brunetière's Law of the Theatre," in Barrett H. Clark, *European Theories of the Drama.* New York: Crown Publishers, 1947.

Krows, Arthur Edwin. *Playwriting for Profit.* New York: Longmans, Green & Co., Inc., 1928.

Langfeld, Herbert Sidney. *The Aesthetic Attitude.* New York: Harcourt, Brace & Company, Inc., 1920.

Lawson, John Howard. *Theory and Technique of Playwriting.* New York: G. P. Putnam's Sons, 1949.

Lessing, Ephraim Gotthold von. *Hamburgische Dramaturgie,* No. 34 in Barrett H. Clark, *European Theories of the Drama.* New York: Crown Publishers, 1947.

Lund, F. H. "The Psychology of Belief: A Study of Its Emotional and Volitional Determinants" in *Journal of Abnormal Psychology,* Vol. 20 (1925).

Martin, Everett Dean. *The Behavior of Crowds.* New York: Harper & Brothers, 1920.

Matthews, Brander. *The Development of the Drama.* New York: Charles Scribner's Sons, 1904.

Matthews, Brander. *Playwrights on Playmaking.* New York: Charles Scribner's Sons, 1923.

Matthews, Brander. *A Study of the Drama.* New York and Chicago: Houghton Mifflin Company, 1910.

McDougall, William. *The Group Mind.* New York and London: G. P. Putnam's Sons, 1920.

Monroe, Alan H. *Principles and Types of Speech,* Rev. Ed. New York: Scott, Foresman & Company, 1939.

Nicoll, Allardyce. *The Theory of Drama.* New York: The Thomas Y. Crowell Company, n.d.

Poffenberger, Albert T. *Psychology in Advertising.* New York and London: McGraw-Hill Book Company, Inc., 1932.

BIBLIOGRAPHY

Price, W. T. *Analysis of Play Construction.* New York: W. T. Price, Publisher, 1908.

Priestley, J. B. *Johnson Over Jordan.* New York and London: Harper & Brothers, 1939.

Racine, Jean. "First Preface to Britannicus" in Barrett H. Clark, *European Theories of the Drama.* New York: Crown Publishers, 1947.

Sandford, William Phillips and Yeager, Willard Hays. *Practical Business Speaking.* New York: McGraw-Hill Book Company, Inc., 1937.

Sandford, William Phillips and Yeager, Willard Hays. *Principles of Effective Speaking.* New York: Thomas Nelson and Sons, 1934.

Sarcey, Francisque. "Essai d'une esthetique de théâtre," in Barrett H. Clark, *European Theories of the Drama.* New York: Crown Publishers, 1947.

Sarcey, Francisque. *Quarante Ans de Théâtre.* Paris: Bibliothèque des Annales Politiques et Litteraires, 1900.

Sarett, Lew and Foster, William Trufant. *Basic Principles of Speech.* New York: Houghton Mifflin Company, 1936.

Schlegel, August Wilhelm. *Lectures on Dramatic Art and Criticism,* translated by John Black. London: George Bell and Sons, Ltd., 1894.

Stanislavski, Constantin. *An Actor Prepares.* New York: Theatre Arts, Inc., 1936.

Starch, Daniel. *Principles of Advertising.* Chicago and New York: A. W. Shaw Company, 1925.

Starch, Daniel, Stanton, Hazel M., and Koerth, Wilhelmine. *Controlling Human Behavior.* New York: The Macmillan Company, 1936.

Thompson, Alan Reynolds. *The Anatomy of Drama.* Berkeley and Los Angeles: University of California Press, 1942.

Wilde, Percival. *The Craftsmanship of the One-Act Play.* Boston: Little, Brown & Company, 1938.

Young, Paul Thomas. *Emotion in Man and Animal.* New York: John Wiley and Sons, Inc.; London: Chapman Hall, Ltd., 1943.

Zucker, E. A. *Ibsen the Master Builder.* New York: Henry Holt and Company, Inc., 1929.

BIBLIOGRAPHY

LIST OF PLAYS

Abe Lincoln in Illinois. Robert Sherwood. New York: Dramatists Play Service, 1939.

Allison's House. Susan Glaspell. In *Pulitzer Prize Plays*, Ed., Kathryn Coe and William H. Cordell. New York: Samuel French, Inc., 1931.

Angel Street. Patrick Hamilton. New York: Samuel French, Inc., 1942.

Anna Christie. Eugene O'Neill. New York: Cape, 1923.

Antigone. Sophocles. In *The Complete Greek Drama*, Ed. Oates and O'Neill. New York: Random House, 1938.

Awake and Sing. Clifford Odets. In *Six Plays of Clifford Odets*. New York: Random House, 1938.

The Bat. Mary Roberts Rinehart and Avery Hopwood. New York: Samuel French, Inc., 1932.

The Beggar on Horseback. George S. Kaufman and Marc Connelly. New York: Boni and Liveright, 1924.

The Bluebird. Maurice Maeterlinck, translated by Alexander Teixeira de Mattos. New York: Dodd, Mead & Company, Inc., 1911.

Born Yesterday. Garson Kanin. New York: The Viking Press, Inc., 1946.

Both Your Houses. Maxwell Anderson. New York: Samuel French, Inc., 1933.

Broken Dishes. Martin Flavin. New York: Samuel French, Inc., 1930.

Bury the Dead. Irwin Shaw. In *Thirty Famous One-Act Plays*, Ed. Bennett Cerf and Van H. Cartmell. Garden City, New York: Garden City Publishing Company, 1943.

Caesar and Cleopatra. George Bernard Shaw. New York: Brentano, 1914.

The Cassilis Engagement. St. John Ervine. New York: Samuel French, Inc., 1907.

Cathleen ni Houlihan. William Butler Yeats. In *Collected Works*. Stratford-on-Avon: The Shakespeare Head Press, 1908.

353

The Cherokee Night. Lynn Riggs. In *Russet Mantle and The Cherokee Night.* New York: Samuel French, Inc., 1936.

The Cherry Orchard. Anton Chekov. In *Chief Contemporary Dramatists,* Ed., T. H. Dickinson. New York: Houghton Mifflin Company, 1930.

Children of the Moon. Martin Flavin. New York: Brentano, 1923.

The Children's Hour. Lillian Hellman. In *Twenty Best Plays,* Ed., John Gassner. New York: Crown Publishers, 1946.

The Circle. Somerset Maugham. New York: Doran, 1921.

Cock Robin. Philip Barry and Elmer Rice. New York: Samuel French, Inc., 1930.

Counsellor-at-Law. Elmer Rice. New York: Samuel French, Inc., 1931.

The Criminal Code. Martin Flavin. New York: H. Liveright, 1929.

Cyrano de Bergerac. Edmond Rostand, translated by Brian Hooker. New York: Henry Holt and Company, Inc., 1924.

The Damask Cheek. John Van Druten and Lloyd Harris. New York: Random House, 1943.

Dark of the Moon. Howard Richardson and William Berney. Manuscript controlled by Select Theatres Corporation, 234 West 44th St., New York.

The Devil's Disciple. George Bernard Shaw. In *Collected Works,* Ed., Ayot St. Lawrence. New York: Wise, 1930-1932. Vol. 9.

A Doll's House. Henrik Ibsen. In *Collected Works,* Ed., William Archer. New York: Charles Scribner's Sons, 1908-1927.

Dream Girl. Elmer Rice. New York: Coward-McCann, 1946.

East Lynne. Mrs. Henry Wood. *Spencer's Universal Stage,* No. XLVII. Boston: Walter H. Baker Company, 1869.

Electra. Sophocles. In *The Complete Greek Drama,* Ed., Oates and O'Neill. New York: Random House, 1938.

Elizabeth the Queen. Maxwell Anderson. New York: Longmans, Green & Co., Inc., 1931.

The Enchanted Maze. Paul Green. New York: Samuel French, Inc., 1939.

An Enemy of the People. Henrik Ibsen. In *Collected Works,* Ed., William Archer. New York: Charles Scribner's Sons, 1908-1927.

354

Faust. Johann Wolfgang von Goethe, translated by Alice Raphael. New York: R. O. Ballou, 1930.

The Field God. Paul Green. New York: Robert M. McBride & Company, 1927.

Flight To The West. Elmer Rice. New York: Coward-McCann, 1941.

From Morn to Midnight. George Kaiser, translated by Ashley Dukes. London: Henderson's, 1920.

Ghosts. Henrik Ibsen. In *Collected Works,* Ed., William Archer. New York: Charles Scribner's Sons, 1908-1927.

The Glass Menagerie. Tennessee Williams. New York: Dramatists Play Service, 1945.

Golden Boy. Clifford Odets. In *Six Plays of Clifford Odets.* New York: Random House, 1939.

Great Catherine. George Bernard Shaw. In *Collected Works,* Ed., Ayot St. Lawrence. New York: Wise, 1930-1932.

Green Grow the Lilacs. Lynn Riggs. New York: Samuel French, Inc., 1931.

The Green Pastures. Marc Connelly. New York: Farrar & Rinehart, Inc., 1929.

The Guardsman. Ferenc Molnar, translated by Grace I. Colbrun and Hans Bartsch. New York: Boni and Liveright, 1924.

Gypsy. Maxwell Anderson. In Burns Mantle, *Best Plays of 1928-1929.* New York: Dodd, Mead & Company, Inc., 1933.

Hamlet. William Shakespeare. In *Shakespeare's Complete Works,* Ed., William Allen Neilson. New York: P. F. Collier and Son, 1925.

Hedda Gabler. Henrik Ibsen. In *Collected Works,* Ed., William Archer. New York: Charles Scribner's Sons, 1908-1927.

Holiday. Philip Barry. New York: Samuel French, Inc., 1929.

Hotel Universe. Philip Barry. New York: Samuel French, Inc., 1930.

The House of Connelly. Paul Green. New York: Samuel French, Inc., 1931.

Idiot's Delight. Robert Sherwood. New York: Charles Scribner's Sons, 1936.

In Abraham's Bosom. Paul Green. In *Pulitzer Prize Plays,* Ed., Kathryn Coe and William H. Cordell. New York: Samuel French, Inc., 1931.

BIBLIOGRAPHY

In A Garden. Philip Barry. New York: Doran, 1926.

I Remember Mama. John Van Druten. New York: Harcourt, Brace & Company, Inc., 1945.

Jacobowsky and the Colonel. Franz Werfel, translated by Gustave O. Arlt. New York: The Viking Press, Inc., 1944.

John Gabriel Borkman. Henrik Ibsen. In *Collected Works*, Ed., William Archer. New York: Charles Scribner's Sons, 1908-1927.

Johnny Johnson. Paul Green. New York: Samuel French, Inc., 1937.

Johnson Over Jordan. J. B. Priestley. New York and London: Harper & Brothers, 1939.

King Lear. William Shakespeare. In *Shakespeare's Complete Works*, Ed., William Allen Neilson. New York: P. F. Collier and Son, 1925.

Ladies in Retirement. Edward Percy Smith and Reginald Denham. New York: Dramatists Play Service, 1941.

Lady in the Dark. Moss Hart. New York: Random House, 1941.

Lady of the Rose. Martin Flavin. New York: Samuel French, Inc., 1925.

Lady Windemere's Fan. Oscar Wilde. In *Chief Contemporary Dramatists*, Ed., T. H. Dickinson. Boston and New York: Houghton Mifflin Company, 1930.

The Late Christopher Bean. Sidney Howard. New York: Samuel French, Inc., 1933.

The Left Bank. Elmer Rice. New York: Samuel French, Inc., 1933.

Life With Father. Howard Lindsay and Russel Crouse. New York: Alfred A. Knopf, Inc., 1940.

The Little Foxes. Lillian Hellman. In *Four Plays by Lillian Hellman*. New York: Random House, 1942.

Lysistrata. Aristophanes. In *The Complete Greek Drama*, Ed., Oates and O'Neill. New York: Random House, 1938.

Macbeth. William Shakespeare. In *Shakespeare's Complete Works*, Ed., William Allen Neilson. New York: P. F. Collier and Son, 1925.

Man of Destiny. George Bernard Shaw. In *The Man of Destiny and How He Lied to Her Husband*. New York: Brentano, ca. 1898.

Mary of Scotland. Maxwell Anderson. Garden City, New York: Doubleday, Doran & Company, Inc., 1934.

The Master Builder. Henrik Ibsen. In *Collected Works,* Ed., William Archer. New York: Charles Scribner's Sons, 1908-1927.

Murder in a Nunnery. Emmet Lavery. New York: Samuel French, Inc., 1944.

Night Over Taos. Maxwell Anderson. New York: Samuel French, Inc., 1932.

Oedipus Rex. Sophocles. In *The Complete Greek Drama,* Ed., Oates and O'Neill. New York: Random House, 1938.

Of Mice and Men. John Steinbeck. New York: Covici, Friede, Inc., 1937.

Oklahoma! Oscar Hammerstein and Richard Rodgers. New York: Random House, 1943.

The Old Maid. Zoe Aikins. New York: D. Appleton-Century Company, Inc., 1935.

Once in a Lifetime. George S. Kaufman and Moss Hart. New York: Farrar and Rinehart, Inc., 1930.

One-third of a Nation. Arthur Arent. In *Federal Theatre Plays.* New York: Random House, 1938.

Othello. William Shakespeare. In *Shakespeare's Complete Works,* Ed., William Allen Neilson. New York: P. F. Collier and Son, 1925.

Our Town. Thornton Wilder. New York: Coward-McCann, 1938.

Outside Looking In. Maxwell Anderson. New York: Longmans, Green & Co., Inc., 1928.

Paradise Lost. Clifford Odets. In *Six Plays of Clifford Odets.* New York: Random House, 1939.

Paris Bound. Philip Barry. New York: Samuel French, Inc., 1929.

The Patriots. Sidney Kingsley. New York: Random House, 1943.

Peter Pan. James M. Barrie. New York: Charles Scribner's Sons, 1928.

Pillars of Society. Henrik Ibsen. In *Collected Works,* Ed., William Archer. New York: Charles Scribner's Sons, 1908-1927.

The Playboy of the Western World. J. M. Synge. Boston: Luce, 1911.

Porgy and Bess. George Gershwin and Dubose Heyward. New York: Gershwin, 1935.

Potter's Field. Paul Green. In *The House of Connelly and Other Plays.* New York: Samuel French, Inc., 1931.

Prologue to Glory. Ellsworth P. Conkle. New York: Samuel French, Inc., 1938.

The Return of Peter Grimm. David Belasco. In *Six Plays of David Belasco.* Boston: Little, Brown & Company, 1929.

Richelieu. Edward Bulwer Lytton. Philadelphia: David McKay Company, 1901.

Rocket to the Moon. Clifford Odets. In *Six Plays of Clifford Odets.* New York: Random House, 1939.

Roll Sweet Chariot. Paul Green. New York: Samuel French, Inc., 1935.

Romeo and Juliet. William Shakespeare. In *Shakespeare's Complete Works,* Ed., William Allen Neilson. P. F. Collier and Son, 1925.

Saint Joan. George Bernard Shaw. New York: Brentano, 1924.

Saturday's Children. Maxwell Anderson. New York: Longmans, Green & Co., Inc., 1927.

The School for Scandal. Richard Brinsley Sheridan. In *The Plays and Poems of Richard Brinsley Sheridan,* Ed., Crompton Rhodes. New York: The Macmillan Company, 1929.

See Naples and Die. Elmer Rice. New York: Samuel French, Inc., 1929.

Shroud My Body Down. Paul Green. Iowa City: Clio Press, 1935.

The Silver Cord. Sidney Howard. New York: Charles Scribner's Sons, 1927.

The Skin of Our Teeth. Thornton Wilder. New York and London: Harper & Brothers, 1942.

State of the Union. Howard Lindsay and Russel Crouse. New York: Random House, 1946.

Street Scene. Elmer Rice. New York: Samuel French, Inc., 1929.

Sumpn Like Wings. Lynn Riggs. New York: Samuel French, Inc., 1928.

Three Men On A Horse. George Abbot and J. C. Holm. In *Twenty Best Plays,* Ed., John Gassner. New York: Crown Publishers, 1946.

Thunder Rock. Robert Ardery. New York: Dramatists Play Service, 1942.

Tomorrow and Tomorrow. Philip Barry. New York: Samuel French, Inc., 1931.

Tread the Green Grass. Paul Green. In *The House of Connelly and Other Plays.* New York: Samuel French, Inc., 1931.

The Truth About Blayds. A. A. Milne. London: French, 1923.

Under the Gaslight. Augustin Daly. New York: W. C. Wemyss, 1867. Also in *French's Standard Drama,* Vol. 48, 1895.

Valley Forge. Maxwell Anderson. Washington, D. C.: Anderson House, 1934.

The Vikings. Henrik Ibsen. In *Collected Works,* Ed., William Archer. New York: Charles Scribner's Sons, 1908-1927.

The Voice of the Turtle. John Van Druten. New York: Random House, 1944.

Waiting for Lefty. Clifford Odets. In *Six Plays of Clifford Odets.* New York: Random House, 1939.

The Weavers. Gerhardt Hauptmann, translated by Mary Morrison. New York: B. W. Huebsch, 1911.

Welded. Eugene O'Neill. In *Plays,* Vol. 2. New York: Random House, 1941.

White Wings. Philip Barry. New York: Samuel French, Inc., 1929.

Winterset. Maxwell Anderson. Washington, D. C.: Anderson House, 1936.

A Winter's Tale. William Shakespeare. In *Shakespeare's Complete Works,* Ed., William Allen Neilson. P. F. Collier and Son, 1925.

You and I. Philip Barry. New York: Brentano, 1923.

The Youngest. Philip Barry. New York: Samuel French, Inc., 1925.

INDEX